The Nature
of
Managerial
Work

The Nature of Managerial Work

HENRY MINTZBERG
McGill University

■ HarperCollins*Publishers*

To Susie and Lisa
. . . who manage me

Quotations on pages 63, 67, 200, and 201, from G. C. Homans, *The Human Group,* are reprinted by permission of Harcourt Brace Jovanovich, Inc. Copyright 1950. Quotations on pages 17, 61, 94, 110, and 124, from Daniel Katz and Robert L. Kahn, *The Social Psychology of Organizations,* are reprinted by permission of John Wiley & Sons, Inc. Copyright © 1966 by John Wiley & Sons, Inc. The quotation on page 112 and Table 4 on page 113, from N. H. Martin, "Differential Decisions in the Management of an Industrial Plant," *Journal of Business, 29* (1956), are reprinted by permission of the University of Chicago Press. Copyright © 1956 by the University of Chicago. Quotations on pages 42 and 133, from Desmond Morris, *The Naked Ape,* are reprinted by permission of McGraw-Hill Book Company and Jonathan Cape Ltd. Copyright © 1967 by Desmond Morris. Quotations on pages 14, 36, 50, 64, 65, 66, 69, 199, and 200, from R. E. Neustadt, *Presidential Power: The Politics of Leadership,* are reprinted by permission of John Wiley & Sons, Inc. Copyright © 1960 by John Wiley & Sons, Inc. Quotations on pages 20, 37, 65, 67, 79, 85, 91, 218, 219, and 220, from Leonard R. Sayles, *Managerial Behavior: Administration in Complex Organizations,* are reprinted by permission of McGraw-Hill Book Company. Copyright © 1964 by McGraw-Hill Book Company, Inc. Quotations on pages 107, 108, 114, 115, 118, 123, 206, 207, and 208, from Rosemary Stewart, *Managers and Their Jobs,* are reprinted by permission of St. Martin's Press and Macmillan London and Basingstoke. Copyright 1967.

Chapter 7 appeared in somewhat different form as a pamphlet entitled "The Future of Managerial Work."

Contents

List of Figures

List of Tables

Preface

The origin of this book should really be traced back about twenty-seven years to the time when, as a child, I wondered what my father did at the office. He was the president of a small manufacturing firm, but his job was not at all clear to a six-year-old. Some people operated machines, others typed letters. All he ever seemed to do was sit in his office, sign an occasional letter, and talk. What did managers do?

This question was lost in my memory through some nineteen years of schooling, including two years of a master of science program in management and the first year of a Ph.D. program in the same field. It never occurred to me (nor, apparently, to many of those who taught me) that nothing was said about the job of the manager—even though the master's program was ostensibly designed to train managers! Only when I was in search of a thesis topic did the old question arise again. A professor of mine had visited a well-known government administrator who thought it might be interesting to have his job studied. The professor approached me with the idea, but I hesitated—this seemed to be a risky project in the modern, science-based management school.

Gradually, however, the idea took hold, its way prepared by my childhood curiosity and by my growing realization that it was not only six-year-olds who did not know what managers do. I was sure what my thesis topic would be after I attended the conference on the impact of the computer on the manager, cited in Chapter 1. Here I witnessed the frustration of leading thinkers in the field who were blocked by an ignorance of the top manager's job. *The Manager at Work—Determining his Activities, Roles, and Programs by Structured Observation* was completed at the MIT Sloan School of Management in 1968, based on study of the work of five chief executives.

For the next two years, I did not touch this material. Then, in 1970, I returned to it. I could now approach it as a university professor reviewing the work of a doctoral student. When I felt that his work was superficial or irrelevant, I had no qualms about deleting it. Also, from this distance I could better understand his conclusions and better see their relevance for both manager and management scientist. However, the book I was to write was not to be the publication of a thesis. It was to be a new work, dealing not only with my own study of the work of five chief executives, but with empirical studies of many other managers as well. I also decided that I would endeavor to create a book with wide appeal, one that would have an impact on practicing managers and staff people as well as on academics and their students. I felt that there were too many misconceptions in the field, that managers had had enough of the fact-free wisdom of the armchair, and that they were ready for a new look at their job, substantiated by systematic research.

In developing a book, one concentrates on a single element at a time, and in due course everything gets done. But now that it is all finished and I sit back and review the whole process, I am surprised at the intricacy of it and at the large number of people who provided significant help along the way. At the start there was Ned Bowman, who volunteered to see me into a somewhat unconventional doctoral program at MIT, and Jim Hekimian, who saw me through it. Jim, Charles Myers, and Don Carroll served on my dissertation committee; each helped me in a significant way, both during and after the writing of the thesis. Thanks to them, my topic turned out to be not at all risky. The five chief executives who allowed me to shadow them for a week and who so freely gave of their time and thoughts must also be thanked, unfortunately not by name.

A number of people made very helpful comments while I was preparing this manuscript. At the McGill University Faculty of Management, I must acknowledge especially my colleagues Pradip Khandwalla, Stan Shapiro, and Harvey Thomson. Harvey, in particular, helped me to work out the section in Chapter 7 on skills and traits. A number of my students at McGill have provided useful feedback. I cite the works of Irving Choran and Liong Wong in the book, and I must also mention Danny Miller and Tony Frayne. John Bex of Phillips Industries in the U.K. and Hans Wirdenius, and his colleagues Kjell Martvall, and Mats Kullstedt of the Personaladministrativa Council in Stockholm all made comments on early drafts which led to significant improvements. I owe a special thanks to Len Sayles, not only for his foreword, but also for his comments on the next-to-final draft of the manuscript that led to a very thorough restructuring and improvement of it.

Amina Rajabalee typed more drafts of these chapters than she or I care to remember; at times the pressure was intense but she never complained or let the high quality of her work suffer. I am particularly grateful to her. At Harper & Row I must express my special appreciation to Jim Campbell for his support. Bill Litwack has been a true friend throughout—ready to pitch in on everything from cleaning up the grammar of a dissertation to proofreading galleys. With the possible exception of the author, no one knows this manuscript more intimately.

In my doctoral dissertation, I expressed my love and appreciation to Yvette, who suspended her career and left her contact "with the reality of city life in Boston for an extended period of hybernation in the 'cabin by the lake' in Ste. Agathe des Monts, while her husband gradually wrote a four-hundred-page thesis." Books turn out to be even more gradually written than theses, and wives make their contributions in hundreds of small ways. But Yvette's real contribution has been in a larger and different sense—in developing an open-minded way of life for us, one that has been rich in emotion and certainly never dull. I believe this has had a significant influence on the book.

Finally, to the two little girls to whom this book is dedicated, let me simply say that they shall never wonder what their father does. They well know that he writes books in the basement and that he is not to be disturbed. Shhh . . .

H. M.

Montreal
September 1972

Foreword

Organizations have no doubts about the value of managerial skills. In good times and bad, there are shortages of managers. While the nonprofit sector may have discovered the critical contribution of management more recently, the constant frustrating searches for deans, agency heads, hospital administrators, and city managers testifies to the scarcity of this human resource.

As economists have told us—often with condescension—such scarcity will reflect itself in market prices, and good executives are indeed well paid. Regrettably our wider society does not assign the same recognition and status to managers. After all, many otherwise informed citizens reason, what's involved in being a boss? Isn't it easier than doing the work yourself? Aside from simple equity and social justice, such failures to comprehend the profound and difficult behavioral and cognitive skills involved in administration impact the labor market. Bright students often forswear managerial careers in favor of the greater challenges of traditional professions. Further, in our haste to evolve new programs to cope with social and environmental problems (now that some naïvely believe the economic ones have all been solved), we have wasted little thought on the need for managerial and organizational talent to implement such program. Our society's efforts are thus biased toward policy decision making: What is the right answer to a nagging problem? It is then implicitly assumed that the answer will be magically converted into satisfying results.

The ease with which the difficulty of management is underestimated must also reflect the simplicity of most studies of managers. Given the popularity of attitude surveys, it is hardly surprising that most prescriptions for managerial success emphasize a narrow range of simplistic orientations: attitudes toward employee welfare, groups, high performance, and risk taking. One often concludes from the traditional leadership surveys that the manager who can think "right" wins the day. (If this were true, it would be even more difficult to explain this perpetual shortage of skilled managers.)

Dr. Mintzberg has sought to remedy a good deal of this excessive simplicity and this reliance on what people think and say about their superiors and themselves. Regrettably, the rush to easy quantification —to the questionnaire that can be administered by a graduate student and evaluated by a computer—dissuades most social scientists from painstaking and painful examination of what human beings do as distinct from their perceptions, whimsies, and wishes. (It is always easier to ask than to see.)

Further problems with attitude surveys stem from their tendency to verify the researcher's predispositions. Thus, some years ago in our own more primitive investigations of managerial behavior we noted the rather obvious amount of time and effort managers devoted to lateral relationships. But because there had been so few behavioral studies (although everyone asserts *behavioral* science), almost all leadership studies neglect all but the hierarchical relationships. Those few who are willing to observe behavior, such as Dr. Mintzberg, are likely to see the real system and not the mythology of organizations. They are also less likely to get caught up in the imputations of causality. Recently we have come to hear more about effective workers who encourage democratic leadership styles to counter the earlier assertions of reverse causation. Behavioral observation emphasizes *process* and *systems,* the regularities of human interaction, and thus is unlikely to founder on this classical problem of which is the chicken and which is the egg.

The willingness to evaluate behavior as distinct from attitudes does not settle the problem for the researcher. What do you observe and categorize? I recall some years ago a presumably serious study of supervisors that included how much time they were standing, how much sitting, and how much walking! Whole volumes could be (and have been) written in seeking to describe everything a human being did during one day! Like the historian, then, the behavioralist must decide what to include, what to measure, and what categories of action to develop. And the answers to these ought to be based on some significant conceptual analysis of the nature of organizations as human systems, not on what is easiest to count or get recorded in diaries. And again, Dr. Mintzberg has sought to integrate his managerial actions with his knowledge of organizations as dynamic entities.

We are indebted to Dr. Mintzberg for seeking to encompass and integrate that small body of behavioral research relating to his study. His own studies go significantly beyond the earlier work and provide both the student and the executive with a rich storehouse of data that should contribute significantly to their knowledge of what makes an effective manager. And, in the process, he provides some additional proof for an old bias of mine. I would assert that those studies that are the most theoretically sound also turn out to be the most practical. Dr. Mintzberg has sought to identify the whole range of relationships comprising the manager's world in the contemporary organization, and as a result his conclusions have great worth in a world dependent on leadership skills. Ironically we have been content to know more about the components of athletic prowess than of managerial skill, and much that has been written about managers implied that there *was* less skill involved than in athletics. But behavioral skills cannot be learned if they are not first identified (which may say something about the aforementioned scarcities). This overview of how managers manage is surely the place to begin.

Leonard R. Sayles
Graduate School of Business
Columbia University

1
Introduction

Observer. Mr. R_____, we have discussed briefly this organization and the way it operates. Will you now please tell me what *you* do.
Executive. What *I* do?
Observer. Yes.
Executive. That's not easy.
Observer. Go ahead, anyway.
Executive. As president, I am naturally responsible for many things.
Observer. Yes, I realize that. But just what do you do?
Executive. Well, I must see that things go all right.
Observer. Can you give me an example?
Executive. I must see that our financial position is sound.
Observer. But just what do you do about it?
Executive. Now, that is hard to say.
Observer. Let's take another tack. What did you do yesterday?

C. L. Shartle [1]

"What do managers do?" This is a simple question, posed to managers by their children, by the staff specialists who work for them, and by the university students who hope one day to replace them. Ask it and you are likely to be told, in Henri Fayol's words of 1916, that managers plan, organize, coordinate, and control. "Fine," you may reply, "but what do managers really do?" If you are intent on getting the answer, you may bury yourself in one of America's better management libraries for a good part of one year. After having read perhaps two hundred books and articles, you will emerge and be able to cite the more recent literature:

[1] Opening quotation: C. L. Shartle, 1956: 82.

The manager, then, plans, organizes, motivates, directs, and controls. These are the broad aspects of the work. He adds foresight, order, purpose, integration of effort, and effectiveness to the contributions of others. That is the best use of the word "manage." That is the work of the manager (Strong, 1965: 5).

So remains the state of our understanding. The manager is the folk hero of contemporary American society. Yet we know so little of what he does. We are told that in him lies the American genius for efficiency—that it is to this corp of ten or more million individuals that America owes her material and organizational success.[2] Hence we look to the manager for leadership. Yet we are concerned about his ability to lead us. "Is the Presidency actually too much for one man?" asks a popular periodical.[3] The question is echoed in the corridors of a thousand government and industrial bureaucracies.

The manager is ostensibly trained in M.B.A. and M.P.A. programs throughout the world. He is written to in magazines such as *Fortune* and *Business Week* and written about in journals such as *Administrative Science Quarterly* and *The Journal of Management Studies*. He is tempted with hundreds of courses supposedly designed to help him manage better and, if he works in any of the larger public or private organizations of America, he has probably been exposed to an in-house management development program as well. Furthermore, he is surrounded by teams of management scientists—the planners, information system designers, operations researchers, an so on—who exist simply to make organizations and especially their managers more efficient in carrying out their work. All this and still we do not really know what managers do.

The problem was brought into sharp focus at a conference called a few years ago at the MIT Sloan School of Management to assess the impact of the computer on the manager. After hours of roundabout discussion by some of the best-known names in management science, one participant [4] posed a question that pointed precisely at the key problem of the conference—and the problem encountered by all management scientists who try to influence the work of the manager:

> I'd like to return to an earlier point. It seems to me that until we get into the question of what the top manager does or what the functions are that define the top management job, we're not going to get out of the kind of difficulty that keeps cropping up. What

[2] Nealey and Fiedler (1968) estimate that there are 3 to 5 million managers at the second level of supervision alone.

[3] *U.S. News and World Report* (June 13, 1966) "A Look at the Inner Workings of the White House," p. 78.

[4] Emmanuel G. Mesthene, Director of the Harvard Program on Technology and Society.

I'm really doing is leading up to my earlier question which no one really answered. And that is: Is it possible to try to arrive at a specification of what constitutes the job of a top manager? (Myers, 1967: 198).

His question was not answered at the conference, and it has remained essentially unanswered in the literature of management.

If we do not understand what constitutes the top manager's job, how can we measure the impact of the computer on his work? In fact, how can we design useful *management* information systems or planning systems for him? If we do not know what managers do, how can we claim to teach management to students in business schools? How can we expect management development programs to improve the performance of practicing managers? And, if we cannot influence the way managers work, how can we hope to enable our large bureaucracies to cope with problems that today appear insurmountable?

We must be able to answer a number of specific questions before we can expect managerial training and management science to have any real impact on practice:

What kinds of activities does the manager perform? What kinds of information does he process? With whom must he work? Where? How frequently?

What are the distinguishing characteristics of managerial work? What is of interest about the media the manager uses, the activities he prefers to engage in, the flow of these activities during the workday, his use of time, the pressures of the job?

What basic roles can be inferred from a study of the manager's activities? What roles does the manager perform in moving information, in making decisions, in dealing with people?

What variations exist among managerial jobs? To what extent can basic differences be attributed to the situation, the incumbent, the job, the organization, and the environment?

To what extent is management a science? To what extent is the manager's work programmed (that is, repetitive, systematic, and predictable)? To what extent is it programmable? To what extent can the management scientist "reprogram" managerial work?

The purpose of this book is to begin to answer these questions and to stimulate others to seek more precise answers to them. It is a book about managers—those people formally in charge of organizations or their subunits. This excludes many of those in "middle management," but includes people with titles such as president, prime minister, foreman, dean, department head, and archbishop.

This is not a book about what effective managers do or what

styles they exhibit. It focuses on the basic question—what do managers do? The aim, in different words, is to develop a job description that will have meaning to those who believe that management can be approached as a science.

Unlike virtually all of its predecessors this book is based exclusively on the evidence from empirical studies of managerial work. The vast majority of books on the manager's job make no reference to systematic evidence. We must reject their conclusions not only because they are unsupported but because many of them are in fact directly contradicted by the evidence of research.

Hence, this book was written without preconceptions of the manager's job. The results of empirical research do the talking—the diary studies of senior and middle managers in business; extended observation of street gang leaders, hospital administrators, and production supervisors; analyses of the working records of U.S. Presidents; activity sampling of foremen's work; structured observation of the work of chief executives. By bringing all of these results together for the first time, we are able to develop a new view of the work of the manager and reach some major conclusions, including the following:

1. Managers' jobs are remarkably alike. The work of foremen, presidents, government administrators, and other managers can be described in terms of ten basic roles and six sets of working characteristics.

2. The differences that do exist in managers' work can be described largely in terms of the common roles and characteristics—such as muted or highlighted characteristics and special attention to certain roles.

3. As commonly thought, much of the managers' work is challenging and nonprogrammed. But every manager has his share of regular, ordinary duties to perform, particularly in moving information and maintaining a status system. Furthermore, the common practice of categorizing as nonmanagerial some of the specific tasks many managers perform (like dealing with customers, negotiating contracts) appears to be arbitrary. Almost all of the activities managers engage in—even when ostensibly part of the regular operations of their organizations—ultimately relate back to their roles as manager.

4. The manager is both a generalist and a specialist. In his own organization he is a generalist—the focal point in the general flow of information and in the handling of general disturbances. But as a manager, he is a specialist. The job of managing involves specific roles and skills. Unfortunately, we know little about these skills and, as a result, our management schools have so far done little to teach them systematically.

5. Much of the manager's power derives from his information. With access to many sources of information, some of them open to no

one else in his organizational unit, the manager develops a data base that enables him to make more effective decisions than his employees. Unfortunately, the manager receives much information verbally, and lacking effective means to disseminate it to others, he has difficulty delegating responsibility for decision-making. Hence, he must take full charge of his organization's strategy-making system.

6. The prime occupational hazard of the manager is superficiality. Because of the open-ended nature of his job and because of his responsibility for information processing and strategy-making, the manager is induced to take on a heavy load of work, and to do much of it superficially. Hence, his work pace is unrelenting and his work activities are characterized by brevity, variety, and fragmentation. The job of managing does not develop reflective planners; rather it breeds adaptive information manipulators who prefer a stimulus-response milieu.

7. There is no science in managerial work. Managers work essentially as they always have—with verbal information and intuitive (nonexplicit) processes. The management scientist has had almost no influence on how the manager works.

8. The manager is in a kind of *loop*. The pressures of his job force him to adopt work characteristics (fragmentation of activity, emphasis on verbal communication, among others) that make it difficult for him to receive help from the management scientist and that lead to superficiality in his work. This in effect leads to more-pronounced work characteristics and increased work pressures. As the problems facing large organizations become more complex, senior managers will face even greater work pressures.

9. The management scientist can help to break this loop. He can provide significant help for the manager in information-processing and strategy-making, provided he can better understand the manager's work and can gain access to the manager's verbal data base.

10. Managerial work is enormously complex, far more so than a reading of the traditional literature would suggest. There is a need to study it systematically and to avoid the temptation to seek simple prescriptions for its difficulties. We shall improve it significantly only when we understand it precisely.

This book analyzes the managers' work in four dimensions. Chapter 3 describes the common work characteristics of managers, and Chapter 4 presents a description of ten roles that all managers appear to perform. Chapter 5 contains the research findings on differences in managers' work, and Chapter 6 takes up the issue of science in the manager's job. Chapter 7 summarizes these findings and their implications. As a preamble to this description of managerial work, Chapter 2 reviews the current literature. Eight schools of thought are discussed; the last section of the chapter defines more precisely the four bodies of theory presented in Chapters 3 through 6—characteristics, roles, differences, and science.

A Note to the Reader. My objective has been to write this book so that it could be read from beginning to end by the manager, the student of management, the staff person, and the teacher and researcher in management. I see no reason why a book on management cannot be both clear to the layman and rigorous to the academic. In order to approach these two goals, some of the detailed materials—reviews of major studies, outlines of various research methodologies, and presentation of my own empirical study—are reserved for appendices at the back of the book; also, the format chosen provides for proper referencing without breaking the flow of the text.

The casual reader will find at the end of each of the four basic chapters (3 through 6), a summary in the form of numbered "propositions." In addition, it is recommended that the last section of Chapter 2 be read as a more detailed introduction to the theoretical framework of this book. Additional summary materials appear in the section on *The Manager's Basic Purposes,* late in Chapter 4, and the section on *Eight Managerial Job Types,* late in Chapter 5.

Chapter 7 opens with an integrated summary of all the findings, which ties together the theoretical materials of Chapters 3 through 6. This summary is followed by a brief section in which it is suggested that the manager is caught in a loop of work pressures and difficult job characteristics. The last four sections analyze the implications of these findings—one section is written expressly for the manager, one for the teacher of managers, one for the management scientist (a summary of the material of Chapter 6), and one for the researcher in management.

2
Contemporary Views of the Manager's Job

We know more about the motives, habits, and most intimate arcana of the primitive peoples of New Guinea or elsewhere, than we do of the denizens of the executive suites in Unilever House. . . .

Roy Lewis and Rosemary Stewart [1]

Although an enormous amount of material has been published on the manager's job, we continue to know very little about it. Much of the literature is of little use, being merely endless repetition of the same vague statements. "It must be admitted that most managers both manage and do, but at the times they are doing, they are not managing," an academic wrote recently (Goodman, 1968: 31). Descriptions like this—abstract generalities devoid of the hard data of empirical research—persist despite repeated warnings over the years that we know almost nothing about what managers do.

[1] Opening quotation: Roy Lewis and Rosemary Stewart, 1958: 17.

Virtually every scholar who has undertaken to review some part of the literature or to study the work of managers seriously has emphasized this gap in our knowledge.[2] In introducing his famous study of the way nine Swedish managers allocated their time, Sune Carlson claimed, in 1951, "This literature is more concerned with general speculations regarding the functions of the executives than with actual descriptions of their work" (p. 23). Carlson's point was later repeated by Mason Haire in 1959: "Attention still falls largely on the behavior and motives of hourly paid and clerical workers in the organization. . . . we have virtually no studies of what management actually does" (p. 15). And when Campbell and his collaborators published their extensive report on managerial effectiveness in 1970, they found no change:

> The fly in the ointment, of course, is our present inability to define and measure managerial task demands. The description of managerial job behavior is still at an abysmally primitive level. The domain of management behavior remains an essentially undifferentiated mass (1970: 476).

Another difficulty with the literature—even when it is based on systematic study—is the tendency to focus on one aspect of the manager's job to the exclusion of all others. In particular, there is much interesting material on the manager as leader and on the manager as decision-maker, but seldom are these two areas brought together in a comprehensive view of the job.[3]

The task I set for myself in this book is to extract the useful findings from the literature and blend them with the findings of my own study to present a comprehensive description of managerial work. As a beginning, this chapter describes eight major schools of thought on the manager's job. Certain of the more important studies referred to along the way are summarized in Appendix A; the seven research methods mentioned here are described and compared in Appendix B.

THE CLASSICAL SCHOOL

The first and most prevalent view of the manager's job comes from writers of what we here refer to as the "classical school." They

---

[2] Unfortunately, we do not even have a comprehensive review of the literature, although Campbell et al. (1970) and Dubin (1962) cover some of the more important empirical studies.

[3] Katz and Kahn point out that "March and Simon (1958) wrote a major book on formal organization [a book well-known for its theories of decision-making] in which the word *leadership* appears neither in the table of contents nor in the index" (1966: 300). Typical of the newer and more significant books on leadership is Campbell *et al.* (1970) in which the term *decision-making* appears not at all in the table of contents and only once in a tangential way in the index ("Decision-Making Approach Scale").

describe managerial work in terms of a set of composite functions. In 1916 the father of this school, Henri Fayol, introduced his five basic managerial functions—planning, organizing, coordinating, commanding, and controlling.[4] His work received impetus in the 1930s from Luther Gulick who gave managers one of their early acronyms:

"What is the work of the chief executive? What does he do?"

The answer is POSDCORB.

POSDCORB is, of course, a made-up word designed to call attention to the various functional elements of the work of a chief executive because "administration" and "management" have lost all specific content. POSDCORB is made up of the initials and stands for the following activities:

Planning, that is working out in broad outline the things that need to be done and the methods for doing them to accomplish the purpose set for the enterprise;

Organizing, that is the establishment of the formal structure of authority through which work subdivisions are arranged, defined and coordinated for the defined objective;

Staffing, that is the whole personnel function of bringing in and training the staff and maintaining favorable conditions of work;

Directing, that is the continuous task of making decisions and embodying them in specific and general orders and instruction and serving as the leader of their enterprise;

Coordinating, that is the all important duty of interrelating the various parts of the work;

Reporting, that is keeping those to whom the executive is responsible informed as to what is going on, which thus includes keeping himself and his subordinates informed through records, research and inspection;

Budgeting, with all that goes with budgeting in the form of fiscal planning, accounting and control.

This statement of work of a chief executive is adapted from the functional analysis elaborated by Henri Fayol in his "Industrial and General Administration." It is believed that those who know administration intimately will find in this analysis a valid and helpful pattern, into which can be fitted each of the major activities and duties of any chief executive (Gulick and Urwick, 1937: 13).

POSDCORB took hold and lives on. It continues to dominate the writings on managerial work to the present day. For example, the *Harvard Business Review* chose to include in its closing issue of the 1960s "The Management Process in 3-D," an article described as providing "a way to fit together all generally accepted activities of management" (Mackenzie, 1969: 87). Coming more than half a century

---

[4] Actually, there is evidence that Fayol was extending similar works of economists dating back as far as 1770. See C. S. George, Jr., *The History of Management Thought* (Englewood Cliffs, N.J.: Prentice–Hall, 1968), p. 65.

after Fayol, this article tells the reader that managers plan, organize, staff, direct, and control. Further detail is provided. The *function* "direct," for example, comprises the *activities:* delegate, motivate, coordinate, manage differences, and manage change. Curiously, the article claims as one of its benefits "a move toward standardization of the terminology," an achievement that it demonstrates is clearly attributable to Fayol's work of 1916!

POSDCORB permeates the writings of popular theorists such as Peter Drucker and industrial leaders such as Ralph Cordiner; it appears when managers are asked to describe their work or when their job descriptions are read; it reappears in a multitude of recent articles, reports, and textbooks.[5] Apparently, POSDCORB has embedded itself in the minds of managers, teachers, and students of management.

How useful is it? If we observe a manager at work and then attempt to link his specific activities with the functions of POSDCORB, we quickly find out. Consider a chief executive who is approached by a group of dissatisfied employees threatening to resign unless a senior executive is fired, and who must spend the next few days collecting information and working out a means of dealing with this crisis. Or a manager who presents a plaque to a retiring employee. Or a chief executive who carries to a subordinate some useful information from an external board meeting.

Which of these activities may be called planning, and which may be called organizing, coordinating, or controlling? Indeed, what relationship exists between these four words and managers' activities? These four words do not, in fact, describe the actual work of managers at all. They describe certain vague objectives of managerial work; ". . . they are just ways of indicating what we need to explain" (Braybrooke, 1963: 537).

It is from those who have studied managerial work systematically that we get the most lucid criticisms of POSDCORB. In his diary study Sune Carlson writes:

> If we ask a managing director when he is coordinating, or how much coordination he has been doing during a day he would not know, and even the most highly skilled observer would not know either. The same holds true of the concepts of planning, command, organization and control, and also for most of the concepts used by Barnard in his analysis of the executive functions [6] (1951: 24).

---

[5] For examples, see Drucker (1954: 343–344), Cordiner (1965), Goodman (1969), Strong (1965: 5), Courtois (1961) and Stieglitz (1968).

[6] In *The Functions of the Executive* Barnard defined the executive functions as, "first, to provide the system of communication; second, to promote the securing of essential efforts; and, third, to formulate and define purpose" (1938: 217).

R. T. Davis, who studied the work of field sales managers, makes the following comment about planning:

> Some sales executives regarded *planning* as a field management activity. But is planning any more of an activity than are analytical, technical, and human relations skills? Does a manager really sit down periodically and announce, "Now I shall plan," without reference to such specific problems as developing and supervising salesmen, anticipating product needs, running the office, and so forth? (1957: 47).

Thus, we can find little of use in the writings of the classical school. They have served to label our areas of ignorance, and may have fulfilled the need of telling managers what they should be doing (even if it did not tell them what they did). But the classical school has for too long served to block our search for a deeper understanding of the work of the manager.

THE GREAT MAN SCHOOL

When the reader tires of the generalities of POSDCORB, he can turn to the hard facts of the biographical and autobiographical literature on managers. Here he will find a wealth of details and anecdotes, but little general theory about managerial work. The "great man school" can be followed monthly in periodicals such as *Fortune* and *Forbes*.[7] The reader in search of greater depth can study books on the great leaders of history—business, military, and political. He will learn here about "the governing elite—those who direct and control the established network of relationships in the major organized activities in our society" (Collins, Moore, and Unwalla, 1964: 3).

This large body of literature can be divided into two parts. One part analyzes managers in groups—their families, educations, social affiliations, careers, personalities. Particularly interesting examples are *The Big Business Executive* by Mabel Newcomer (1955) and *The Boss* by Roy Lewis and Rosemary Stewart (1958). These books provide a mixture of views worthy of study—the first on American corporate executives, the second on their British counterparts. No

---

[7] In its March 15, 1971, issue, *Forbes* promoted an upcoming issue with the following words: "It struck the editors of *Forbes* that while dozens and dozens of books had been written on the science of management and the psychology of management, few people had a clear idea of what the boss actually *does*" (p. 9). Then, on May 15, 1971, appeared an issue devoted to "The Role of the Chief Executive Officer." In fact, it contained 25 interesting short articles about the chief executives of as many major corporations (such as General Electric, Coca-Cola, Bank of America). The articles dealt with their current problems, strategies, philosophies, and concerns, but not with their work.

matter how interesting, this literature is of little use to us here since it does not focus on the men's work.

Slightly closer to the mark are the case studies of individual managers. Typical of these is *My Years at General Motors* by Alfred P. Sloan (1963). Often the writers focus on the time of crisis—what the protagonist did while the world watched. They also tell about the man's habits—literally everything from how he invested the enormous resources he controlled to why he skipped breakfast. This is a vast and fascinating body of literature, but it says little about the work these managers actually performed. Instead, such books concentrate on a man's styles and strategies, building their descriptions on anecdotes. Often they are devoid of generalization. The reader is occasionally told about a manager's working hours, his methods of obtaining information and making decisions, and, perhaps, something of the details of one working day. But the accounts are generally too sketchy to be used in the construction of a descriptive framework of managerial work.

Thus the "great man" literature, although interesting to the general reader and of use to the historian and perhaps the psychologist, reveals almost nothing about managerial work. It is rich in specific anecdotes, poor in general theory.

THE ENTREPRENEURSHIP SCHOOL

In this, the first of two schools that deal with the manager exclusively as decision-maker, we consider the writings of economists. In the traditional theory of microeconomics, the manager does not have decisional discretion. Faced with the need to make a decision, he acts "rationally"—he simply maximizes profit.

> Although theoretical economists have made room for the entrepreneur as a decision-maker and actor in economic events, the entrepreneur has typically been cast in the role of a rational man who makes optimal choices in an environment of very limited and highly specified dimensions. As such, his function is confined to that of a kind of computational link between impersonal forces on the one hand and foregone conclusions on the other (Collins and Moore, 1970: 7–8).

Decision-making begins with a problem, explicit goals, and all possible courses of action—as well as their consequences—laid out before the manager. He merely evaluates all these consequences, ranks alternatives in terms of goal achievement, and chooses the best one. Ambiguous problems, ill-defined and conflicting goals, and unpredictable consequences simply do not exist. Thus, the manager holds little importance for the economist. It is the founder-entrepreneur who has held his attention, for this man has one degree of freedom—he can start organizations.

Joseph Schumpeter, the economist most well-known for his views on entrepreneurship, stressed that the entrepreneur's key role was innovation at the outset: "Everyone is an entrepreneur only when he actually 'carries out new combinations,' and loses that character as soon as he has built up his business" (quoted in Collins and Moore, 1970: 10). Other economists have written of risk bearing, and various debates have ensued in the literature.[8] Is the entrepreneur simply the Innovator? Is he the supplier of capital? Or is he a broker bringing together money and ideas? No conclusion appears to have been reached, not only because the theorists could not agree on terminology, but also because these writers do not seem to concern themselves with the operational meanings of the entrepreneurial function. One is told that the entrepreneur innovates, but never how he does so.[9] Thus the entrepreneur has come to be surrounded by a mystique, as Collins, Moore, and Unwalla note:

> In some respects, the entrepreneur is an heroic figure in American folklore akin, perhaps, to Davy Crockett and other truly indigenous epic types—stalwart independents who hewed forests, climbed over the tops of mountains, built new communities, rose from nothing to something, and did all the things American heroes must have done to build a great nation (1964: 4–5).

We can conclude that the entrepreneurship school contributes to our understanding by the specification—but not by the description —of innovation (the creation of new combinations) as one component of the manager's job.

THE DECISION THEORY SCHOOL

A number of management theorists have devoted their attention to the study of the *unprogrammed* decision, thought to be the kind most commonly faced by the senior manager. To call a decision "unprogrammed" is to maintain that it is complex and poorly understood, and that the manager can use no predetermined method in its solu-

[8] Three items in our bibliography—Harbison and Myers (1959), Collins and Moore (1970), and Papandreou (1962)—discuss these debates. The reader interested in primary sources can turn to Schumpeter (1947 and 1961) and Knight (1934).

[9] A recent study reported by a sociologist and a dean of industrial relations fills this gap. In a fascinating book called *The Enterprising Man: A Behavioral Study of Independent Entrepreneurs,* based on 150 depth interviews with entrepreneurs, Collins and Moore (1970) describe these men's personalities, their backgrounds, and the means by which they projected and created their enterprises.

tion. N. H. Martin concludes from his study of managers at four organizational levels that the decisions of higher-level managers are characterized by longer time horizons and duration, greater discontinuity, more elastic time limits, more abstract data and casual relationships, and greater uncertainty.

> It is up to the executive himself to determine whether the situation warrants a change. He must search for and construct possible alternative courses of action: he must work out administrative procedures to implement the decision. Such situations may be termed "unstructured" (Martin, 1956: 254).

It is to Herbert A. Simon that this school owes its origin and much of its development. Drawing on Chester Barnard's early work (1938), Simon published *Administrative Behavior* in 1947. He then gathered together a group of researchers at Carnegie Institute of Technology (now Carnegie-Mellon University). Most important among these were James G. March, with whom he wrote *Organizations* in 1958, and Richard M. Cyert, who collaborated with March on *A Behavioral Theory of the Firm* (1963), possibly the most significant study of organizational decision-making yet published.

In essence, these researchers view decision-making, not in the economist's terms of rational choice from known alternatives, but in terms that they feel reflect more accurately the manager's real limitations. They argue that managers do not have explicit goal systems or preference functions; that a most important and neglected part of the decision-making process is the step to define a problem; that alternatives and their consequences are seldom known with clarity; and, finally, that choices are made to satisfy constraints, not to maximize objectives (that is, managers "satisfice," not maximize). Their world being complex, managers usually act in a reactive way, primarily to avoid uncertainty. Furthermore, the manager's organization is subject to a wide variety of pressures from a coalition of interest groups with differing goals. Maximization is simply not possible; the manager hopes no more than to avoid conflict. This he does by "sequential attention to goals."

> Just as the political organization is likely to resolve conflicting pressures to "go left" and "go right" by first doing one and then the other, the business firm is likely to resolve conflicting pressures to "smooth production" and "satisfy customers" by first doing one and then the other. The resulting time buffer betweeen goals permits the organization to solve one problem at a time, atttending to one goal at a time (Cyert and March, 1963: 118).

Extending their framework, these theorists depict the organization as a loosely coupled set of programs (established procedures) arranged in hierarchical order so that the high-level programs do the work of constructing and modifying the low-level programs that perform the basic work. This suggests that the manager's job is essentially one of "programming"—designing and modifying the procedures to be used by subordinates. In the words of two advocates of the Carnegie view:

> This conception [ill-defined tasks at top, well-defined at bottom] seems consonant with the way in which tasks flow into and through organizations. They often enter at the top in ill-defined, new forms. The top works them over, defines and operationalizes them, and then, if they are to become continuing tasks, *passes them down the hierarchy,* where they are again converted from their now partially operational states into highly defined states, and again passed down to specially created or adapted substructures. Presumably the top, in the interim, has turned its attention to other new, ill-defined issues (Klahr and Leavitt, 1967: 112).

This suggests—as does Martin's research cited at the opening of this section—that the work of managers is essentially unprogrammed. At the lowest end of the organization, work is routinized or programmed—familiar stimuli (customer orders, for example) are reacted to with predictable and organized responses. Managerial work is more complex—the stimulus is often ambiguous and the response is essentially one of groping for a solution. "There is no cut-and-dried method for handling the problem because it hasn't arisen before, or because its precise nature and structure are elusive or complex, or because it is so important that it deserves a custom-tailored treatment" (Simon, 1965: 59; see also March and Simon, 1958: 139–142).

But what appears to the observer to be disorganized and "unprogrammed" may simply not be understood. In other words, managers may in fact be using higher-order programs in their work—a program to define problems, a program to search for alternatives, a program to make choices.[10] This exciting possibility has led some management researchers to consider the possibility of programming managerial work—that is, of describing it systematically as a set of programs.

To date most of the interesting research on programming complex decisional processes has been concerned with contrived or simplified decisions, such as those in playing chess and proving geometric theorems (Simon, 1965, and Newell and Simon, 1972). However, a few attempts have been made to describe managerial work itself in terms of programs. These are discussed in Chapter 6.

---

[10] These correspond to Simon's trichotomy of decision-making behavior —intelligence activity, "searching the environment for conditions calling for decision"; design activity, "inventing, developing, and analyzing possible courses of action"; and choice activity, "selecting a partciular course of action from those available" (Simon, 1965: p. 54).

To conclude, the Carnegie theorists describe the manager as un-programmed decision-maker who programs the work of others. Also from them comes the intriguing noton that managerial work, which on first glance may appear to be completely unstructured, may in fact be amenable to precise description; that is, it may be programmed.

An additional and most interesting voice in this school is that of Yale economist Charles Lindblom. He presents a view of the manager as decision-maker that supplements that of the Carnegie group. In a series of publications (1959, 1965, 1968, and Braybrooke and Lindblom, 1963), Lindblom presents "disjointed incrementalism" (more simply called "the science of 'muddling through' " in his first article) as the policy-making system used by the public administrator. Arguing in the same manner as the Carnegie group, Lindblom begins by attacking the economist's rational or "synoptic" approach. In Lindblom's opinion, this approach fails because it does not recognize man's inability to cope with complex problems, the usual lack of information, the cost of analysis, the problems of timing, and the difficulties of stating realistic goals.

Lindblom's manager acts in remedial fashion, moving away from ills rather than toward goals. Only marginal alternatives—those that will not result in unanticipated change—are considered, and few consequences are investigated. Goals are flexible, being revised continually to adjust to the means available. Most significantly, the manager acts in serial, or stepwise fashion, making an incremental change, interpreting the feedback, making another change, and so on. In Lindblom's view, "policy making is typically a never-ending process of successive steps in which continual nibbling is a substitute for a good bite" (1968: 25). Lindblom's view of the manager contrasts sharply with that of the economist presented earlier:

> Man has had to be devilishly inventive to cope with the staggering difficulties he faces. His analytical methods cannot be restricted to tidy scholarly procedures. The piecemealing, remedial incrementalist or satisficer may not look like an heroic figure. He is nevertheless a shrewd, resourceful problem-solver who is wrestling bravely with a universe that he is wise enough to know is too big for him (Lindblom, 1968: 27).

Lindblom's views, although not yet substantiated by systematic empirical evidence, are thought-provoking and important. This is especially so when one considers that the economist's view of rational man has maintained its popularity. Fixed in the minds of many technocrats (operations researcher or long-range planner, for example) is the view of the manager as a rational profit-maximizer. Clearly this must change, and clearly the view of the manager "muddling through" must be married to the view of the manager as entrepreneur, so that a realistic picture of decision-making can emerge.

THE LEADER EFFECTIVENESS SCHOOL

While the last two schools focus on decision-making to the exclusion of all other managerial activities, the next three focus on leadership to the exclusion of decision-making and other activities.

The study of leadership is the study of interpersonal behavior, specifically that between the leaders and the led. "Leadership is a relational concept implying two terms: the influencing agent and the persons influenced. Without followers there can be no leader" (Katz and Kahn, 1966: 301). Researchers of the leader effectiveness school —many of them social psychologists—focus not so much on the job of managing as on the man in the job. They seek to discover what set of personality traits or managerial styles lead a manager to effective performance.

Early workers in this field looked for particular traits or constellations of traits that could be found in all successful leaders. On the whole, these researchers met with little success—significant correlations were not found for many traits, and where they were, the traits were so general (empathy, self-confidence) that they were of little help in predicting managerial performance.

In the 1960s, another group of writers—let us call them the "humanists"—focused their attention on managerial styles, criticizing the autocratic, task-oriented style and advocating the participative, people-oriented style. More recently empirical social psychologists have been arguing for situational or contingency theories of leader effectiveness. As they see it, no one style of managing is always best; the effectiveness of a particular style of leadership—autocratic or participative—depends on a number of situational factors, including the reward structure of the particular organization, the power of the manager's position, the nature of the work he supervises, the climate in his organization, and his own skills, personality, and expectations.[11]

To conclude, the leader effectiveness school is only beginning to say something about those factors that produce successful leaders. Excessive attention to two basic styles—autocratic and participative —and a lack of understanding of the interpersonal behaviors of leaders have slowed its progress.

[11] Cecil Gibb (1969) presents a thorough review of the literature on leadership, with special attention to theories of leader effectiveness, in his paper in *The Handbook of Social Psychology*. For typical examples of the humanist view, see McGregor (1960) and Likert (1961); for statements of contingency theories, see Fiedler (1966) and Campbell *et al.* (1970).

THE LEADER POWER SCHOOL

A school of leadership different from the one just discussed concerns itself with power and influence—with the manipulative prerogatives of the leader. Writers of this school ask: To what extent can the leader control his environment? To find out, they study the leader's ability to use power to evoke desired responses from subordinates and peers. Some studies focus on the position and the discretion it allows the incumbent; others focus on particular individuals and how they use this discretion.

Melville Dalton, in his famous study of middle managers, uses the former approach. As a sociologist, he collected his data while living in organizations as a participant observer. His key conclusion is that the informal social forces of bureaucracy tend to dominate individual action.

> The individual in the large organization or mobile society, like the uncalculating animals, is also a defenseless creature who calculatingly practices deception for safety's sake against the invisible threats around him (Dalton, 1959: 270).

In another well-known study, political scientist Richard Neustadt (1960) analyzes the American Presidency and three men who held that office, and draws somewhat different conclusions. His book, appropriately titled *Presidential Power: The Politics of Leadership,* exposes the informal intrigue and cunning required to deal with power, but Neustadt makes clear that the effective power of the President is largely dependent on the style of the man and on how he approaches his job. (Neustadt's study is reviewed briefly in Appendix A.)

There is, in addition, some interesting general theory on leader power. Much of it is reviewed in a paper entitled "Influence, Leadership, and Control" by Darwin Cartwright (1965) in *The Handbook of Organizations.* His review focuses on the means by which one man (O) influences another (P). The review is long and difficult, with the terms *authority, persuasion, power, influence, control,* and *leadership* sprinkled throughout. The theme, repeated at many points, is the categorizing of forms of power. The five-part scheme of French and Raven that Cartwright cites appears to be most comprehensive:

> *Reward power* is based on P's belief that O has the ability to mediate rewards for him.
>
> *Coercive power* is based on P's belief that O has the ability to mediate punishments for him.
>
> *Referent power* is based on P's identification with O. By identification French and Raven mean "a feeling of oneness of P with O, or a desire for such an identity."
>
> *Legitimate power* stems from internalized values in P which dic-

tate that O has the right to influence P and that P has an obligation to accept this influence. In formal organizations legitimate power is usually attached to an office, and the occupant of the office then has the right to exert influence over a specified domain of people and range of activities.

Expert power is based on P's belief that O has some special knowledge or expertness (Cartwright, 1965: 28–30).

Clearly, to understand the work of the leader it is necessary to study his sources of power and the extent to which he is able to control his own job. In some of the literature on leadership, a distinction is made between informal leadership, where the leader is chosen by the followers (as in a street gang), and formal leadership, or "headship," where the leader is appointed from above (as in most business organizations). Whereas the informal leader can rely on referent power, managers must rely basically on legitimate power and the reward and coercive power it generates (such as the right to promote, increase salary, terminate employment).

THE LEADER BEHAVIOR SCHOOL

A number of writers and researchers have analyzed the actual content of the manager's job by studying the behavior of the incumbents. Although they are here brought together under the title "leader behavior school," their writings are alike only in a concern for a common issue. Their methods vary widely; they have not built on each other's work; and, most important, no central theme or common thread of conclusions has emerged from their studies. Hence, one must study them one by one, extracting from each what appears to be useful.

A brief look at some of the more interesting studies should give the reader the flavor of the literature of this school. Each study is reviewed in more detail in Appendix A.

In his analysis of leader behavior, George Homans (1950) develops a number of interesting conclusions from William F. Whyte's study of a street gang. He finds, for example, that the leader is the best-informed member of his group, and that even in street gangs there emerges a hierarchy of leader authority. The analysis of the manager's job in Chapters 3 and 4 draws on the remarkable similarity between many of Homan's conclusions, based on a study of a most informal leadership situation, and conclusions based on studies of formal managers.

Hodgson, Levinson, and Zaleznik (1965) analyze the three-member top management team of a hospital and draw interesting conclusions concerning the way members of the team share the work along task and emotional dimensions. Their work provides the basis for theory on job variations presented in Chapter 5. Stieglitz (1969) questioned 280 chief executive officers in American and foreign businesses and produced an eight-part job description strongly reminiscent of POSDCORB; he talks, for example, about things like formulating policy, determining overall objectives and plans. In two studies of foreman behavior, Wikstrom (1967) describes erosion of the foreman's authority and means for reversing the trend, while Walker, Guest, and Turner (1956) delve into a number of specific aspects of the foreman's work (meeting emergencies, staffing, and so on).

Finally, two items in the appendix are described in particular detail. The Ohio State Leadership Studies represent the most ambitious examination of managerial behavior yet undertaken. Spanning three decades, these studies comprise investigations of a great number of managers in business, the military, labor unions, and many other situations. Similar methods were used in all—managers were given questionnaires that asked them to rate a large number of statements in terms of their own jobs. Statistical techniques were used to group the answers in categories that would describe different aspects of leader behavior. Considering the enormous amount of effort expended in these studies, they provide relatively little of use in describing the work of managers. As noted in Appendix A, the categories they came up with seldom went far beyond POSDCORB technology. Perhaps this reflects the ways in which the questions were produced in the first place; perhaps it reflects the fact that these researchers were studying the managers' *perceptions* of their jobs rather than the jobs *themselves*. (See Appendix A for details on these points.)

The final study in our review of the leader behavior school is that of Leonard Sayles (1964). Sayles lived within an organization for a period of time, recording whatever seemed of interest "with no pretence of having conducted a scientific experiment" (p. vii). His subsequent description of the behavior of lower and middle-level managers is certainly the most significant statement about managerial work among those reviewed. Sayles describes the manager as monitor, as leader, and as participant in external work flows. Perhaps the most interesting theme of the analysis is the notion of "moving equilibrium." Sayles claims that managers must react to pressures and introduce short-term adjustments or long-term structural changes, balancing stability and change so as to achieve "a dynamic type of stability" (1964: 163). We return to Sayles's study repeatedly in our discussion of the manager's roles in Chapter 4.

Each of these studies (treating the Ohio State group as an entity) is distinct in its orientation and conclusions. Nevertheless, conclusions extracted from some of them, when worked into a framework of managerial roles, indicate a number of basic features in the content of the manager's job. Chapter 4, which describes the manager's working roles, draws on these conclusions.

THE WORK ACTIVITY SCHOOL

This last school of study on the manager's job stands at the other extreme from the classical school. This is the school of inductive research, in which the work activities of managers are analyzed systematically; conclusions are drawn only when they can be supported by the empirical evidence. Furthermore, unlike those of the leader behavior school, these studies are most decidedly linked together. The research methods used are largely similar, and in most cases there are explicit attempts to incorporate the findings of previous studies in the development of new conclusions.

The more significant group of studies were carried out by the "diary method"; the managers themselves recorded various aspects of each activity (duration, place, participants) on a precoded pad. A number of diary studies are reviewed in the appendix; particular attention is given to two—Sune Carlson's study of nine Swedish managing directors, which set the pattern for all subsequent studies, and Rosemary Stewart's study of 160 senior and middle managers in Britain, certainly the most extensive and the most useful of the diary studies. Figure 1 reproduces a sample of Carlson's diary recording form.

Another group of studies use two observational techniques— activity sampling, in which the researcher records the manager's activities at random time intervals, and structured observation, in which the data of the diary pad (perhaps other data as well) are recorded by the researcher instead of the manager. The observation studies reviewed in Appendix A generated essentially the same conclusions as those by the diary method.

Table 1 lists many of the published diary and observation studies. In all, ten diary studies and four by observation are included.[12] At least 579 different managers, primarily in business organizations, but at all levels in the hierarchy, were studied for periods ranging from one day to one month.

In discussing the results of the work-activity studies, we must draw a basic distinction between the *content* (mentioned in the previous section) and the *characteristics* of managerial work. A researcher studying the job of the manager may wish to know such things as where managers work, with whom they do so, how long they

---

[12] Wirdenius (1958) also reviews a number of Scandinavian studies (by observation, diary, and activity sampling) which have not been published in English.

Date: 3/11 49   Telephone: In ☐   Out ☐

Time: 10:45 – 11.05

Place (other than own office): _____

Person: _____

_____

Manuf. dir.	☐	Comptr.	☐	Adv. dir.	☐
Works man. A		Account.		Pers. dir.	
Works man. B	X	Sales dir. Swed.		Assistant	
Organ. dir.		Sales dir. exp.		Secr.	

A. Question handled		Kind of action	
Finance, legal	☐	Getting information	X
Accounting		Systematizing information	
Buying		Taking decisions	
Production	X	Confirming or correcting decisions of others	
Product research	X		
Sales		Giving orders	
Personnel		Advising, explaining	
Public relations		Inspecting, reviewing	
Organiz. planning		Executing	
_____		_____	
_____		_____	
_____		_____	
Private		Personal development	

B. Question handled		C. Question handled	
Development	X	Policy	
Current operations		Application	X

Figure 1. Diary Recording Form Designed by Carlson for Use by the Managers

Source: Carlson, 1951: 46.

work, what media they use (telephone, for example). Answers to questions like these give the *characteristics* of managerial work. Or, the researcher may wish to know what managers do in their work— that is, what activities they carry out and why. Answers to these questions describe the *content* of managerial work. Categorizations of work

Table 1. Empirical Studies of Managerial Work Activities

Researcher	Year Reported	Method Used	Subjects	Period of Study (Days)	Special Interests
Carlson	1951	Diary	9 Senior managers (managing directors)	216	Finding common behavior patterns (particularly communication) in the work of managing directors
Burns	1954	Diary	4 Middle managers	103	Relationship of managers in one departmental group
Burns	1957	Diary	76 Senior and middle managers	1520[a]	How managers spend their time
Copeman	1963	Diary	58 Senior and middle managers	290(?)	Comparison of the work of chief executives and department heads
Dubin, Spray	1964	Diary	8 Senior and middle managers	80	How managers spend their time
Brewer, Tomlinson	1964	Diary	6 Senior managers	105	Decision-making behavior
Horne, Lupton	1965	Diary	66 Middle managers	330[b]	How managers spend their time
Thomason	1966-67	Diary	Various configurations of managers	not reported	Communication centers
Lawler, Porter, Tennenbaum	1968	Diary	105 Middle and lower level managers	525	Manager's reactions toward interaction episodes
Stewart	1967	Diary	160 Senior and middle managers	3200[b]	Variations in managerial jobs
Kelly	1964	Activity sampling	4 Foremen (section managers)	60[b]	How section managers spend their time
Ponder	1957	Observation	24 Foremen	48	Foreman effectiveness
Landsberger	1962	Observation	3 Middle managers	6	Horizontal relationships
Guest, Jasinski	1956	Observation	56 Foremen	56	How foremen spend their time

[a] Estimated; Burns only states that each was studied for three, four, or five weeks.
[b] Assumes an average work week of five days.

content and purpose lead to statements of *functions* or *roles*. The first type of analysis would tell us, for example, that a manager worked long hours in a given week, whereas the second would show that he did so because he was deeply involved in labor negotiations.

Drawing this distinction makes it clear from the outset that work-activity studies of managers' jobs provide a number of significant conclusions about characteristics of managerial work but almost nothing about work content.

A number of researchers, including Sune Carlson, have attempted to collect data on job content. Their diary pads include sections where the manager can code their activities in categories such as "getting information" and "regulating." The conclusions they have drawn are, however, of such a meager nature that when Rosemary Stewart came to conduct her extensive diary study in the middle 1960s, she explicitly avoided recording job content. She explains:

> There is no problem if one is asking unambiguous questions such as "Where is he working?" "Is he alone or with someone else?" and "Who is he with?" . . . Such investigations tell one something about how the manager spends his working day, but little about the content of his work, which is the most interesting part of what he does. Those who have sought to describe it have usually thought in terms of the classic management functions, such as planning and organizing, or of activities like giving information or making decisions. The objection to these descriptions is that such activities cannot be defined so unambiguously that different managers recording the same tasks will necessarily classify them in the same way. This is even true for such apparently less ambiguous classifications of work as production or sales. It may be a mixture of the two, or production looked at from one point of view and sales looked at from another (1968a: 81).

The difficulty appears to be with the diary method itself. It requires that managers who do the recording be armed with precoded pads so that they can code each activity quickly (see Figure 1). To design the form, therefore, one must have a few unambiguous categories to be checked off by the manager. As Burns notes:

> The use of a simplified diary schedule of this kind means that the amount of information contained in each is extremely limited; it amounts to a description of one's behavior in a language of less than fifty verbs and nouns . . . (1957: 46).

Thus, to design the form the researcher must have some idea what managers do. For a factor such as "place of work," one need merely list: own office, office of associate, plant, outside company, and so forth. But what words could be used to describe the content of managerial activities? As a matter of fact, nowhere in the literature is content categorized, except in the vague words of POSDCORB. The challenge for the work-activity researchers was to find the words that belonged on the diary form, that is, to develop a useful statement of the content of the manager's activities. In the words of Hodgson, Levinson, and Zaleznik, who used the same argument in discussing the questionnaire method:

> To construct questionnaires, we had to know the salient dimensions of the situation we were studying. It took about a year of field work to find them out, and by that time we were already obtaining so much data that questionnaires would have been of no incremental value . . . (1965: 481).

My own study of five chief executives (Mintzberg, 1968), which is described in detail in Appendix C, also falls into the work activity school. However, because the prime objective was to describe work content, and because the diary studies had failed to do so, a different methodology was used. The study used structured observation, but with one important distinction from previous uses. The categories were developed during and after observation. An attempt was made to describe the "purpose" of each of the events observed (as well as other features, such as place, participants, duration) in the words that seemed appropriate at the time of observation. The formal categorization was carried out at a later time, when all data were in and when there was time to do it carefully. This approach retained the basic advantage of the diary method—systematic recording of field data—but also maintained the flexibility to develop content categories inductively. As a result, the study develops a new description of managerial work content as well as a number of conclusions on work characteristics that reinforce the findings of earlier work-activity studies.

Chapter 3 presents in detail the findings on managerial characteristics. Let us note at this point that the work-activity studies produced evidence of some remarkable similarities that cut across all levels of management, from chief executives to foremen. For example, virtually all the studies emphasize the importance of face-to-face communication; they note, as well, the high incidence of horizontal and lateral transfers of information in managerial jobs. The characteristics of fragmentation and interruption at the chief executive level are pointed out by Carlson (1951), and, for the foreman level, by Guest (1955–1956). Both Guest and Stewart, studying different levels of management, emphasize the variety and lack of repetition in managerial work; Guest and Carlson, researching the two ends of the hierarchy, note the hectic pace. No doubt some managers do not fit these patterns, but there would be little theory in the social sciences if researchers were restricted to conclusions that had no exceptions.

We have evidence of differences as well. Thomason (1966,

1967) notes the existence of specialized centers of information. Carlson's finding about long working hours at the chief executive level contrasts with the findings of Horne and Lupton (1965) for the middle manager level. And Burns (1967) points out that higher-level managers tend to be less specialized than those at lower levels.

There has been some discussion in the literature on whether different managerial jobs are characterized by their essential similarities or by their differences.[13] Surely, the ultimate answer must be that there are certain essential features common to all manager's jobs, and that there are also uniquenesses that distinguish every type of managerial job. We must seek first to isolate the common features and describe the basic job of managing; only then can we understand the differences. Fortunately, the work-activity studies provide a rich base of hard data to help isolate important similarities and differences in the characteristics of managerial work.

FOUR ASPECTS OF MANAGERIAL WORK

We have reviewed eight schools of thought on the manager's job. They comprise a variety of approaches and research methods, and they reach a variety of conclusions. Most of them tell us little about the job of managing, but by taking them as a group we can begin to piece together some reasonable description. The next four chapters, which constitute the heart of this book, combine evidence from the published literature with evidence from my own study to describe the job of the manager from four points of view.

The next two chapters deal with the basic job. Chapter 3 focuses on job characteristics and draws its findings from the work-activity studies, the results of which suggest six important sets of work characteristics common to all managers' jobs.

Chapter 4 describes the content of the manager's job in terms of ten basic roles. This framework derives from my own study of the work of five chief executives, but it is supported by the evidence of a number of empirical studies of the behavior of different types of managers. It draws in particular on the findings of two decision-making and three leadership schools of thought on managerial work.

In Chapter 5, we turn our attention to variations in managers' work, using the common roles and characteristics as a basis for investigating the differences. A contingency theory is suggested in which variations are attributed to the job environment, the job itself (its level and function in the organization), the person in the job, and the

[13] Campbell et al. (1970) and Nealey and Fiedler (1968) discuss this issue. Comments on their conclusions appear in the opening section of Chapter 5.

situation of the moment. Chapter 5 generates propositions about job differences, drawing on almost all of the empirical studies of managerial work that can be found.

Chapter 6 takes up the interesting question of programming the manager's job, as suggested in the work of the decision theory school. It deals, in more detail, with the concept of programming, and then presents preliminary descriptions of some of the programs managers apparently use. Chapter 6 also discusses at some length the role of the management scientist and those areas in which he can influence the manager's effectiveness.[14]

The final chapter opens with an integrated review of the four bodies of theory—characteristics, roles, variations, and programs. It concludes with an assessment of the implications of our findings—for managers, teachers of managers, management scientists, and researchers.

[14] We describe the relationship between these four bodies of theory and the research data in more detail at the end of Appendix C. See in particular Figure 19.

3
Some Distinguishing Characteristics of Managerial Work

I don't want it good—
I want it Tuesday!

Contemporary adage

In this chapter we focus our attention on various characteristics of the manager's work as a first step toward a
comprehensive description. We shall examine six sets of
characteristics, dealing with (1) the quantity and pace
of the manager's work, (2) the patterns in his activities,
(3) the relationship, in his work, between action and reflection, (4) his use of different media, (5) his relationship to a variety of contacts, and (6) the interplay between his rights and duties.

The conclusions of this chapter are based primarily on the findings of the empirical studies of work
activities discussed at the end of the previous chapter.
These studies, carried out primarily by direct observa-

tion and by having managers record their activities on diary pads, have generated a number of findings that show remarkable similarities for managers at all levels of the hierarchy. Work-activity studies have been undertaken on foremen, middle and senior managers, and chief executives. For some of the illustrative and anecdotal materials I drew on my own study of the chief executives of five middle- to large-sized organizations.

The reader should note that in this chapter and the next the term *organization* describes that unit directly under the manager's formal authority. Therefore, the words "manager" and his "organization" can mean a "president" and his "company," a "supervisor" and his "branch," or a "foreman" and his "shop." The manager's organization may in fact be a subunit of a larger organization (a division of a company, for example), and "outsiders" may in fact be other members of the larger organization who are not in a direct line relationship with the manager in question.

MUCH WORK AT UNRELENTING PACE

How hard do managers work? Studies of chief executives suggest that they seldom stop thinking about their jobs. In "How Hard Do Executives Work?" Whyte reports that the chief executives he interviewed claimed to work four nights out of five. One night was spent at the office; and one entertaining; and "on two other nights he goes home, not to a sanctuary so much as to a branch office" (1954: 109). Carlson discusses the effects of this pace:

> For the chief executives themselves this excessive working load has many unpleasant effects. It means that their opportunities to be with their families or to see their private friends are severely curtailed, and it entails travelling in night trains and evenings and weekends spent away from home. In some cases it also causes a certain intellectual isolation. . . . They seldom have time to read anything but technical and economic literature or to go to a theatre or a concert (1951: 75).

Studies of middle- and lower-level managers have, significantly, not found evidence of long hours on the job (for example, see Horne and Lupton, 1965). But there is evidence from these studies that the amount of work the managers feel compelled to do during regular hours is great and the pace is unrelenting. Guest found that foremen engaged in between 237 and 1073 incidents per day without a break in the pace:

Obviously, these foremen had little idle time. They had to handle many pressing problems in rapid-fire order. They had to "take" constant interruption, to retain many problems in their minds simultaneously, and to juggle priorities for action (1956: 480).

In their study of senior and middle managers, Dubin and Spray commented that " . . . the level of work activity was pretty constant throughout the day" (1964: 102). And Davis quotes one of his students, on the job of the field sales manager, "He does one damn thing after another!" (1957: 21)

My own study of chief executives found no break in the pace of activity during office hours. The mail (average of 36 pieces per day), telephone calls (average of 5 per day), and meetings (average of 8) accounted for almost every minute from the moment these men entered their offices in the morning until they departed in the evenings. A true break seldom occurred. Coffee was taken during meetings, and lunchtime was almost always devoted to formal or informal meetings. When free time appeared, ever-present subordinates quickly usurped it. If these managers wished to have a change of pace, they had two means at their disposal—the observational tour and the light discussions that generally preceded scheduled meetings. But these were not regularly scheduled breaks, and they were seldom totally unrelated to the issue at hand—managing the organization.

Thus the work of managing an organization may be described as taxing. The quantity of work to be done, or that the manager chooses to do, during the day is substantial and the pace is unrelenting. After hours, the chief executive (and probably many other managers as well) appears to be able to escape neither from an environment that recognizes the power and status of his position nor from his own mind, which has been well trained to search continually for new information.

Why do managers adopt this pace and workload? One major reason is the inherently open-ended nature of the job. The manager is responsible for the success of his organization, and there are really no tangible mileposts where he can stop and say, "Now my job is finished." The engineer finishes the design of a casting on a certain day, the lawyer wins or loses his case at some moment in time. The manager must always keep going, never sure when he has succeeded, never sure when his whole organization may come down around him because of some miscalculation. As a result, the manager is a person with a perpetual preoccupation. He can never be free to forget his job, and he never has the pleasure of knowing, even temporarily, that there is nothing else he can do. No matter what kind of managerial job he has, he always carries the nagging suspicion that he might be able to contribute just a little bit more. Hence he assumes an unrelenting pace in his work.

ACTIVITY CHARACTERIZED BY BREVITY, VARIETY, AND FRAGMENTATION

Most work in society involves specialization and concentration. Machine operators may learn to make one part and then spend weeks doing so; engineers and programmers often spend months designing a single bridge or a computer program; salesmen often spend their working lives selling one line of products. The manager can expect no such concentration of efforts. Rather, his activities are characterized by brevity, variety, and fragmentation.[1] Guest, whose foremen averaged 583 incidents each day, comments:

> Interestingly enough, the characteristics of a foreman's job—interruption, variety, discontinuity—are diametrically opposed to those of most hourly operator jobs, which are highly rationalized, repetitive, uninterrupted, and subject to the steady, unvarying rhythm of the moving conveyor (1955–1956: 481).

In my own study, the chief executives averaged 36 written and 16 verbal contacts each day, almost every one dealing with a distinct issue. Figure 2 provides an indication of the great variety in the content of verbal contacts and mail.[2]

A subordinate calls to report a fire in one of the facilities; then the mail, much of it insignificant, is processed; a subordinate interrupts to tell of an impending crisis with a public group; a retiring employee is ushered in to receive a plaque; later there is discussion of bidding on a multi-million-dollar contract; after that, the manager complains that office space in one department is being wasted. Throughout each working day the manager encounters this great variety of activity. Most surprising, the significant activity is interspersed with the trivial in no particular pattern. Hence the manager must be prepared to shift moods quickly and frequently.

The data of this study were analyzed to see whether there were activity patterns, but with minor exceptions,[3] none was evident. In other words, it cannot be argued, based on the data available, that mornings differed from afternoons, that certain activities took place at special times of the day, or that certain days of the week differed from others.[4] Certain monthly and seasonal patterns exist in some

---

[1] Guest (1955–1956), Ponder (1957), Carlson (1951), and Stewart (1967), all draw attention to these characteristics in their empirical studies.

[2] See Appendix C for a description of each of these work-content categories.

[3] For example, days usually started and ended with desk work, and activities of long duration almost always were followed by sessions of desk work.

[4] It was, however, possible to classify five kinds of days. (1) "Catch-up" days, generally following trips or extremely heavy schedules, find the manager

Distribution of Incoming Mail by Purpose

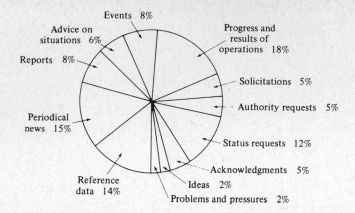

Distribution of Hours in Verbal Contact by Purpose

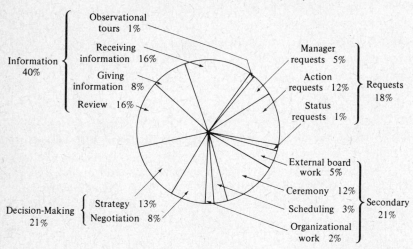

Figure 2. The Purposes of Managerial Activities *a*

a Based on five weeks of observation of chief executives' work.

spending much time at his desk catching up on the mail, returning telephone calls, scheduling appointments, and making himself available informally to subordinates who have been looking for him. (2) "Crisis days" find the manager delaying all that can be delayed so that he can concentrate on a major disturbance that has suddenly developed. (3) A "free day" sees few scheduled meetings; instead, old mail is processed, tours may be taken, and subordinates, who abhor an activity vacuum, are received. (One such day was the busiest of the 25, when one chief executive had only 3 scheduled meetings, but 14 desk work sessions, 17 unscheduled meetings, and 5 tours.) (4) "Heavily scheduled days" find the manager in scheduled meetings most of the day, wedging in only important telephone calls and urgent mail. (5) "Normal days" bring the usual heavy load of mail, callers, and meetings (scheduled and unscheduled).

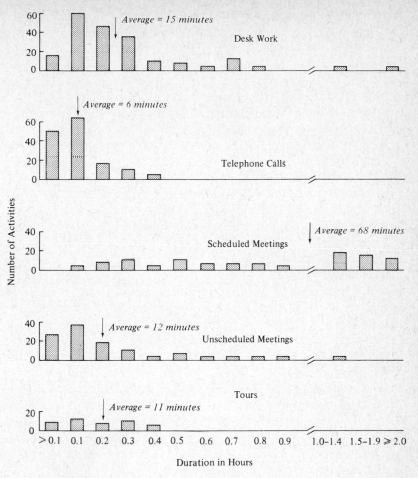

Figure 3. Frequency Distribution of Managerial Activities by Duration (in hours) [a]

[a] Based on five weeks of observation of chief executives' work.

managerial jobs, but there is little evidence of shorter-term patterns in this study or in others.

The brevity of many of the manager's activities is also most surprising. Figure 3 shows the distribution of activities by duration for the chief executives of our study. Half of the observed activities were completed in less than nine minutes, and only one-tenth took more than an hour. In effect, the managers were seldom able or willing to spend much time on any one issue in any one session. Telephone calls were brief and to the point (averaging 6 minutes), and desk work sessions and unscheduled meetings seldom lasted as long as half an hour (they averaged 15 and 12 minutes, respectively). Only scheduled meetings, usually dealing with a multitude of issues or one complex issue, commonly took more than an hour. But even an average duration of 68 minutes seems meager, given the nature of the issues discussed. The same characteristic of brevity was reflected in the treatment of mail. A few of the men expressed dislike for long memos, and most long reports and periodicals were skimmed quickly.

The characteristic of brevity, notable at the chief executive level, becomes more pronounced as one moves down the hierarchy. At the foreman level both Guest (1955–1956) and Ponder (1957) found extreme brevity, in the first case 48 seconds average duration per activity, in the second, in the vicinity of 2 minutes.

Both Carlson (1951) and Stewart (1967) emphasize the characteristics of fragmentation and interruption in managerial work. Rosemary Stewart, who studied 160 managers for four weeks by the diary method, found that they averaged only nine periods of at least one-half hour without interruption. And 12 out of the 25 contacts per day were recorded in the "fleeting contacts" section of her diary. Carlson analyzes one managing director's work in particular and notes that only 12 times in the 35 days of the study did he work undisturbed in his office for intervals of at least 23 minutes. "All they knew was that they scarcely had time to start on a new task or to sit down and light a cigarette before they were interrupted by a visitor or a telephone call" (1951: 73–74).

Carlson draws the conclusion that managers can easily lengthen the average duration of their activities. This would simply involve freeing themselves from interruption by making better use of their secretaries and by being more willing to delegate work. But Carlson begs one important question—do managers *choose* to have brevity, variety, and fragmentation in their work?

The five chief executives of my own study appeared to be properly protected by their secretaries, and there was no reason to believe that these men were inferior delegators. In fact, there was evidence that they *chose* not to free themselves of interruption or to give themselves much free time. To a large extent, it was the chief executives themselves who determined the durations of their activities. For example, the tours that they chose to take could not be interrupted by the telephone, yet they lasted, on an average, only 11 minutes. Furthermore, the managers, not the other parties, terminated many of the meetings and telephone calls, and the managers frequently left meetings before they ended. They frequently interrupted their desk work to place telephone calls or to request that subordinates come by. One chief executive located his desk so that he could look down a long hallway. The door was usually open, and his subordinates were continually coming into his office. He fully realized that by moving his desk, closing his door, or changing the rules his secretary used to

screen callers, he could easily have eliminated many of these interruptions.

Why, then, is there indication that managers prefer brevity and
interruption in their work? To some extent, certainly, the manager
tolerates interruption because he does not wish to discourage the flow
of current information. Furthermore, the manager may become ac-
customed to the variety in his work, and he may find that boredom develops easily. But it would appear that these factors can only partly
explain the manager's behavior.

A more significant explanation might be that the manager becomes conditioned by his workload. He develops a sensitive appreciation for the *opportunity cost* of his own time—the benefits forgone
by doing one thing instead of another. Thus, he takes on much work
because he realizes his own worth to the organization. In addition, he
is aware of the ever-present assortment of obligations associated with
his job—the mail that cannot be delayed, the callers that must be attended to, the meetings that require his participation. In other words,
no matter what he *is* doing, the manager is plagued by what he *might*
do and what he *must* do.

In effect, the manager is encouraged by the realities of his work
to develop a particular personality—to overload himself with work, to
do things abruptly, to avoid wasting time, to participate only when the
value of participation is tangible, to avoid too great an involvement
with any one issue. To be superficial is, no doubt, an occupational
hazard of managerial work. In order to succeed, the manager must,
presumably, become proficient at his superficiality.[5]

PREFERENCE FOR LIVE ACTION

There is strong indication that the manager gravitates toward
the more active elements of his work—activities that are current, specific, and well-defined, and those that are nonroutine.

This was demonstrated in a number of ways in my study—in
the treatment of mail, for example. Despite the fact that only 22 percent of the five chief executives' time was spent on desk work, a number of comments suggested that mail processing was considered to be
a burden. This can be explained, in part at least, by the age of the information in the mails, by the dullness of a medium that lacks immediate feedback, and by the fact, to be discussed at a later point,
that only a small part of the mail in this study tended to be of specific

[5] To the manager who has left the job of specialist, this may create
problems of adjustment. For example, the chief executive of the school system
in my study expressed regret that he could not become more deeply involved
in curriculum development. No doubt, those who remain in the job have, or
develop, particular personality traits. These merit careful study.

and immediate use to the managers. The treatment of the information sent to these managers suggests that they did little with routine information. Of the 40 routine operating reports received during the 5 weeks, only 2 elicited written reactions. And the 104 periodicals received evoked only 4 pieces of output mail. In contrast, replies to written requests accounted for about half the managers' total output mail. Finally, it might be noted that the mail categorized as "advice on situations"—that related to live problems and opportunities—tended to be handled in the most active way. In summary, the chief executives seemed to react to the active, ad hoc mail that dealt with concrete, live situations, and seemed to be less concerned with the routine reports and regular periodicals.

The managers' desire to have the most current information was strongly and frequently demonstrated. An outstanding example was one chief executive's receipt of the ratings of a sponsored television show less than 24 hours after its broadcast. A most interesting phenomenon was that of "instant communication"—the very current, "hot" information that flowed frequently and informally, by telephone or unscheduled meeting. It received top priority, often interrupting meetings, and it easily satisfied the secretaries' criteria for entry to the chief executives' offices. Often they redesigned workdays or redirected meetings because of some "instant communication" they received.

Thus there is evidence in this study that the manager demonstrates a strong thirst for current information and, conversely, that he tends to do little with the many routine reports that his organization provides for him. Because he wants his information quickly, the manager seems willing to accept a high degree of uncertainty. In other words, gossip, speculation, and hearsay form a most important part of the manager's information diet.

Definiteness and lack of routine were suggested also by the way the chief executives scheduled their time. One surprising statistic to emerge from the study is that only 1 verbal contact in 14 was held on a regular or "clocked" basis, the other 13 being ad hoc. Carlson and Neustadt note in their empirical studies of chief executives that these men reacted first to what was definite and concrete in their schedules. To Neustadt, "Deadlines rule his personal agenda" (1960: 155), and to Carlson:

> There is a tendency for business executives to become slaves to their appointment diaries—they get a kind of "diary complex." One can seldom see two business executives talking together without their diaries in their hands, and they feel rather lost unless they know that they have these diaries within easy reach. When they start their working day they will look up what they have to do, and whatever is in the diary they will fulfil punctually and efficiently. If one wants to be sure of getting something done by this group of

people, one has to see that it gets into their diaries. One should never ask a busy executive to promise to do something e.g. "next week" or even "next Friday." Such vague requests do not get entered into his appointment diary. No, one has to state a specific time, say, Friday 4.15 P.M., then it will be put down and in due course done. The more exactly the time is specified, the more certain it will be that the task will be attended to (1951: 71).

Finally, with few exceptions managerial activities in my study concerned specific rather than general issues. During working hours it was rare to see a chief executive participating in abstract discussion or carrying out general planning.[6] "Observational tours"—the one totally open-ended activity of this study—accounted for only 1 percent of the managers' time.

Clearly, the classic view of the manager as planner is not in accord with reality. If the manager does indeed plan, it is not by locking his door, puffing on his pipe, and thinking great thoughts. Rather, in the words of Leonard Sayles:

We thus prefer not to consider planning and decision making as separate, distinct activities in which the manager engages. They are inextricably bound up in the warp and woof of the interaction pattern, and it is a false abstraction to separate them.
A good example of this is Dean Acheson's description of what he believed to be the naïveté of the then new Secretary of State Dulles' expectations concerning his job:
"He told me that he was not going to work as I had done, but would free himself from involvement with what he referred to as personnel and administrative problems, in order to have more time to think.
"I did not comment, but was much struck by the conjunction of ideas. I wondered how it would turn out. For it had been my experience that thought was not of much use without knowledge and guidance, and that who should give me both and how competent they would be must depend on who chose, dealt with, assigned and promoted these people and established the forms of organization within which they worked."
Later in this same essay, Acheson expresses criticism of the view that even the President (Eisenhower at that time) needs more time for isolated contemplation:
"This absorption with the Executive as Emerson's 'Man Thinking,' surrounded by a Cabinet of Rodin statues bound in an oblivion of thought . . . seemed to me unnatural. Surely thinking is not so difficult, so hard to come by, so solemn as all this." (1964: 208–209)

---

[6] There was only one real case of this in the 5 weeks. The superintendent held a regular meeting with a group of teachers to discuss general educational problems and ideas.

To conclude, we have further indication that the manager adopts particular behavior patterns as a result of the nature of his work. The pressure of the managerial environment does not encourage the development of reflective planners, the classical literature notwithstanding. The job breeds adaptive information-manipulators who prefer the live, concrete situation. The manager works in an environment of stimulus-response, and he develops in his work a clear preference for live action.   •

ATTRACTION TO THE VERBAL MEDIA

The manager uses five basic media: the mail (documented communication), the telephone (purely verbal), the unscheduled meeting (informal face-to-face), the scheduled meeting (formal face-to-face), and the tour (visual). Certain fundamental differences exist among these. Documented communication requires the use of a formal subset of the language, and involves long feedback delays. All verbal media can transmit, in addition to the messages contained in the words used, messages sent by voice inflection and by delays in reaction. In addition, face-to-face media carry information transmitted by facial expression and by gesture.[7]

The most significant finding concerning media is that managers demonstrate very strong attraction to the verbal media. Virtually every empirical study of managerial time allocation draws attention to the great proportion of time spent in verbal communication, with estimates ranging from 57 percent of time spent in face-to-face communication by foremen (Guest, 1956) to 89 percent of episodes in verbal interaction by middle managers in a manufacturing company (Lawler, Porter, and Tennenbaum, 1968). Rosemary Stewart (1967), who collected the most extensive data, found that her middle and senior managers averaged only 34 percent of their time alone, most of the rest in informal communication, and Burns (1954) found that conversation consumed 80 percent of the middle managers' time. My own findings bear this out. Figure 4 indicates that verbal interaction accounted for 78 percent of the five managers' time and 67 percent of their activities.

We turn now to a detailed examination of each medium. The figures cited are drawn from my study of five chief executives.

---

[7] One manager recounted an interesting story that highlights the differences between face-to-face and documented communication. At head office, a number of people had developed a dislike for a Swiss employee. She used the word "demand" instead of "ask" in her memos. Only when she visited the head office was the problem resolved. In face-to-face contact, it became clear that she was simply using the word that seemed most appropriate to her. The verb "to ask" in French is *demander!*

Distribution of Hours

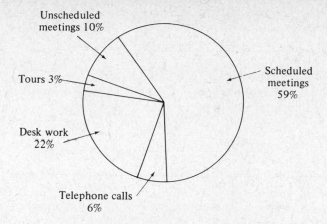

Unscheduled
meetings 10%

Tours 3%

Scheduled
meetings
59%

Desk work
22%

Telephone calls
6%

Distribution of Number of Activities

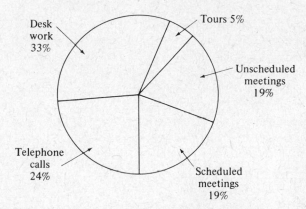

Desk
work
33%

Tours 5%

Unscheduled
meetings
19%

Telephone
calls
24%

Scheduled
meetings
19%

Figure 4. Distribution of Time and Activities by Media [a]

[a] Based on five weeks of observation of chief executives' work.

Mails. The outstanding feature about the incoming mail was the cursory treatment it received from the managers. Mail processing appeared to be a chore, something to be done but not enjoyed. Frequently, mail was processed so quickly that one could wonder if this was some sort of ritual. Processing rates frequently exceeded 30 pieces per hour, and one man came in on Saturday to read 97 pieces of mail and react to 45 in a period of just over 3 hours. An average of 20 periodicals were received per week. Most were skimmed (often at the rate of 2 per minute), and an average of only 1 in 25 elicited a reaction. The treatment of routine reports was often similar. One manager looked at the first piece of "hard" mail he received all week—a standard cost report—and quickly put it aside with the comment, "I never look at this."

During the week of observation, one chief executive repeatedly sifted through his mail, hesitant to process it, yet searching for items that could not be left unattended. From Monday to Friday he found 32 pieces worthy of immediate attention. Then he came in for a period of 3 hours on Saturday to process the rest, to "get rid of all this stuff." This activity reflects a general concern; no matter how inconsequential the contents, the flow of mail cannot be impeded or the manager will be swamped with paper.

The incoming mail in this study was divided into 12 distinct "purpose" categories.[8] Four among these, accounting for 36 percent of the mail, dealt with relatively inconsequential matters—*acknowledgments, status requests* (inconsequential requests made because of the manager's status), *solicitations,* and *reference data.* Another 51 percent, representing six categories—*reports, periodicals, events, internal operations,* and *ideas*—informed the manager about his organization and its environment. Much of this mail was skimmed; relatively little elicited reaction. Only 13 percent of the mail fits a third grouping, that of specific and immediate use to the manager. This included the *requests for his authorization,* the *advice on current situations,* and the *pressures and problems* specifically brought to his attention in the mail. Thus, the managers' treatment of the mails may be explained by the fact that 87 percent of the input mail did not, by and large, deal with issues of "live action."

Outgoing mail followed the same patterns. Carlson reports similar findings:

> One of the most noticeable [characteristic features in common between the different executives] was the limited use of letters as a means of communication. There were chief executives who signed not more than one or two letters a week, and the maximum was two or three letters a day. The picture of the chief executive as a man who is busy dictating and signing letters was not borne out by any of our studies (1951: 83).

The chief executives of my study sent considerably more mail than those in Carlson's study, but almost all of it was in reaction to mail received. They originated on their own initiative an average of only 1 piece per day. Of the 9 pieces of outgoing mail averaged per day, almost half acknowledged incoming mail or replied to written requests. Most of these requests were inconsequential, but the executives felt obliged to reply. Another 30 percent consisted of incoming mail forwarded to subordinates.

Comments by these executives bore out their treatment of the

[8] See Appendix C for a description of each category.

mail. One said, "I don't like to write memos, as you can probably tell. I much prefer face-to-face contact." Another repeated the same sentiments. "I try to write as few letters as possible. I happen to be immeasurably better with the spoken word than with the written word." Their reasons are clear. Contrasted with verbal communication, letter writing is time-consuming, primarily since words to be documented must be chosen carefully. Furthermore, the information moves slowly to the target, and much time elapses before there is feedback. This presents no difficulty for formal documents, for lengthy or routine reports, or for general information. But for much of his important information, the manager must use other media. Mail as a medium does not fit well with the manager who prefers live action.

Telephone Calls and Unscheduled Meetings. During the study, telephone calls and unscheduled meetings were generally of short duration, averaging 6 and 12 minutes, respectively. Together they accounted for two-thirds of the chief executives' verbal contacts. They were used when both parties were well known to each other, could dispense with formalities, and had to transmit information quickly or make requests briefly. Thus, the records show that most verbal status requests and solicitations came on the telephone or in the unscheduled meeting. The managers and their subordinates also used the telephone and the unscheduled meeting for certain important requests and for the passing of information, especially for "instant communication." Occasionally, when a problem arose suddenly, strategy was developed during a telephone call or an unscheduled meeting.

Subordinates who were within walking distance of the chief executives' offices and who had frequent contact with them, tended to prefer the unscheduled meeting to the telephone call. If the manager made himself inaccessible, they used the telephone. Those who did not work in the immediate vicinity of the manager, but who interacted with him frequently enough to have ready and informal access, used the telephone for informal verbal contacts.

Scheduled Meetings. Scheduled meetings consumed 59 percent of the managers' time. These contacts were relatively long ones and provided the managers with the opportunity to meet with large groups and to meet people away from their organizations.

Scheduled contacts were sometimes used for the same purposes as informal contacts—to deliver status and action requests and to transfer information. More characteristically, however, these contacts differed in kind. The scheduled meeting was often held with someone who did not have a close working relationship with the chief executive—a newspaper reporter, a salesman, a student. Furthermore, the issue under discussion was often formal in nature. Scheduled meetings were used instead of unscheduled meetings when large quantities of information had to be transferred. Thus, when a close peer wished to send a small quantity of information, he used the telephone. When the two men wished to discuss various events in the trade, they scheduled a meeting, perhaps over dinner.

Three kinds of activities took place primarily at scheduled meetings—*ceremony, strategy-making,* and *negotiation.* The reasons are clear. All three are time-consuming and involve many participants, often from diverse places. Scheduling the meeting was the only way to bring these people together.[9]

The scheduled meeting appears to follow a particular pattern which, regardless of its ostensible purpose, makes it, in part at least, a vehicle for trading information. Three stages of the scheduled meeting can be distinguished—an opening period of pleasantries and gossip, the discussion of the core issue, and the closing discussion of side issues. An interesting account of this pattern is provided by Desmond Morris in his popular book, *The Naked Ape.*

> It is an amusing game to plot the course of grooming talk during a social encounter. It plays its most dominant role immediately after the initial greeting ritual. It then slowly loses ground, but has another peak of expression as the group breaks up. If the group has come together for purely social reasons, grooming talk may, of course, persist throughout to the complete exclusion of any kind of information, mood or exploratory talk. The cocktail party is a good example of this. . . .
>
> If we switch our observations now to the more formal business encounter, where the prime function of the contact is information talking we can witness a further decline in the dominance of grooming talk, but not necessarily a total eclipse of it. Here its expression is almost entirely confined to the opening and closing moments. Instead of waning slowly, as at the dinner party, it is suppressed rapidly, after a few polite, initial exchanges. It reappears again, as before, in the closing moments of the meeting, once the anticipated moment of parting has been signalled in some way. Because of the strong urge to perform grooming talk, business groups are usually forced to heighten the formalization of their meetings in some way, in order to suppress it. This explains the origin of committee procedure, where formality reaches a pitch rarely encountered on other private social occasions (Morris, 1967: 179–180).

[9] By taking one further step and scheduling meetings on a regular or "clocked" basis, the managers could substantially decrease the time they spent in making scheduling arrangements. As the data of Appendix C indicate, Managers C and E, who had a substantially higher incidence of clocked meetings spent much less time scheduling their activities. The price, of course, was the risk of wasted time. There may have been nothing of importance to discuss and certain participants may have had more important work to do elsewhere.

Our observations verify this, except that the early ritualistic discussion often leads to the trading of information that may prove to be important to the manager, even though it is unrelated to the purpose of the meeting. Gossip about peers in the industry is exchanged; comments are made on particular encounters the participants have recently had or on published materials they have recently read; important political events are discussed and background information is traded. It seems reasonable to conclude that the manager collects much important information in these discussions, and that this fact alone makes the formal, face-to-face meeting a powerful medium. Similarly, at the close of meetings, important side issues will often be raised:

Manager: I just remembered; a friend called looking for a job; do you need an engineer in your department?

Manager: By the way, I just bought a company!

Subordinate: There was quite a reaction at the plant over your decision to end the program.

Peer: By the way, a top-ranking civil servant will be in country next week; you may want to meet him.

These are side issues, of secondary concern at the time; yet they may be important ones to the manager. He may accomplish something that needs to be done, or he may receive or transmit some important information. In particular, it was interesting to notice the skills the managers of the study displayed in using this third stage of meetings to pry information from available sources, oftentimes when participants did not appear to be likely sources of information.

The characteristics of verbal communication, and these features of meetings in particular, raise a question about differing treatment of subordinates. Those working in the vicinity of the manager have the opportunity of attending many meetings with him. Executives in nearby cities can have frequent telephone contact. But those far away, overseas for example, must communicate largely by mail. Thus one would expect those executives within walking distance of the manager to be best informed, and those beyond the reach of the routine telephone call to be less well-informed about current issues facing the organization. They are forced to use the mails, a medium for which the manager has little regard, and they miss the general trading of information that takes place at scheduled meetings.[10]

Tours. The tour provides the manager with a unique opportunity. He can observe activity without prearrangement. The contacts

[10] This raises a question about whether the "multinational" enterprise can really ever reach the point where subsidiaries become equal partners. Unless they are entirely independent, it would appear that the bulk of the power would rest with head office, where the information is.

he makes are completely informal: Contrast stopping a man in the halls to mention something to him with telephoning or making a formal appointment to see him.

The surprising feature about this powerful tool is that it was used so infrequently. Tours in my study accounted for only 3 percent of the chief executives' time.[11] Carlson found that the Swedish chief executives spent 10 percent of their time in visits and inspection tours, while Rosemary Stewart's senior and middle managers averaged 6 percent of their time in inspection tours. However, the chief executives of my study recognized the value of the tour, and cited instances of important discoveries made during strolls through their organizations, but still they gave little time to this relatively open-ended activity. Managers appear hesitant to leave their offices unless they have specific reasons for doing so.

To summarize, the manager demonstrates a strong preference for the verbal media of communication. He seems to dislike using the mail, and consequently it is used primarily for formal correspondence and for lengthy documents. The informal means of communication—the telephone call and the unscheduled meeting—are used to transmit pressing information and to deliver informal requests. Scheduled meetings are used for formal delivery of information and requests, and for time-consuming events that involve a number of people, notably events concerned with ceremony, strategy-making, and negotiation.

One further point merits emphasis. Unlike other workers, the manager does not leave the telephone or the meeting to get back to work. Rather, these contacts *are* his work. The ordinary work of the organization—producing a product, undertaking research, even conducting a study or writing a report—is seldom undertaken by its manager. The manager's productive output can be measured primarily in terms of verbally transmitted information.

BETWEEN HIS ORGANIZATION AND A NETWORK OF CONTACTS

The manager maintains communication relationships with three groups—superiors (directors or trustees, in the case of chief executives), outsiders (to the unit that he manages), and subordinates. In effect, he stands between subordinates and the others, linking them in a variety of ways. The findings of this and other studies suggest that contacts between managers and outsiders have been underestimated (as to time allocated) and oversimplified in the traditional literature.

[11] During the week of observation only one chief executive made a practice of taking open-ended tours. They consumed 10 percent of his time.

In fact, the manager maintains a complex network of relationships with a great variety of people outside his own organization.

Consistent findings are reported in study after study. The managers spent substantial time with subordinates—generally between one-third and one-half of their total time in verbal contact—whereas contact time with superiors seldom exceeded one-fifth. The other contacts—horizontal (with peers), lateral (with the bosses and subordinates of peers), and external to the larger organization—were always significant. In most studies, they consumed in the vicinity of one-third to one-half of the managers' contact time and often they took more time than did subordinate contacts. Rosemary Stewart, for example, found that senior and middle managers averaged 41 percent of their contact time with subordinates, 12 percent with bosses, and 47 percent with others (19 percent with colleagues, 13 percent with fellow specialists, 8 percent with other internal people, and 8 percent with external people). In studies of foremen, Jasinski found these three figures to be 46 percent, 10 percent, and 44 percent, respectively, while Kelly gives the comparable fractions as one-half, one-fifth, and one-third.

In my study of chief executives, an average of 48 percent of their contact time was with subordinates, 7 percent with directors (superiors), and 44 percent with outsiders. Figures for the mail show similar tendencies—39 percent from, and 55 percent to, subordinates; 1 percent from, and 2 percent to, directors; and 60 percent from, and 43 percent to, outsiders. (See Figure 5.)

What is perhaps more interesting than the proportions is the nature and variety of contacts, particularly those with outsiders. The contacts for the five chief executives of my study included clients, business associates and suppliers, peers who managed their own organizations, government and trade organization officials, codirectors, and independents (those with no relevant organizational affiliation). Many of them had relatively formal relationships with the chief executive. They made the occasional status request and engaged in ceremonial activity with him. Peers asked him to speak, consultants sought contracts, politicians requested advice, consumers wrote for free merchandise.

To gain access to outside information, these chief executives developed networks of informers—self-designed external information systems. Some informers were personal contacts—friends, peers, and codirectors—who sent various reports and told of latest events and opportunities. In addition, the chief executives retained numbers of experts—consultants, lawyers, underwriters—to provide specialized advice. Trade organizations kept them up to date on events in the trade—the unionization of a competitor, the state of impending legislation in Washington, the promotion of a peer. Finally, stemming

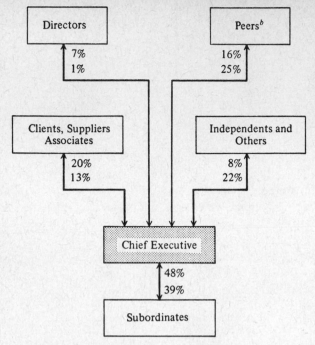

Figure 5. The Chief Executives' Contacts [a]

[a] Figures indicate, respectively, proportion of total contact time spent with each group and proportion of mail from each group. (Figures taken from mail and contact records presented in Appendix C, based on five weeks of observation.)

[b] Includes codirectors and trade organization people.

from their personal reputation and that of their organizations, these managers were fed with unsolicited information and ideas—a suggestion for a contract, a comment on a product, a reaction to an advertisement.

Foremen also deal with complex networks of outsiders. "The average foreman talked with many different individuals, rarely fewer than 25 and often more than 50. He dealt with a wide variety of persons in the operating and service departments and on different levels" (Guest, 1955–1956: 483). Jasinski (discussing the same study as Guest), notes the foreman-to-foreman relationships where they must "get along" rather than exert authority over one another, and the diagonal relationships where "foremen advised and made suggestions to, rather than directed, these non-subordinate operators" (1956: 132). In his study of lower- and middle-level managers, Sayles describes seven types of external relationships, some dealing with the flow of work through the organization, others with the receiving of services and advice, with purchasing and selling, and so on. In all cases, the significance and complexity of nonline relationships are stressed as major characteristics of managerial work.

There is some evidence, however, that despite the wide variety outside contacts, much of the managers' time in nonline relationships is spent communicating with cliques of peers. Both Burns (1954) and Thomason (1966, 1967) note the existence of these managerial cliques at middle levels, and Thomason suggests that they constitute specialized centers of information.

Manager-subordinate relationships are, of course, significant in content and extent. In my own study subordinates accounted for 39 percent of the mail the managers received, 55 percent of the mail generated, 65 percent of the verbal contacts, and 48 percent of the time in verbal contact.[12] Subordinates made a variety of requests of the managers, largely for authorization, information, and advice; they sent a wide variety and a great quantity of information, in the form of operating reports, "instant communication," briefings on problems and opportunities, ideas, trade gossip, and so on. To some extent, they acted as information filters, selectively forwarding letters, memos, and magazine articles from their own mail. In turn, the managers forwarded to subordinates a good part of the information received from the outside, and they delegated a number of tasks to them. Many review sessions—important for information trading— were held with subordinates, as were most strategy-making sessions.

It was clear in this study (as it was in those of Carlson and Burns) that the managers interacted freely with a wide variety of subordinates and seemed not to be concerned when they bypassed formal lines of authority (downward).

> The accepted view of management as a working hierarchy on organization chart lines may be dangerously misleading. Management simply does not operate as a flow of information up through a succession of filters, and a flow of decisions and instructions down through a succession of amplifiers (Burns, 1957: 60).

It would appear that it is more important for the manager to get his information quickly and efficiently than to get it formally.

Finally, managers appear to spend a surprisingly small amount of time with their superiors. In our study, very little material flowed between the chief executives and their directors in the mails, and what did tended to be of a formal nature—status requests and formal

---

[12] It is interesting to note the finding in both this study and the one by Sayles that subordinate contacts were of especially short duration on the average.

reports. Verbal contact was only slightly more common, much of it in terms of formal board meetings. About such meetings, Carlson writes:

> Although most of the executives spent considerable time in preparing the agenda for the board meetings, none of them regarded the communication with the board and its individual members as a particularly time-consuming or difficult task (1951: 85).

And Brewer and Tomlinson (1964) who used diaries to study senior executives were surprised by the "absence of contact with a superior." Even at lower levels, where one would expect more contact, the amount of time spent with superiors was not great. For example, Stewart found it to be 12 percent of contact time for senior and middle managers and Jasinski, 10 percent for foremen. Aguilar notes with surprise "the relatively infrequent mention of superiors as a source of important external information." (1967: 70) [13]

We may summarize by characterizing the manager's position as the neck of an hourglass. Information and requests flow to him from a wide variety of outside contacts. He sits between this network of contacts and his organization, sifting what is received from the outside and sending much of it into his organization. Other informational inputs and requests come from below, some to be used by him, others to be sent back to different parts of the organization or outside to the manager's contacts.

BLEND OF RIGHTS AND DUTIES

To what extent can the manager control his own affairs? Peter Drucker appears to have no doubt about the answer:

> The manager has the task of creating a true whole that is larger than the sum of its parts, a productive entity that turns out more than the sum of the resources put into it. One analogy is the conductor of a symphony orchestra, through whose effort, vision and leadership individual instrumental parts that are so much noise by themselves become the living whole of music. But the conductor has the composer's score; he is only interpreter. The manager is both composer and conductor (1954: 341–342).

---

[13] The reader may wonder about an apparent inconsistency here. Since some managers are themselves subordinates, the relatively little time spent with superiors must be reconciled with the greater time spent with subordinates. An example will clarify the issue. If a manager supervises six people and spends 48 percent of his time with these six subordinates, then each of these subordinates spends 8 percent of his time with the boss. This assumes that all work equal hours and that the boss never sees two subordinates at once. It is probably reasonable to assume that he sees his subordinates most often in two-person, informal meetings.

But Sune Carlson, who carried out a systematic study of managers, is not so sure:

> Before we made the study, I always thought of a chief executive as the conductor of an orchestra, standing aloof on his platform. Now I am in some respects inclined to see him as the puppet in the puppet-show with hundreds of people pulling the strings and forcing him to act in one way or another (1951: 52).

The empirical data are equally inconclusive. Guest's data indicate that the foremen he studied initiated 60 percent of their contacts, and in the Lawler, Porter, and Tennenbaum (1968) study of middle- and lower-level managers, the figure was closer to one-half. Burns (1954) presents more specific data on four middle managers to suggest that they initiated about half of all contacts with peers, fewer with superiors, and more with subordinates. Our data (shown in Figure 6) indicate that the five chief executives initiated only 32 percent of their verbal contacts. And of the 890 pieces of mail analyzed, the managers sent only 231 of them (26 percent) and almost every one of these was in response to one of the 659 pieces received.

Our study provides one other possible measure of the extent to which the manager can control his own work. We can categorize verbal activities according to whether the manager was actively or passively involved. In 42 percent of them—including ceremonial activities and all those where requests were made of him—his involvement was ostensibly passive. In 31 percent, including *strategy, negotiation, informing, touring,* and *requests* made by him, his involvement was more active. And in 27 percent, including *review, scheduling,* and *external board work,* his involvement can be con-

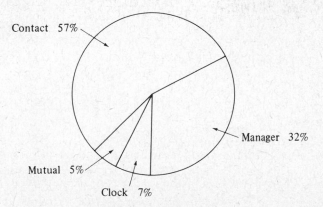

Contact 57%

Manager 32%

Mutual 5%

Clock 7%

Figure 6. Initiation of Verbal Contacts [a]

[a] Based on five weeks of observation of chief executives' work.

sidered neither active nor passive. Again the manager appears to be in active control of a relatively small proportion of his activities.

The two important students of the work of chief executives—Carlson and Neustadt—argue that in fact managers spend most of their time *re*acting. Carlson refers to the "diary complex" (p. 71), and Neustadt expresses his conclusion in this way:

> A President's own use of time, his allocation of his personal attention, is governed by the things he *has* to do from day to day: the speech he has agreed to make, the fixed appointment he cannot put off, the paper no one else can sign, the rest and exercise his doctors order. These doings may be far removed from academic images of White House concentration on high policy, grand strategy. There is no help for that. A President's priorities are set not by the relative importance of a task, but by the relative necessity for him to do it. He deals first with the things that are required of *him* next. Deadlines rule his personal agenda (1960: 155).

Thus, there is evidence to support the thesis that the manager is unable to decide on the majority of his own activities. The telephone rings, the calendar pad calls for a battery of meetings, subordinates drop in, problems arise unexpectedly, and underlying all this is the constant fear of falling behind on the processing of mail. Surely the job is designed to swallow the weak man and cage the strong one.

But do the figures tell the true story? Do the facts that many of the manager's meetings are set up by others, that he receives more mail than he generates, that requests are more often made of him than by him, that he is a slave to his diary, indicate that the manager cannot control his affairs? Status requests are never self-initiated, yet their frequency may be a good measure of the self-developed status of the manager. The number of requests for authorization, all initiated by others, may reflect the manager's control over organizational decision-making. The extent to which meetings are set up by others or by the clock may be a measure of the manager's organizing ability, and the quantity of unsolicited information he receives may measure his ability to build effective lines of communication.

Thus, a manager may be depicted as a conductor or a puppet, depending on how he manages his own affairs. In particular, he has two important degrees of freedom:

1. The manager is able to make a set of initial decisions that define many of his own long-term commitments. For example, he can choose to join an external board of directors or a committee, although once done, associated activities are largely planned for him. He can initiate a project that, once underway, may demand his time, on and off, for years. He has the power to develop his own information channels, although, having done so, he does not control the day-to-

day information that flows to him. Clearly, control is exerted in terms of a few crucial decisions, many of them made shortly after the manager assumes office.

2. The manager exerts his own will by controlling, or using for his own ends, those activities in which he *must* engage. In other words, he can take advantage of his obligations. A ceremonial occasion provides the shrewd manager with an opportunity for collecting information. A request for authorization allows him to inject his values into the organization. And an obligation to speak provides an opportunity to lobby for a cause. A problem may be more than simply solved, and a pressure may be more than simply removed. Steps may be taken to turn problems into opportunities by exploiting new ideas in their solution.

Perhaps it is these two factors that most clearly distinguish successful and unsuccessful managers. All managers appear to be puppets. Some decide who will pull the strings and how, and they then take advantage of each move that they are forced to make. Others, unable to exploit this high-tension environment, are swallowed up by this most demanding of jobs.

PROPOSITIONS ABOUT MANAGERIAL WORK CHARACTERISTICS

1. Because of the open-ended nature of his job, the manager feels compelled to perform a great quantity of work at an unrelenting pace. Little free time is available and breaks are rare. Senior managers, in particular, cannot escape from their jobs after hours, because of the work they take home and because their minds tend to be on their jobs during much of their "free" time.

2. In contrast to activities performed by most nonmanagers, those of the manager are characterized by brevity, variety, and fragmentation. The vast majority are of brief duration, on the order of seconds for foremen and minutes for chief executives. The variety of activities to be performed is great, and the lack of pattern among subsequent activities, with the trivial interspersed with the consequential, requires that the manager shift moods quickly and frequently. In general, managerial work is fragmented and interruptions are commonplace.

3. The manager actually appears to prefer brevity and interruption in his work. He becomes conditioned by his workload; he develops an appreciation for the opportunity cost of his own time; and he lives continuously with an awareness of what else might or must be done at any time. Superficiality is an occupational hazard of the manager's job.

4. The manager gravitates to the more active elements of his work—the current, the specific, the well-defined, the non-

routine activities. Mail processing is viewed as a burden, with the little "action" mail receiving the most careful attention. Very current information (gossip, hearsay, speculation) is favored; routine reports are not. Time scheduling reflects a concern with the definite and the concrete, and activities tend to focus on specific rather than general issues. The pressure of the job does not encourage the development of a planner, but of an adaptive information manipulator who works in a stimulus-response environment and who favors live action.

5. Verbal and written contacts are the manager's work and his prime tools are five media—mail (documented), telephone (purely verbal), unscheduled meetings (informal face-to-face), scheduled meetings (formal face-to-face), and tour (observational). The manager clearly favors the three verbal media, spending most of his time in verbal contact.

6. Mail receives cursory treatment, although it must be processed regularly. The mail tends to contain little "live action" material; processing is time-consuming; and it moves slowly and involves long feedback delays. The mail contains much general data and lengthy documents (reports, periodicals, and so on) and numbers of formal communicatons and inconsequential requests that must, nevertheless, be answered. The manager generates much less mail than he receives, most of it necessary responses to input mail. The manager's treatment of mail suggests that subordinates beyond his routine verbal reach tend to be at an information disadvantage compared with those who work in closer proximity.

7. The informal media (telephone and unscheduled meeting) are generally used by the manager for brief contacts when the parties are well known to each other, and when information or requests must be transmitted quickly.

8. The scheduled meeting consumes more of the manager's time than any other medium. It allows for contacts of long duration of a formal nature, with large groups of people, and away from the organization. Activities for the purposes of ceremony, strategy-making, and negotiation generally take place at scheduled meetings. Of special interest in scheduled meetings is the general discussion at the beginning and end of each, which frequently involves the flow of important information.

9. Tours provide the manager with the opportunity to observe activity informally without prearrangement. But the manager spends little of his time in open-ended touring.

10. The manager may be likened to the neck of an hourglass, standing between his own organization and a network of outside contacts, linking them in a variety of ways. External contacts generally consume one-third to one-half of the manager's contact time. These are of great variety and include clients, suppliers, associates, peers, and others. These people serve, in effect, as a network of informers. Nonline relationships are a significant and complex component of the manager's job.

11. Subordinates generally consume one-third to one-half of the manager's contact time, most often for purposes of making requests, of sending or receiving information, and of making strategy. The manager interacts freely with a wide variety of subordinates, bypassing formal channels of communication to do so.

12. The manager spends relatively little of his time with his superior (or directors in the case of the chief executive)—generally on the order of 10 percent.

13. The manager's job reflects a blend of duties and rights. Although superficial study of managers' activities suggests that they often control little of what they do, closer analysis suggests that the manager can exert self control in two important ways. The manager is responsible for many initial commitments, which then lock him into a set of ongoing activities; and the manager can take advantage of his obligations by extracting information, by exercising his leadership, and in many other ways.

4
The Manager's Working Roles

A good theory is one that holds together long enough to get you to a better theory.

D. O. Hebb [1]

Wﬁe now come to the crux of our study, the theory of *what* managers do. Here we use the concept of role, a term that has made its way from the theatre to management via the behavioral sciences. A role is defined as an organized set of behaviors belonging to an identifiable office or position (Sarbin and Allen, 1968). Individual personality may affect *how* a role is performed, but not *that* it is performed. Thus, actors, managers, and others play roles that are predetermined, although individuals may interpret them in different ways.[2]

[1] Opening quotation from *Psychology Today* (November, 1969).
[2] Readers interested in more detail on the role concept are advised to see Sarbin and Allen (1968) and Thomas and Biddle (1966).

THE SET OF TEN ROLES

It should be made clear at the outset that the view of managerial roles presented in this chapter is one among many that are possible. The delineation of roles is essentially a categorizing process, a somewhat arbitrary partitioning of the manager's activities into affinity groups. The result must ultimately be judged in terms of its usefulness.

This statement of roles was derived initially from the observational study of the work of five chief executives reported in Appendix C. Each contact and piece of mail observed during this study was analyzed in terms of one basic question—why did the manager do this? The answers, gathered together in logical groupings, emerged as a statement of ten roles. (The reader interested in more detail on this process may turn to the section on the derivation of the roles near the end of Appendix C.)

Despite the basis for these results, there is a logical argument as well as considerable empirical evidence to support the contention that these ten roles are common to the work of all managers. As shown in Figure 7, each manager stands between his organizational unit and its environment. The president guides his firm and looks out to an environment consisting of competitors, suppliers, governments, and so on. The foreman guides his shop and looks out to other foremen and staff groups within the firm, and to suppliers (and others) outside the firm. Each must manage an organization within a complex environment. To do so, the incumbent manager must perform a set of managerial roles and the requirements of these roles lead to certain common work characteristics.

Various studies—of production foremen, field sales managers, and so on—provide support for this argument. Each makes reference to one or more of the roles presented in this chapter; between them the ten roles are mentioned in one form or another for managerial jobs ostensibly quite different from that of chief executives. Furthermore, there is evidence from three subsequent empirical studies using

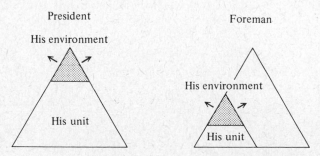

Figure 7. The Manager Between Unit and Environment

this role set to suggest that presidents of small firms and middle managers in business and government perform these ten roles.[3]

Much of the anecdotal material of the chapter is derived from my own study of chief executives, but the findings of other studies are referenced and quoted throughout, both to enrich the theory and to support the contention that these ten roles are performed by all managers. Again (as in Chapter 3), the term *organization* refers to that unit directly under the manager's formal authority, whether it be a foreman's shop or a president's company.

Managerial activities may be divided into three groups—those that are concerned primarily with interpersonal relationships, those that deal primarily with the transfer of information, and those that essentially involve decision-making. It is for this reason that the ten roles are divided into three groups—three *interpersonal* roles, three *informational* roles, and four *decisional* roles.

The manager's position provides the starting point for this analysis. Earlier the manager was defined as that person formally in charge of an organizational unit. This formal authority leads to a special position of status in the organization. And from formal authority and status come the three interpersonal roles. First and most simple is the role of *figurehead*. The manager has the duty of representing his organization in all matters of formality. Status enables the manager also to play the *liaison* role, in which he interacts with his peers and other people outside his organization to gain favors and information. The third interpersonal role, that of *leader,* defines the manager's relationships with his subordinates—motivating, staffing, and so on.

The interpersonal roles place the manager in a unique position to get information. His external contacts bring special outside information and his leadership activities serve to make him a focal point for organizational information. The result is that the manager emerges

---

[3] Choran (1969) used structured observation to study the work of the presidents of three small firms. He concluded that they performed all ten roles (and two additional roles of special importance in their jobs), but that they gave more or less attention to certain roles than did the chief executives of larger organizations. Costin (1970) received questionnaires from 200 middle managers, half in business and half in government, in which they assessed the frequency with which they performed the ten roles. Not only did both groups perceive themselves as performing all ten roles, but there were no significant differences between the two groups in their ranking of nine of the roles. (Both studies are discussed in Chapter 5.) In addition, John Bex of Phillips Industries in Great Britain has undertaken research on the middle manager's job using this role framework. Its applicability at this level is suggested in his preliminary findings, presented in his paper, "Some Observations Regarding the Managerial Role in a Changing Environment," read at the U.K. Operational Research Society Conference, September 1971.

as the key nerve center of a special kind of organizational information. Of the three informational roles, the first—*monitor*—identifies the manager as receiver and collector of information, enabling him to develop a thorough understanding of his organization. The second role, termed *disseminator,* involves the transmission by the manager of special information into his organization. The third, the *spokesman* role, involves the dissemination of the organization's information into its environment.

The manager's unique access to information and his special status and authority place him at the central point in the system by which significant (strategic) organizational decisions are made. Here four roles may be delineated: In the *entrepreneur* role the manager's function is to initiate change; in the *disturbance handler* role the manager takes charge when his organization is threatened; in the *resource allocator* role the manager decides where his organization will expend its efforts; and in the *negotiator* role he deals with those situations in which he feels compelled to enter negotiations on behalf of his organization.

In reading the following detailed statements of these roles, the reader should bear three points in mind.

First, each role is observable. For example, one can witness a manager handling disturbances or performing as *figurehead*. The description of each role will refer back to the set of observable activities from which it derives. It should, however, be noted that some activities may be accounted for by more than one role. (The question of mapping activities onto roles is taken up in Appendix C).

Second, all of the observed contacts and mail in the study of the five executives are accounted for in the role set. There has been a tendency in the literature to exclude certain work that managers do as inherently nonmanagerial. Drucker has written:

> Every manager does many things that are not managing. He may spend most of his time on them. A sales manager makes a statistical analysis or placates an important customer. A foreman repairs a tool or fills in a production report. A manufacturing manager designs a new plant layout or tests new materials. A company president works through the details of a bank loan or negotiates a big contract—or spends dreary hours presiding at a dinner in honor of long-service employees. All these things pertain to a particular function. All are necessary, and have to be done well. But they are apart from that work which every manager does whatever his function or activity, whatever his rank and position, work which is common to all managers and peculiar to them (1954: 343).

If the president *must* negotiate the contract or preside at the dinner, how can one claim that this is not a part of his job? Omissions such as these are arbitrary—they suggest a preconceived notion of the job which may not be in accord with the facts. If a manager engages in an activity, we must begin with the assumption that this is part of his job and seek to understand why he does it in the broadest sense of his responsibilities. This approach leads to a conclusion that is diametrically opposed to that of Drucker.

Third, the roles are described individually but they cannot be isolated. As shown in Figure 8, these ten roles form a *gestalt*—an integrated whole. In essence, the manager is an input-output system in which authority and status give rise to interpersonal relationships that lead to inputs (information), and these in turn lead to outputs (information and decisions). One cannot arbitrarily remove one role and expect the rest to remain intact. A manager who, for example, ceases to perform a *liaison* role loses access to external information, and so cannot disseminate good information or make effective strategic decisions.

THE INTERPERSONAL ROLES

Consider the following activities performed by chief executives: ceremonial work (such as formal dinners), requests to subordinates to follow-up on work, letters acknowledging other letters, replies to inconsequential requests received because of the manager's status (for free merchandise, for example). There are two features common to all these activities. Each one links directly to the manager's status and authority, and each essentially involves the development of interpersonal relationships. Status requests are received and ceremony engaged in because the manager is the highest ranking figure in his organization; the manager has access to certain contacts because of his status as manager; he acknowledges mail to maintain a set of interpersonal relationships; his follow-up requests relate to his legal authority in the organization. In each case, the interpersonal contact is of key significance. Hence these activities describe what can be called the interpersonal roles, of which three can be delineated.

The Manager as *Figurehead*

Most basic and most simple of all managerial roles is that of *figurehead*. Because of his formal authority, the manager is a symbol, obliged to perform a number of duties. Some of these are trite, others are of an inspirational nature; all involve interpersonal activity, but none involves significant information-processing or decision-making. As Carlson notes:

> The Report of the President's Committee on Administrative Management states that the President of the United States, besides being a leader of the political party in power, is "head of the Nation in the ceremonial sense of the term, the symbol of the American national solidarity" (1951: 24).

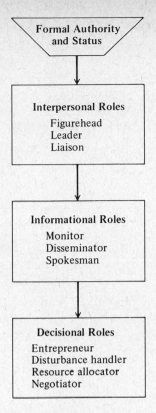

Figure 8. The Manager's Roles

Consider the following incidents, each related to the *figurehead* role:

> In the incoming mail, one manager finds a letter addressed to "The President" in which free merchandise is requested. In the stack of outgoing mail awaiting signatures, different managers find diplomas for graduating nurses, a letter of appreciation to a retiring employee, and a proposal letter to a prospective client dictated by a subordinate.

> A salesman, telling the secretary that he is an old friend, schedules a meeting with the chief executive in order to sell his soap product, and a real friend writes the general director of a hospital to ensure that a relative receive good care there. One manager entertains some clients while another makes a speech to a visiting group.

None of these incidents appears to be central to the job of managing. Yet each is, for in every case the manager—simply because he is manager—must be involved. In some cases—notably the signing of certain documents—his participation is required by law. In other cases, his participation is considered a social necessity; he must preside at certain events to add dignity and status. And in still other cases, he must make himself available (in the words of one of the men studied) "to those whose feeling is that the only way to get something done is to get to the top":

> A distraught parent telephones the superintendent to complain about a teacher. Afterwards the superintendent comments, "As you can see, it is something I don't get involved in except to call the principal and say she called me."

> A hospital chief calls the general director to complain that the ladies auxiliary has taken one of his rooms.

> The chief executive is asked to speak to a group of volunteers, with the comment, "I want them to know that this is a policy clearly endorsed by you."

Such incidents are not restricted to chief executives. In discussing the work of field sales managers, Davis comments:

> Some customers . . . refuse to have any dealings with anyone but the field manager. A small New York State brewer insisted upon purchasing his entire supply of cans from the manufacturer's branch manager even though the local salesman was qualified and authorized to render identical service. The brewer argued that his account deserved the attention of management. Whether the attitude is warranted or not, the fact remains that in this instance the title and prestige of the local manager were needed to maintain customer relations (1957: 43–44).

Other students of managerial work have occasionally mentioned the *figurehead* role, but it has, in general, been largely ignored. Possibly its lack of overt significance did not suit traditional views of managerial work.

The Manager as Leader

The organization looks to its formal head for guidance and motivation. In his *leader* role, the manager defines the atmosphere in which the organization will work.

> The tone of the organization is usually sounded by its top executive, and the success of the enterprise may well depend on whether he infuses the whole hierarchy with energy and vision or whether, through ineptness or neglect, he allows the organization to stagnate (Harbison and Myers, 1959: 15–16).

Leadership involves interpersonal relationships between the leader and the led. In the informal group, the leader is usually followed because of his physical or charismatic power. In formal organizations, where the he is most often appointed from above, the manager must frequently rely on the powers vested in his office.

There can be a power structure in primitive groups in terms of the superior personality force of a leader, whether because of physical prowess, mental alertness, or persuasiveness. This is not, however, the same as authority structure in which the order is followed because it comes from the legitimized position in the structure rather than from a certain personality. The soldier salutes the uniform of the superior officer, not the man (Katz and Kahn, 1966: 46).

The *leader* role is clearly among the most significant of all roles, and has received far more attention than any other. The literature of leadership dwells on a number of themes, such as the requirement for the leader to give his organization direction and purpose, various styles of leaders and their impact on subordinates, and the power of leaders. However, as noted in Chapter 2, little has been written on the actual leadership activities of managers, and it is here that we focus our discussion.

In analyzing the activities that make up the *leader* role, we must note first that leadership permeates all activities; its importance would be underestimated if it were judged in terms of the proportion of a manager's activities that are strictly related to leadership. Each time a manager encourages or criticizes a subordinate he is acting in his capacity as *leader*. Most often, he does these things when he is engaged in activities that have other basic purposes—to transmit information or to make strategic decisions. But in virtually everything he does, the manager's actions are screened by subordinates searching for leadership clues. In answering a request for authorization, he may encourage or inhibit a subordinate, and even in his form of greeting, messages (perhaps nonexistent ones) may be read by anxious subordinates.

Some activities may be categorized as concerned primarily with leadership. A special class are those associated with staffing—hiring, training, judging, remunerating, promoting, and dismissing subordinates. Another class of activities includes those primarily motivational in nature, as illustrated by the following anecdotes:

> A subordinate turns to the manager for advice on a personal problem and for reassurance that his work is adequate.

> The manager uses his authority in a memo to a subordinate: "I was thinking about the lead; wonder if we shouldn't follow up more aggressively."

> During a tour of the organization, the manager calls on an employee who has been ill; he greets another employee, asks about his work, and compliments him on his achievements.

In addition to these activities, one finds another set in which the manager probes (one might say "meddles") into the actions of his subordinates. Although not recognized in the literature on leadership, the study of the five executives shows clear evidence of this activity. In touring, in reading the company magazine, in much of what he does, the manager seeks information on his organization. When he is exposed to something he does not like, the manager does not hesitate to act.

> Noting a company advertisement on the back of a magazine, the manager forwards it to one of his vice-presidents with the comment: "Notice we are still using this for advertising instead of PR . . . when do we get back on track?"

> Having received a request for additional office space, the manager takes an early-morning trip to the department concerned. Later he gets in touch with the head of the department and tells him that if his people would arrive for work on time, they would be able to perform their work in the available space.

The manager looks for operations that are going wrong, problems in need of attention, and subordinates who require encouragement or criticism. In effect, it is up to him to maintain a certain degree of alertness in the organization. The manager is able to probe freely because he alone is not constrained by well-defined bounds of authority within his organization. He is the only one in the organization with a very broad mandate—to put this another way, he is the only one who can meddle at will—and his activities clearly reflect this.

In concluding the discussion of the *leader* role, two points should be noted. First, the key purpose of the *leader* role is to effect an integration between individual needs and organizational goals. The manager must concentrate his efforts so as to bring subordinate and organizational needs into a common accord in order to promote efficient operations. Second, it is in the *leader* role that managerial power most clearly manifests itself. Formal authority vests the manager with great potential power; leadership activity determines how much of it will be realized. William F. Whyte in his study of a street gang provides an apt illustration of the extent of this power.

> The leader is the focal point for the organization of his group. In his absence, the members of the gang are divided into a number of small groups. There is no common activity or general conversation. When the leader appears, the situation changes strikingly. The small units form into one large group. The conversation becomes general, and unified action frequently follows. The leader becomes the central point in the discussion. A follower starts to say something, pauses when he notices that the leader is not listening, and begins again when he has the leader's attention. When the leader leaves the group, unity gives way to the divisions that existed before his appearance (1955: 258).

Thus, through the *leader* role the manager welds diverse elements into a cooperative enterprise.

The Manager as *Liaison*

One of the major findings of the empirical studies of managerial work is the significance of horizontal relationships. While vertical or authority relationships have received much attention in the literature —specifically in terms of the *leader* role—horizontal relationships have been largely ignored.

The *liaison* role deals with the significant web of relationships that the manager maintains with numerous individuals and groups outside the organization that he heads. These are what Homans (1958) refers to as "exchange" relationships—the manager gives something in order to get something in return. Presidents join external boards for contacts that will provide favors and information; in return they pledge their time and expertise.

Homans hypothesizes about these relationships as follows: " . . . the higher a man's social rank, the more frequently he interacts with persons outside his own group. . . . social equals tend to interact with one another at high frequency." (1950: 185–186). For the manager, whose status is unmatched within his own organization, this means the development of outside contacts.

> First, a manager has status. He is set apart from nonmanagerial employees, and he is accepted in the managerial class. He stops eating lunch with nonmanagerial associates and starts eating lunch with other managers, often in a private dining room. Many of his nonmanagerial friendships dissolve and are replaced by friendships within the managerial group. He is admitted to membership in social clubs which were formally closed to him, by convention if not by fiat. He is invited to be an officer in charitable and professional organizations (Starbuck, 1965: 512).

Thus, the diary and observational studies have indicated that foremen spend much time with other foremen, middle managers with other middle managers, presidents with presidents.

Chief executives build and maintain their system of status contacts in a variety of formal and informal ways—by joining external boards and performing public service work, by attending conferences and social events, by "keeping in touch," by answering requests simply (in the words of one man studied) "to keep the channels open." The following anecdotes illustrate this:

> The head of a large transportation system calls the chief executive of a consulting firm to request a copy of a published report. The contact is significant, the request is not.
>
> A manager, upon reading in a magazine of the promotion of a peer, writes to congratulate him.
>
> A chief executive calls an official of a foreign embassy to thank him for arrangements he made related to an overseas trip. It is sug-

gested by the official during the conversation that the chief executive try to meet a member of that country's planning office who will be visiting the United States. A contract could result.

And, of course, the chief executive strengthens his *liaison* role through the development of his reputation. This was most clear in the study of one chief executive who used the word "exposure" to link his televised appearance at congressional hearings with his position as head of a consulting firm. The results of this exposure were frequently in evidence during the week of observation, specifically in his access to top governmental people in Washington and foreign capitals. His firm did a considerable amount of consulting work for government.

The *liaison* role represents the beginning of a key part of the manager's job—the linking of the environment with his organization. The *spokesman, disseminator,* and *negotiator* roles further this linkage. In the *liaison* role the manager establishes his web of external relationships; in the other roles he makes use of it in terms of the favors and the information that such contacts bring.

The *liaison* role has not received wide recognition in the literature of management, although there have been three important exceptions. In analyzing the power of U.S. Presidents, Neustadt speaks of Roosevelt's skill at this role:

> His personal sources were the product of a sociability and curiosity that reached back to the other Roosevelt's time. He had an enormous acquaintance in various phases of national life and at various levels of government; he also had his wife and her variety of contacts. He extended his acquaintanceships abroad; in the war years Winston Churchill, among others, became a "personal source." Roosevelt quite deliberately exploited these relationships and mixed them up to widen his own range of information. He changed his sources as his interests changed, but no one who had ever interested him was quite forgotten or immune to sudden use (1960: 156–157).

At the other extreme, we have the views of William F. Whyte on the *liaison* role in the leadership of the street corner gang:

> The leader is better known and more respected outside his group than are any of his followers. His capacity for social movement is greater. One of the most important functions he performs is that of relating his group to other groups in the district. Whether the relationship is one of conflict, competition, or cooperation, he is expected to represent the interests of his fellows. The politician and the racketeer must deal with the leader in order to win the support of his followers. The leader's reputation outside the group tends to support his standing within the group, and his position in the group supports his reputation among outsiders (1955: 259–260).

Leonard Sayles, who studied lower- and middle-level managers, probes most deeply into the *liaison* role. To Sayles, "The one enduring objective of the manager is the effort to build and maintain a predictable, reciprocating system of relationships . . ." (1964: 258). Whereas we here stress the maintenance of such relationships at the chief executive level as necessary for gaining special favors and information, Sayles describes them at lower levels as relating primarily to the maintenance of external work flows. In other words, the lower- and middle-level manager develops his system of horizontal relationships so as to better deal with those who feed his organization with its input work, and those to whom his organization sends its output. Such relationships may involve purchasing and selling, service and advisory activities, evaluation, control, and innovation.

To sum up, in the *liaison* role the manager, by virtue of his authority and associated status, is able to develop a special kind of external linkage system. He connects his organization to its environment, using his array of contracts to further the intelligence and the position of his organization. To develop this system, he makes a series of commitments. Sayles's study finds that lower-level managers perform the same role, although their activities are primarily concerned with the more routine flow of work.

THE INFORMATIONAL ROLES

A second set of managerial activities in the study of chief executives relates to the receiving and transmitting of information. Much of their mail was strictly informational in nature—reference data, reports, news of events, ideas, and other items. Similarly, a number of verbal contacts were informational, such as making requests, passing along fresh bits of information, receiving briefings, taking tours. Interpersonal interaction was incidental in most of these activities; the information was simply moved or recombined and was not used at the time in making significant decisions. Hence, the second set of managerial roles is classed as informational.

Consider the following accounts, two from my own study and one from Neustadt's work:

> A company vice-president must leave a meeting on the west coast early. He and some colleagues were in the process of negotiating an acquisition. Shortly after the meeting ends, the vice-president, anxious to know the result, calls across the country to the president at headquarters in Boston. The president, who has just spoken to the other negotiators, describes the outcome. Later, in reply to the observer's comment, "So you are in Boston, they are both out west, yet you are in a better position to tell the vice-president what went on," the president comments, "I usually am!"

Someone in need of organizational information who does not know where to turn will call the manager or his secretary. An outsider, who has been switched from one telephone extension to another, finally asks for the secretary of the chief executive. Afterwards, she comments on her role, "If they can't answer a question from any part of the organization, call Jane—she can answer it!" In another similar case, a manager comments after a meeting with a woman, "She didn't know where to go so she came to me."

The essence of Roosevelt's technique for information-gathering was competition. "He would call you in," one of his aides once told me, "and he'd ask you to get the story on some complicated business, and you'd come back after a couple of days of hard labor and present the juicy morsel you'd uncovered under a stone somewhere, and *then* you'd find out he knew all about it, along with something else you *didn't* know. Where he got his information from he wouldn't mention, usually, but after he had done this to you once or twice you got damn careful about *your* information." (Neustadt, 1960: 157)

What do these accounts tell us about managerial work? They indicate that, to his subordinates, to the observer, and to the man himself, the manager clearly occupies the central position in the movement of a certain kind of information within his organization. In effect, the manager is his organization's "nerve center." The flow of nonroutine information in an organization focuses on its manager.

This reflects two features of the manager's job—his unique access to external information and his all-embracing access to internal information. Consider, first, the manager's access to internal information. In all but the least structured of organizations, each man below the manager is a specialist, and the manager, relatively speaking, a generalist. At the top of the corporate hierarchy, the president oversees vice-presidents charged with such specialist functions as marketing, production, and finance. Reporting to the foreman are lathe operators, milling machine operators, and so on. With formal lines of communication to each of these specialists, the manager develops a broad base of information, and emerges as nerve center of internal information. He may not know as much about any one function as the specialist charged with it, but he is the only one to know a significant amount about all functions. As a result a variety of outsiders turn to the manager when the information that they need from his organization involves more than one function, or when they don't know which specialist can answer their questions.

Because of his status and its manifestation in the *liaison* role, the manager has unique access to a variety of knowledgeable outsiders including other managers who are, themselves, nerve centers of their own organizations. Hence he has unique access to a network of nerve centers. The result is that the manager becomes the focal point in his organization for special external information. His sources ensure that he is best informed about events in his organization's environment.

For illustration of this in another context, let us turn again to the study of street gangs. Homans, who reviews Whyte's study, stresses both the internal and external aspects of nerve-center information, as follows:

> Since interaction flowed toward [the leaders], they were better informed about the problems and desires of group members than were any of the followers and therefore better able to decide on an appropriate course of action. Since they were in close touch with other gang leaders, they were also better informed than their followers about conditions in Cornerville at large. Moreover, in their position at the focus of the chains of interaction, they were better able than any follower to pass on to the group the decisions that had been reached (Homans, 1950: 187).

Three roles characterize the manager as nerve center. In the *monitor* role, he informs himself about his organization and its environment, and in the *disseminator* and *spokesman* roles, he transmits his information to others.

The Manager as Monitor

The manager as *monitor* (a term used by Sayles [3]) is continually seeking, and being bombarded with, information that enables him to understand what is taking place in his organization and its environment. He seeks information in order to detect changes, to identify problems and opportunities, to build up knowledge about his milieu, to be informed when information must be disseminated and decisions made. Observation clearly indicates that the manager receives a wide variety of information from a wide variety of sources,

---

[3] Sayles (1964) uses the term more broadly, to cover not only information collecting but problem defining and problem solving as well. He distinguishes six stages in monitoring activity.

1. Methods of detecting disturbances in the work systems in which the manager participates.
2. Development of criteria for evaluating the significance of disturbances that are detected.
3. Patterns of corrective action to be applied and the assessment of their effects.
4. Detection of continuing (resistant) sources of disturbance in the work systems and their analysis.
5. Formulation of strategies of organizational or structural change to cope with these.
6. Implementation and validation of these structural modifications.

Points 2, 3, 5, and 6 apply to the decisional roles (especially *entrepreneur*) described later in this chapter.

both inside and outside his organization. One man commented, "I have to sift through about forty rumors every day!" The information received by the chief executives of my study falls into five categories: [4]

Internal Operations. Information on the progress of operations in the organization, and on events that take place related to these operations, comes in many forms: standard operating reports, ad hoc inputs from subordinates, observations from touring the organization.

External Events. The chief executive seeks and receives information concerning clients, personal contacts, competitors, associates, and suppliers, as well as information on market changes, political moves, and developments in technology. His personal contacts keep him informed on various events and gossip of the trade; subordinates act as his filter, sending in information on external events; trade organizations routinely feed the chief executive special trade information by way of reports and newsletters; the chief executive subscribes to a wide variety of periodicals, which carry a steady flow of information on events in the trade, in technology, in business in general, and in the world at large.

Analyses. Analyses and reports of various issues, solicited and unsolicited, come to the chief executive from various sources. From time to time, the chief executive expresses an interest in a particular subject; subordinates then provide him with clippings and reports on the subject. Trade organizations and other groups send the chief executive reports they feel will interest him or his organization. And frequently the chief executive will request a report or briefing on factors associated with an upcoming decision; subordinates and outsiders, hired or retained because of a special expertise, produce these analyses.

Ideas and Trends. The chief executive uses a number of means to develop a better understanding of the trends in his environment, and to learn about new ideas. He attends conferences, pays attention to unsolicited letters from clients, glances at trade organization

---

[4] In *Scanning the Business Environment,* Aguilar (1967) presents a most extensive analysis of the manager's external information. His study, based on interview and the analysis of critical incidents, categorizes information by kind, source, and method of finding (solicited, unsolicited, and so on). Aguilar breaks the data down for managers at three levels in the hierarchy: in general management, marketing, and technical and other functional areas; in small, medium, and large companies; and for experienced (more than three years) and inexperienced (less than one year) managers.

reports, receives ideas from contacts and subordinates—a suggestion for a promotion, a lead for a contract, notice of a man who seeks employment.

Pressures. In addition to the usual types of information, the chief executive's channels also bring information in the form of pressures of various kinds. Subordinates, seeking greater power or various changes, attempt to influence the chief executive's decisions— to appoint a local man, to set up a new committee. Outsiders make a variety of demands—a client seeks special arrangements, a charity organization writes to ask why no donation was made. Directors express opinions and the public-at-large may become involved in certain issues. A letter addressed to "President, ABC Company" reads, "A group in Detroit has decided not to buy any ABC products because you used that anti-flag, anti-American pinko, Johnny Lindell, upon your Thursday night TV show."

It is evident from the discussion to this point that the manager's advantage lies, not in the documented information that is widely available, and which takes much time to process, but in the current, nondocumented information transmitted largely by word of mouth. As discussed in Chapter 3, managers seem to indicate strong preferences for current information, much of which is necessarily unsubstantiated (gossip), and for information on events rather than on trends. The following comments in a memo to a chief executive, although documented, are in other ways typical of this kind of information.

> I hear via the grapevine that George will be transferred to Atlanta within a few months. I presume that he will be in charge of Wojeck's interests in the Atlanta area, but I will try to develop more information about this. In any event, this concern with special projects would indicate he might need our services from time to time. He has always been a good friend of ours and he should be a good man to know in the Wojeck organization.

This kind of information, not that carried in formal reports, forms the heart of the manager's information system. The manager develops an understanding of his milieu by piecing together all the scraps of data he can find. Neustadt makes this point eloquently:

> It is not information of a general sort that helps a President see personal stakes; not summaries, not surveys, not the *bland amalgams*. Rather . . . it is the odds and ends of *tangible detail* that pieced together in his mind illuminate the underside of issues put before him. To help himself he must reach out as widely as he can for every scrap of fact, opinion, gossip, bearing on his interests and relationships as President. He must become his own director of his own central intelligence (1960: 153–154; italics added).

As a result, the manager can expect little help in the performance of his *monitor* role from the traditional formal information system. It provides largely historical, aggregated information, whereas he seeks current, trigger information. The manager must, therefore, design his own information system. This he does by developing his own contacts and by establishing special communication channels within his organization. As Aguilar notes in his analysis of where the manager finds external information:

> Findings showed that personal sources greatly exceed impersonal sources in importance (71 percent versus 29 percent), and thus indicated the relatively heavy reliance that managers place on their personal networks of communication (both private and organizational) (1967: 94).

Aguilar's further finding that 62 percent of the manager's information from outside sources was "unsolicited" suggests just how well developed this personal network is.

As I found in my study and in my survey of others, the internal information channels of the manager do not coincide with the formal lines of authority. He needs certain kinds of information, and he has no qualms about bypassing subordinates (or training their subordinates to bypass superiors) to get it. Wrapp explains why managers form these internal channels and why they seek the kind of information they do.

> Top-level managers are frequently criticized by writers, consultants, and lower levels of management for continuing to enmesh themselves in operating problems, after promotion to the top, rather than withdrawing to the "big picture." Without any doubt, some managers do get lost in a welter of detail and insist on making too many decisions. Superficially, the good manager may seem to make the same mistake—but his purposes are different. He knows that only by keeping well informed about the decisions being made can he avoid the sterility so often found in those who isolate themselves from operations. If he follows the advice to free himself from operations, he may soon find himself subsisting on a diet of abstractions, leaving the choice of what he eats in the hands of his subordinates (1967: 92).

What does the manager do with his information? Clearly, he simply transfers a good part of it. As shown in Figure 9, he may transfer information between environment and subordinates in four ways. The two means of transferring information outside the organization are discussed in terms of the *spokesman* role, the two means of transferring information to subordinates, in terms of the *disseminator* role. In addition, the manager processes information in more complex ways. He integrates the information that comes to him in the form of pressures and statements of preference to develop value

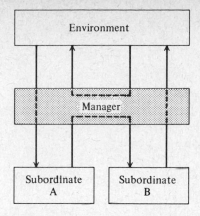

Figure 9. The Manager in the Information Flow

positions for his organization. And he uses information to find problems and opportunities. Finally, he uses information to develop mental images—"models" of how his organization and its environment function and "plans" of where it must go.

Figure 10 shows the manager's roles in the processing of information. This diagram makes clear that it is the informational roles that tie all managerial work together—linking status and the interpersonal roles with the decisional roles. The interpersonal roles ensure that information is provided; the decisional roles make the most significant use of it. We now turn to the description of the manager's output of information.

The Manager as *Disseminator*

His special access to information allows the manager to play the important role of *disseminator,* sending external information into his organization and internal information from one subordinate to another. The information is of two distinguishable types—factual and value.[5]

Factual information can be tested as to its validity; on some recognized scale it is either correct or incorrect. The manager receives much factual information simply because of his formal authority. A good part of this is quickly forwarded to the appropriate subordinates:

> An invitation to a technical conference is forwarded to a vice president with the comment, "Anyone interested?" An offer by a financial firm for sale and leaseback arrangements is sent to a financial

[5] See Simon (1957), Chapter 3, for a discussion of factual and value information.

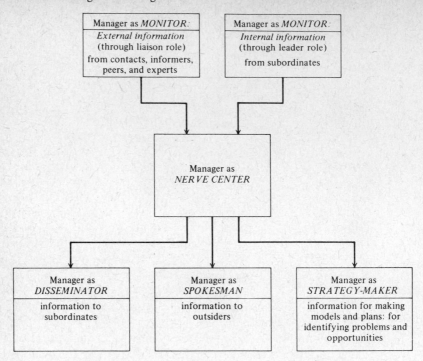

Figure 10. The Manager as Information Processing System

executive, and a report on a nursing conference is sent to a nursing chief. The manager arranges to have published in the staff letter a complaint by the librarian that journals are not being returned.

More significant for dissemination is information from outside contacts in the form of ideas, trade gossip, and instant communication:

> A discussion at an external board meeting is reported to a subordinate who is in the process of developing a proposal for that organization.
>
> A telephone conversation with a client is transcribed by the chief executive's secretary and the transcription sent to a subordinate.
>
> The chief executive tells a subordinate about a distraught customer, and another manager briefs members of his organization on the results of a trip.

Value information deals with preferences—someone's arbitrary belief of what "ought" to be. A statement of values can be neither correct nor incorrect; it merely reflects the needs of those who wish to exercise power over decision-making. A significant function of the

disseminator role is to transmit value statements into the organization to guide subordinates in making decisions. Value information
can be communicated by the manager whenever significant issues are
discussed:

> When asked to authorize the development of a new industrial rela-
> tions policy manual, the manager expresses a set of preferences on
> labor policy.
>
> The editor of the school system's newspaper is asked to revamp
> the periodical. She meets with the superintendent first to ask him a
> variety of questions: How often does he think it should appear?
> What role should PTA play? Should the first issue contain a letter
> from the superintendent? What ideas does he have for format and
> content?
>
> At a meeting with a new executive, the manager comments, "I
> wanted to ease any thought in your mind that I had anything speci-
> fic in mind. . . . Whatever happens in it is up to you; it's your
> [department]." The manager goes on to state other value positions
> and then answers various questions concerning organizational goals.

What do the manager's statements of value actually represent?
In categorizing the chief executive's information earlier, we saw that
some comes in the form of pressures. Subordinates seek to extend
their own influence; directors attempt to impose their opinions on
decisions; members of the public bring special pressures to bear. In
addition, the government, labor unions, trade organizations, and
various other pressure groups attempt to influence organizational
decisions from time to time. These pressures form a special part of
the organization's information system. They represent the value positions of those who seek some measure of control over the actions of
the organization in order to satisfy special needs. Since the manager
has broad powers of authority in the organization, people direct their
statements of preference to him. The manager assimilates these
statements, combines them according to the influence of the source,
determines overall organizational preferences, and then disseminates
these as organizational values.

The chief executives of my study clearly saw themselves this
way. One commented, "One of the principal functions of this position
is to integrate the hospital interests with the public interests." Another stated, "I've always perceived the superintendent's role as
relating the community to the professional staff."

The economist Andreas Papandreou describes the manager in
this way, referring to him as "peak coordinator":

> It is a major thesis of this essay that the preference function maxi-
> mized by the peak coordinator is itself a resultant of the influences

which are exerted upon the firm. The peak coordinator is conceived as performing the integrating function; he is conceived as formulating the preference system of the enterprise. He does so, however, under the "weight" of the unconscious and conscious influences exerted upon him (1952: 211).

While there is evidence to support Papandreou's basic point, there is no evidence to suggest that managers deal with preference functions per se. Value statements are made by the manager, not in terms of global preferences, but as specific answers to specific questions. For example, it is unlikely to find a manager saying, "Here, we prefer profit to growth." More commonly one will hear, "I like the second option; it has a better return on investment even though it is smaller." Furthermore, there is no reason to believe that the manager enters into all situations with well-defined preferences. Sometimes preferences develop as issues develop, as new information and new alternatives appear. Lindblom uses the phrase "adjustment of objectives to policies" (Braybrooke and Lindblom, 1963: 93) to refer to this process—ends (values) are not absolute, but change as means (alternatives) change.

The chief executives studied appeared to be personally responsible for many of the organizational preferences that they expressed. Chief executives, particularly those in large organizations with fragmented groups of "influencers," are able to assume much power over organizational values. They have strong mandates, and many of the outside pressures are ambiguous or conflicting. On the other hand, managers that are dominated by one main influencer (for example, the boss of a middle manager), probably exert less influence on the values they express. To a large extent, they merely transmit them unchanged from above to below.

Before leaving the *disseminator* role, let us consider what appears to be a most significant managerial problem, herein referred to as the *dilemma of delegation*. Consider the following incident:

A subordinate calls to ask the chief executive if a certain appointment should be cleared through a particular committee. The executive replies that it should not. To a second question on another appointment, he gives an affirmative reply. Finally, the subordinate asks about a third man, and receives another negative reply. Asked why he did not give consistent decisions, the chief executive replies that his knowledge of the personalities of the three men and of the committee members necessitated that he make individual decisions.

But consider the result of this action. The next time such a situation arises the chief executive will have to be consulted again. Not only did he give the subordinate no basis on which to make a future decision, he actually discouraged him from doing so by providing no rationale for his own decisions. Quite clearly (although perhaps not consciously), he chose not to delegate responsibility for this kind of decision, but to retain it for himself. The obvious reason is that he considered himself better informed.

Tasks involving only one specialist function are easily delegated to the subordinate charged with that function. But what of tasks that cut across specialities or that involve the manager's special information? The manager, as nerve center, has the best command of the relevant factual and value information, and hence is best suited to handle these tasks. Yet he cannot do everything. Some of these tasks must be delegated. There would be no problem if the manager could easily disseminate all relevant information to the subordinate. But he cannot, because so much of it is verbal (and is, therefore, stored only in memory). Documented information can be transmitted easily and systematically; that existing in memory can not. Verbal transmission is time-consuming and crude.

Hence the manager is damned by his own information system either to a life of overwork or to one of frustration. In the first case, he does too many tasks himself or spends too much time disseminating verbal information; in the second case, he must watch as delegated tasks are performed inadequately, according to his standards, by the uninformed. It is altogether too common in our organizations to witness subordinates being blamed for performancees that indicate simply that they have no direct access to the necessary information and that the manager has not realized the need to disseminate the privileged information that he does have. I shall return to this most significant managerial dilemma repeatedly in this study.

The Manager as *Spokesman*

While the *disseminator* role looks into the organization, in the *spokesman* role the manager transmits information out to his organization's environment. As formal authority, the manager is called upon to speak on behalf of his organization; as nerve center, he has the information to do so effectively. The manager may lobby for his organization, he may serve as its public relations head, or he may be viewed as an expert in the trade in which his organization operates.

The *spokesman* role requires of the manager that he keep two groups informed. The first is the organization's set of key influencers —the board of directors in the case of a chief executive and the boss in the case of a middle manager.

> A board meeting opens with a report by the chief executive, in which he briefs the directors on various ongoing programs. Much time is then consumed by the questions that the directors ask the chief executive.[6]

The second group to be informed is the organization's public. In the case of chief executives, this includes suppliers, trade organizations, peers, government agencies, customers, and the press.

> The manager gives a speech to a visiting group on the organization's history and one to a trade organization on its plans. He then grants an interview to a member of the press on the same subject. At the end of the year, he oversees the writing of the annual report, and writes the introductory statement himself.

The manager must keep both groups—influencers and the general public—informed about the organization's plans, policies, and results. Furthermore, he can only maintain his liaison network by sharing his information with his contacts. For both these reasons, it is crucial that the manager's information be current. To speak effectively for his organization, and to gain the respect of outsiders, the manager must demonstrate an up-to-the-minute knowledge of his organization and its environment.

In the *spokesman* role the manager is required to act as expert in those activities in which his organization engages.

> The manager is invited to appear on television to discuss events in his industry. A friend calls to ask the president for his opinion on a firm available for sale. A political leader asks the general director of a hospital for advice on a public health appointment, and a girl who saw him on television writes to ask why she is having so much difficulty becoming a nurse.

In effect, because of his position and the resulting nerve center information, the manager is vested with considerable expert power—special knowledge about his organization's industry. He is, therefore, called upon by various outsiders (and sometimes by his subordinates as well) to give his advice on general problems related, not to his own organization, but to that industry in which his organization is active.

[6] The well-known Berle and Means finding (1968) that control of large corporations tends to rest with management rather than with the shareholders is easily explained in terms of the informational roles. As nerve center, the chief executive simply knows more than anyone else about his organization. Hence his knowledge cannot be matched by shareholder or director, and he assumes great power. This was clearly in evidence in the two board meetings observed during the study. In both cases, the key flow of information was from manager to directors; the *spokesman* role emerged as by far the most important in these contacts.

The dissemination of expert information, ostensibly a minor part of the chief executive's job, can be considered part of his *spokesman* role.[7]

To summarize this discussion of the informational roles, in one role—that of *monitor,* the manager receives information, and in two others—that of *disseminator* and *spokesman,* he is involved in the more or less straightforward transmission of information. In addition, the manager uses his information in his decision-making roles, the subject of the next section.

THE DECISIONAL ROLES

The third and final set of managerial activities categorized in Appendix C involve the making of significant decisions—handling requests for authorization, scheduling his own time, holding meetings to make strategies and handle problems, and negotiating with other organizations.

Probably the most crucial part of the manager's work—the part that justifies his great authority and his powerful access to information—is that performed in his decisional roles. These roles involve the manager in the strategy-making process in his organization. Strategy-making can be defined simply as the process by which significant organizational decisions are made and interrelated.

One clear conclusion emerges from my study: The manager takes full charge of his organization's strategy-making system. To use other words, the manager is substantially involved in every significant decision made by his organization. This is so because (1) as formal authority the manager is the only one allowed to commit his organization to new and important courses of action, (2) as nerve center the manager can best ensure that significant decisions reflect current knowledge and organizational values, and (3) strategic decisions can most easily be integrated by having one man control all of them.

Before discussing the four decisional roles, it is necessary to describe briefly the nature of strategic decisions made by organizations. Decisions range along a continuum, from the purely voluntary innovative ones, to the involuntary reactive ones. At one end there is, for example, the successful company that markets a new product in order to expand its sales volume; at the other extreme, there is the firm that changes its product offerings because competition threatens its survival. At one extreme we have what might be called *entrepreneurial* decisions; at the other extreme, *disturbance* or *crisis* decisions. What are commonly called *problems* fall somewhere in the

---

[7] In Chapter 5, we shall see that this is a crucial part of the job of the staff manager, and merits distinction as a separate role for him.

middle—the organization experiences a mild threat and perhaps it believes it can innovate in its choice of solution.

We shall use a second categorization scheme in describing decisional roles—the Herbert Simon (1965) trichotomy of the decision-making process. The *intelligence* phase is the initiating activity—looking for and selecting situations requiring decisions. The *design* phase is the heart of decision-making analysis—seeking alternatives and evaluating them. The *choice* phase deals with the process of choosing or accepting one alternative from among those available.

Four decisional roles are described below. The *entrepreneur* role is at the proactive, innovative end of the continuum, and includes both intelligence and design phases. The *disturbance handler* role includes the same phases at the reactive end of the continuum. The *resource allocator* role deals with choice-making activities. In the *negotiator* role the manager engages in a distinct type of decisional activity—negotiations with other organizations.

The Manager as *Entrepreneur*

In the *entrepreneur* role the manager acts as initiator and designer of much of the controlled change in his organization. The word "controlled" implies that this role encompasses all activities where the manager makes changes of his own free will—exploiting opportunities, solving nonpressing problems. Thus, although the term *entrepreneur* is borrowed from the economists, we view the entrepreneurial function in a significantly broader context. The economists have tended to focus on the work of starting new organizations; we focus on all managerial work associated with systematic change in ongoing (as well as new) organizations.

Entrepreneurial work begins with scanning activity. As part of his *monitor* role, the manager spends much of his time scanning his organization, looking for opportunities and for situations that may be considered problems.

> The chief executive questions subordinates at random, holds functional review sessions, takes the occasional unannounced tour, searches for possible problems in the mail and in the comments of deputies and others, all the time looking for areas of possible improvement.

Particularly here, in his search for opportunities and problems, the manager has need for tangible information in the form of stimuli—specific events and ad hoc data—rather than the gradual trends displayed in routine reports. This was as clear in our study of chief executives as it was to Sayles in his study of managers at lower levels in the hierarchy:

The usual managerial reporting systems—information flows or paper flows—fail to come to grips with the real purpose of controls. Rather, they naively try to tell the manager what is happening or, more precisely (and less valuably), what *has* happened. Only recently have there been concerted efforts to distinguish significant events for the manager (1964: 163).

Having discovered a problem or opportunity, the manager may decide that it is necessary for his organization to take action to improve an existing situation. At this point the design phase of decision-making begins. What is most interesting about the "decision" to improve a situation is that it is not really just that—rather, it emerges as a series of smaller decisions and other activities sequenced over a period of time. Sequencing of steps and prolongation are the key features of the improvement "decision." The following example, typical of many, illustrates this:

> In reaction to vigorous public debate, a committee of eight people was formed, including the superintendent, a school committee member, and assistant superintendents and principals, to investigate the issue of serving lunches to school children. In the last meeting, the decision was made to begin a pilot program. At this meeting, one of the participants is leading the discussion on methods of measuring the appropriate factors in the pilot program. After some time, the talk shifts to what appears to be the issue at hand— choosing a committee of citizens to oversee the pilot program. Leading the discussion, the superintendent begins to recommend the types of people required and the specific people who seem to fit. Each participant generates more suggestions, until the superintendent announces that enough acceptable names have been suggested. It is decided that the superintendent will write letters inviting these people to join the committee. When the replies are received, the group will meet again. The superintendent comments, "I think we've gone as far as we can go," and the participants prepare to leave.

From this point on, we shall use the term *improvement project* to refer to a sequence of activities designed to improve a particular organizational situation (exploit an opportunity, solve a problem).

The manager may choose to involve himself in the design and choice phases of an improvement project on one of three levels:

Delegation. For some improvement projects—the least consequential ones—the manager delegates all responsibility for both phases. He involves himself only to the extent that he may choose the subordinate who will deal with it and he implicitly retains the right to replace that man should his actions not comply with the manager's expectations.

Authorization. Some improvement projects require closer control, perhaps because they involve large risks or important precedents. In these cases the manager chooses to delegate all responsibility for the design phase, while retaining responsibility for the choice-making phase. When the subordinate has completed design work, he seeks the manager's approval for the proposed course of action in a "request for authorization." By operating in this way, the manager maintains ultimate control over actions without having his time consumed in design work.

Supervision. Finally, the manager chooses to retain responsibility for, and supervises, the design phase of certain improvement projects. He may do so for any of a variety of reasons—because the interests of a powerful organizational group are to be affected; because he has a strong personal interest in the issue; because it involves a major change in a department that reports directly to the manager; because the project involves a major commitment of resources or a significant risk of resource loss; or because sensitive value issues are involved.

Supervision is discussed below in terms of the *entrepreneur* role. Authorization will be discussed later in terms the *resource allocator* role.

Senior managers appear to maintain supervision at any one time over a large inventory of improvement projects in widely differing stages of development.

> Among the improvement projects that the chief executive of one organization was seen supervising during the one week of observation were: an attempt to better the organization's cash position; transferring a weak department to headquarters for a period of time so that the chief executive could strengthen it; the initiation of one public relations program, the continuing development of three others, and the finalization of still another, which had been held up by a ten-year-old technological problem; the seven-year-old problem of dealing with a weak overseas executive and his discouraged staff; the possible acquisition of a consumer-goods manufacturer and concerns about antitrust; the difficulties of reorienting salesmen to the selling of new lines; the need to change one of the professional services retained by the organization; the development of integrated computer operations; the plans to purchase an overseas supplier; the possibility of setting up new overseas manufacturing facilities; a foreign subsidiary's problem with an advertising agency.

The inventory of active projects appears to change continually, as new ones are added, old ones reach completion, and others wait in storage until the manager is able to find time to begin work on them. Furthermore, projects in active inventory are subject to frequent delays between successive steps. A particular project may be held in limbo while the manager waits for information, or a project may be delayed for purposes of timing, as the manager awaits some development before going on to the next step (the retirement of a man blocking progress, the easing of funds, the solution of an engineering difficulty). The overall effect of delays is that the manager is able to maintain a very large inventory of active improvement projects, perhaps as many as fifty in the case of chief executives.

The manager as supervisor of improvement projects may be likened to a juggler. At any one point in time he has a number of balls in the air. Periodically, one comes down, receives a short burst of energy, and goes up again. Meanwhile, new balls wait on the sidelines and, at random intervals, old balls are discarded and new ones added.

These features of managerial decision-making—splitting up of decisions (in the form of improvement projects), sequencing steps, timing, juggling a number of projects—have not generally been recognized by students of the managerial process. Two important exceptions should, however, be noted. As discussed in Chapter 2, Charles Lindblom has emphasized the sequential and disjointed nature of managerial decisions; the present research provides some evidence of the validity of certain of his views. Marples, in reporting his research design for studying decision-making, discusses the notions of juggling and of sequenced episodes. But, unlike Lindblom, Marples sees important threads linking the steps of decision-making.

> The manager's job can usefully be pictured as a stranded rope made of fibres of different lengths—where length represents time—each fibre coming to the surface one or more times in observable "episodes" and representing a single issue. The higher the level of manager the longer the average length of the fibre, the more intertwined the issues become, and the greater the number of episodes per issue. A prime managerial skill may be the capacity to keep a number of "issues" in play over a large number of episodes, and long periods of time (1967: 287).

To summarize, in the *entrepreneur* role the manager functions both as initiator and as designer of important controlled change in his organization. This change takes place in the form of improvement projects, many of which are supervised directly by the manager and all of which come under his control in one way or another.

The Manager as *Disturbance Handler* [8]

Whereas the *entrepreneur* role focuses on voluntary action by the manager to bring about controlled organizational change, the *dis-*

---

[8] I thank Hans Wirdenius for suggesting this term.

turbance handler role deals with involuntary situations and change that is partially beyond the manager's control. An unforseen event may precipitate a disturbance, or a problem too long ignored may generate a crisis. At this end of the continuum, the manager acts because he must, because the pressures brought to bear on his organization are too great to ignore. A disturbance occurs, a correction is necessary.[9]

We can describe the reasons for the manager's involvement in disturbance handling in the vocabulary of the Carnegie school.[10] The organization typically consists of a set of specialized operating programs that are routinely evoked by anticipated stimuli. But some stimuli are unexpected. Perhaps they are not clearly distinguished in terms of one existing program, perhaps they evoke conflicting programs. In special cases they may evoke operating programs that have ceased to function effectively. In all these situations a general program must be applied to the stimulus, one that is designed to handle any type of stimulus. This program will determine where the stimulus belongs, or it may design a new operating program to handle these stimuli in the future as they become more common.

The manager acts as just such a program. When subordinates cannot agree among themselves, they seek the help of the manager; when no one knows how to handle a difficulty, they pass it about until the manager gets it; when a crisis is perceived, the manager must take immediate charge. Specialists do their specialized work; the manager, as generalist, must handle the general disturbance.

The types of disturbances are many—the sudden departure of a subordinate, fire in a facility, the loss of an important customer, or a feud between two subordinates. Three disturbance situations from my study, as typical as any can be, are described below for illustrative purposes.

> A particular professional staffer schedules an appointment with the chief executive for the first time in several years. There is an "explosive situation" in his department, he claims, and he and his colleagues will walk out if their boss is not fired. After the meeting, the chief executive's first action is to open information channels, ad-

---

[9] Although these two roles clearly represent the two ends of our decision-making continuum, there is an area in between where they are not so distinct. In "problem solving," the manager may be reacting to a mild disturbance or he may believe he is acting voluntarily to avoid one. No doubt, the longer he waits to deal with a problem, the more it becomes a disturbance. But much depends on perceptions. What appears necessary to one man may appear voluntary to another. Henry Ford did not perceive a crisis in his firm when others did, whereas Thomas Watson would probably claim that he initiated development of the IBM System 360 because he had to.

[10] See Chapter 2 for a discussion of this school's approach.

vising the board chairman and seeking his advice, asking his deputy to watch for signs of the trouble. Every opportunity during the next few days is used to gain more information, while contact is maintained with the dissidents. Eventually it is decided that their concern is a real one, and a strategy is worked out—to confront the executive with the problem at a social function and point out his need to change.

During a meeting in progress, the deputy comes in quickly and leaves a message. "Harry Jamison will call . . . Elwood man . . . feels that Mr. Flagdale was forced out . . . wishes to object . . . wants a hearing." The issue relates to the ratification of a new executive at the open board meeting to be held that evening. A group associated with the organization, people who favor the previous office holder, are pressuring the directors and the chief executive. That evening, in an informal meeting of the directors preceding the board meeting, the extent of the lobby becomes clear. As each director enters, he tells of pressuring telephone calls, usually from close contacts. They try to develop a picture of the situation—who are the dissidents, what is their exact complaint, what actions might they take? Once the issue is clear, the chief executive immediately takes charge, developing a strategy, and acting to have it carried out. One board member will find the dissidents before the meeting, attempt to understand their position, and explain the possible embarrassment to the resigning executive if the issue is raised at the meeting. If necessary, the resignation can be delayed. At the board meeting there is no incident.

While the chief executive and two of his vice presidents are meeting informally, the secretary receives a telephone call from a purchasing agent in one of the plants. She immediately conveys the message to the chief executive. The note reads, "Heard from grapevine—will ship 2000 [parts to competitor]." To the executives, this means that a supplier who signed an agreement to develop a certain part for the firm, and who has since been bought by a competitor, may be reneging on his commitment, supplying the competitor instead. Discussion of other issues ceases and the office begins to take on the appearance of headquarters of an army under siege. One executive searches for a copy of the contract with the supplier, while the other is on the telephone finding out how many of these parts are called for in the sales plan, and at what times. After intensive discussion a tentative strategy evolves. The firm will attempt to force the supplier to honor the agreement immediately, despite extra holding costs. This will delay the competitor. However, as calmness begins to prevail again, the executives reconsider their position and agree to limit action to a written request to the supplier asking for clarification.

What do these examples tell us about disturbance handling? First of all, they suggest that disturbances may be of three types: (1) *conflicts between subordinates,* because of resource demands, personality clashes, or overlap of specialities; (2) *exposure difficulties* between one organization and another; and (3) *resource losses* or threats thereof. Second, we learn that timing enters importantly into the handling of disturbances. By their very nature, disturbances come up suddenly. Third, we find that disturbances are seldom found in the routine flow of information—in the reports and so on. Rather, they are defined by ad hoc stimuli, generally in the form of "instant communication." Often, the information is carried to the manager by someone who realizes that a disturbance has occurred. In effect, the manager does not appear to find his own disturbances; others recognize them for him. Fourth, the manager apparently allows disturbance handling to take priority over most other kinds of activity. He reworks his schedule and devotes the bulk of his energies to developing short-term solutions. His primary concern appears to be to relieve the pressures acting on him, to "buy time," perhaps so that an improvement project can eventually be initiated on a more leisurely basis. We might add a fifth point, verified by Hamblin in his experimental study of crisis behavior: "Leaders have more influence during periods of crisis than during non-crisis periods" (1958: 322).

While it is fashionable to write about the long-range perspectives of high-level executives and to depict them as reflective planners, it seems evident that every manager must spend a good part of his time reacting very quickly to high-pressure disturbance situations. These arise not only because "poor" managers ignore situations until they reach crisis proportions, but also because "good" managers cannot anticipate the consequences of all actions taken by their organizations. Disturbances are no doubt commonplace in both the innovative and the insensitive organization.

Despite some recognition in the literature of the disturbance-handling duties of the manager (for example, management by exception), seldom do we find insightful, empirically based discussion of this role. Two exceptions should be noted. Walker, Guest, and Turner entitle one chapter of their book "The Foreman Meets Emergencies" and comment:

> A foreman's primary role in the assembly line is to take care of minute-to-minute problems which arise and which are the result of the failure of a highly rationalized work process to operate perfectly (1956: 81).

These authors cite eight causes of emergencies for assembly-line foremen in the auto industry—changes in demand, seasonal fluctuations, model changes, problems with the multiplicity of parts of the products, difficulties in coordinating the many outside suppliers, labor turnover and absenteeism, the need for quick disposal of inventory, and the "hand-operated" nature of the assembly process.

Leonard Sayles, in dealing with disturbance handling, turns around the Drucker analogy presented in the last chapter to create a graphic image of the relationship between voluntary innovation and imposed disturbance:

> The achievement of . . . stability, which is the manager's objective, is a never-to-be-attained ideal. He is like a symphony orchestra conductor, endeavoring to maintain a melodious performance in which the contributions of the various instruments are coordinated and sequenced, patterned and paced, while the orchestra members are having various personal difficulties, stage hands are moving music stands, alternating excessive heat and cold are creating audience and instrument problems, and the sponsor of the concert is insisting on irrational changes in the program (1964: 162).

In Sayles's view, the manager seeks to maintain as much self-regulation as possible in his system. But he can never succeed perfectly—disturbances occur and changes must be initiated. Sometimes short-term adjustments will suffice to bring the system back to equilibrium; when disturbances persist long-term structural changes must be introduced.

The great significance of the *disturbance handler* role is due to the impact that resulting decisions can have on the organization's strategy because of the precedents they set. It is, therefore, unfortunate that this role has not received more attention in the literature.

The Manager as *Resource Allocator*

Resource allocation is the heart of the organization's strategy-making system. For it is in the making of choices involving significant organizational resources that strategies are determined. As formal authority, the manager must oversee the system by which organizational resources are allocated.

> The executive may be conceived to occupy a focal point of responsibility. Above him or beyond him there are his principals who hold him responsible for success: bigger output, more profits, fewer rejects, demonstrable economies, efficient service, victories, a satisfied public. Beneath the executive lies the organization that looks to him as the fount of authorizations (Braybrooke, 1964: 542).

We consider resource allocation here in the broadest context. Among organizational resources are money, time, material and equipment, manpower, and reputation. Each of these can be allocated positively or negatively; that is, decisions can be taken to use up or to protect these resources. When a chief executive decides to have a policy limiting the number of executives allowed in the corporate jet at any one time, he is protecting manpower resources. When he buys that jet, he is using up money resources, and when he refuses to let the airplane manufacturer use his company's name in an advertisement, he is protecting reputation—another kind of resource.

The manager can allocate resources in a variety of ways—by scheduling his own time, by assigning work to subordinates, by implementing a change that will involve new facilities, by making or approving budgets—in fact, by making virtually any decision. In our study, there was evidence that resource allocation comprises three essential elements—scheduling time, programming work, and authorizing decisions made by others in the organization.

Scheduling of Time. Throughout each working day, the manager is faced with a myriad of decisions involving the allocation of his own time.

> Should I make an appointment to see this salesman? Can I afford the time for a tour? Should I call him back or ask my assistant to do so? Is half an hour long enough for our PR man to explain his problem? Is this trip abroad sufficiently important or should I delay it? Should I represent us at the dinner for the trade mission?

Most important, these decisions have effect well beyond the manager and his own schedule. In scheduling his own time, the manager is in fact determining the interests of his organization and setting its priorities for action. In effect the manager announces by his schedule that certain issues are important to the organization and that others, because they receive little or none of his time, are inconsequential. Those issues that receive low priority do not reach the formal authority of the organization and are blocked for want of resources.

Subordinates, it would appear, react strongly to these priorities set implicitly by the manager. They will learn, by their inability to interest him, that certain issues are to be avoided in favor of others. Thus, marketing is sometimes favored by an organization whose president came from the marketing department, and engineering, by an organization whose president is an engineer.

The results of his scheduling decisions indicate how powerful the manager of an organization really is, how much influence he can exert in simple ways over the diverse affairs of his organization. They also indicate the enormous opportunity cost of the manager's time to his organization.

Programming Work. It is the manager's duty to establish the work system of the organization—what is to be done, who will do it, what structure will be operative. Such decisions, involving basic resource allocation, are generally made in the context of improvement projects. Many of them are made when the organization is new, or when a new part is added to the existing organization. But the work system also requires continual readjustment as the organization continues to operate.

This work is essentially that of programming. The manager, by deciding what is to be done, in effect programs the work of his subordinates. In supervising improvement projects, he designs the programs that subordinates will perform, and he links these together in an organizational structure.

Authorizing Actions. The manager maintains continuing control over the allocation of resources by insisting that he authorize all significant decisions before they are implemented. Included are all kinds of decisions—improvement projects supervised by subordinates, actions taken on low-level disturbances, exceptions to existing procedures and policies, contracts negotiated by subordinates, operating budget requests, and so on. In the case of chief executives, that such power can be absolute over choices made in the organizations is illustrated by the following incident from our study, typical of many:

> The meeting to decide whether to enter the joint venture in a foreign country begins as soon as the chief executive arrives. Sides quickly form, the executives on one side of the room arguing for a positive decision, and those on the other side questioning the validity of these arguments. For about fifteen minutes the chief executive is silent. Suddenly he interrupts the discussion, asks three quick questions on capital required, estimated return-on-investment, and risk, and then comments, "It has interesting innovative aspects, and not much financial risk. I'd like to see us go ahead to see what problems we'll encounter." With this, he gets up and leaves the meeting, the decision made.

By retaining the power to authorize important decisions, the manager ensures that he can interrelate decisions. Obvious conflicts between decisions can be avoided; attempts can be made to have decisions complement one another; resource limitations can be respected by choosing only the best of competing projects. To fragment this power is to invite discontinuous decision-making and a disjointed strategy.

As noted previously, the manager may choose to retain for himself supervision of certain improvement projects, and to limit himself to simply authorizing a host of others. In these latter cases, his approval is sought either at the outset or before final action is taken. Here, the manager is not involved in the creative part of the decisional process; he enters the process once a subordinate has identified a desirable course of action. The manager is presented with an alternative and is asked either to approve or to reject it:

> "Jack, how does this strike you? If you have no contrary thoughts, I'd like to see a thing like this go through."

These "requests for authorization" may come to the manager in one of two forms. The term *budgeting* refers to those requests for authorization that involve specific resource demands and that come to him in batches, all choices to be made at one time. In capital or program budgeting, as practiced in industry and government respectively, the manager is faced with a budget of a given size and with a number of well-defined projects requiring the limited funds. Cost and benefit data for each project are presented, with an emphasis on monetary measures. The decision-maker must decide which projects to accept, that is, which to provide resources for.

However, to use formal budgeting as a means of resource allocation, the manager must be dealing with proposals (1) that have clearly discernible costs and benefits, (2) that are competing for specified resources with other known proposals, and (3) that can wait for a certain time of the year for approval. Some proposals—specifically the ones involving definite schedules and massive capital outlays—satisfy these requirements. It appears, however, that in the great majority of cases the conditions for budgeting are not met. Nonmonetary costs often predominate and are ill-defined; many requests require special consideration; the competing requests are not known and the scheduling of the decision is such that the organization cannot wait to find out what they are. In these cases, the manager's approval must be sought on an ad hoc basis. This is common both for many improvement project and for most other requests (for example, to approve a policy exception) as the following examples from our study indicate:

> A nurse asks the hospital director if approval can be given to allow nurses to operate cardiac units when no doctors are available. A subordinate seeks authorization from another chief executive to bring in consultants to begin a study, and another asks if construction can begin on a new building. One chief executive meets with a promoter and one of his own vice presidents and is asked if the firm is willing to sponsor an athletic event.

What are the factors that enter into the manager's choice-making behavior in allocating resources? Because requests for authorization are usually presented individually, they involve particularly difficult choices. The manager must feel sure in his own mind that the organization's resources will not be over extended; he must consider whether the decision is consistent with other decisions; he must somehow test the feasibility of the proposals. Furthermore, the manager must consider factors of timing when deciding on requests for authorization. By authorizing too quickly, he may be denying himself important information—on events that will take place, on consequences of the decision that he did not at first consider, on other possible uses, yet to be suggested, for the same resources. By delaying authorization, the manager may be losing an opportunity, or he may be confusing subordinates who do not know whether to begin taking action or to forget about the request and start something else.

Despite the complexity of these choices that he must make, the very fact that the manager is approving rather than supervising these decisions suggests that he is not prepared to spend much time on them. Yet to make a choice quickly ("with the stroke of the pen" as one subordinate expressed it) is to risk discouraging a subordinate who may see a pet project, which has taken months to develop, destroyed in minutes. Clearly, the manager's success in his *leader* role depends in large part on the extent to which he does not inhibit innovative ideas that come to him in the form of requests for authorization.

Faced with these difficulties, the manager can beg the complexity by choosing the man rather than the proposal. That is, the manager may approve proposals presented by subordinates who are perceived as capable and reject those presented by subordinates who are perceived as incapable.

> One manager comments, "I don't decide on the issues; I have people do that. All I do is ensure that I have good people. If they don't lead me well, I change them."

But most choices must be faced directly. Here the manager calls on his considerable store of information. He must first make sure that a proposal complies with the values of the organization's influencers— that it does not inappropriately violate the wishes of any power group, and that it will carry the organization in the direction in which the influencers would like to see it move. Then the manager can draw on his extensive factual knowledge of the organization and its environment. Some of this is represented in terms of *models* and *plans* which the manager appears to develop in his mind to aid him in making choices.

A *model* is an abstraction of reality, a set of causal relationships by which the effects of given conditions can be predicted. One gets the impression, in listening to managers as they make decisions, that they carry an array of such models in their memories. One manager of my study, for example, reacted to a question about product distribution by giving a detailed description of the distributor network. Had an operations researcher been there with a tape recorder, he would probably have recorded enough information to begin development of a computer simulation of this operation.

In effect, the manager absorbs the information that continually bombards him and forms it into a series of mental models—of the internal workings of his organization, the behavior of subordinates, the trends in the organization's environment, the habits of associates, and so on. When choices must be made, these models can be used to test alternatives. The manager can say to himself, "Does this proposal make sense in terms of my understanding of the distribution network?" "Will the finance people be able to get along with marketing on this?" "What will happen to production if we introduce this one-week delay in shipping?" The effectiveness of the manager's decisions is largely dependent on the quality of his models.

My own impression is that the manager's *plans* are not explicit, documented in detail in the organization's files for all to see. Rather, crude plans seem to exist in the manager's mind in the form of a set of improvement projects that he would one day like to initiate.

> When asked about the future of his organization, the manager replies, "Well, once I get these foreign operations fully developed, I would like to begin to look into a reorganization."

> When a public relations project is proposed to the manager, he accepts it because it will help him to succeed in another public relations project that he has in mind for the future.

Such plans serve as a manager's vision of direction. By making choices with regard to them, the manager is able to interrelate various decisions and to insure that they all lead the organization in one general direction.

It should be stressed that the plans developed by the manager tend to be flexible. Because of unanticipated disturbances, unpredictable timing factors, possible new information and alternatives, the manager often cannot afford the luxury of rigid plans. He must allow himself the flexibility to react to the environment. Thus, his plans are made to be modified. And because they might readily be modified, the manager's plans are seldom made explicit. They remain in his mind, to be used in the making of his choices.

To summarize, the *resource allocator* role has three components —scheduling of time, programming of work, and authorizing of actions. This last component, in particular, involves very complex choice-making behavior. Models and plans which he develops in his mind help the manager to deal with the complexity.

The Manager as *Negotiator*

The manager's final role is that of participant in negotiation activity. From time to time, the organization finds itself in major, non-routine negotiations with other organizations or individuals. It is frequently the manager who leads the contingent from his organization. We see occasional reference in the news to such situations—the chairman of a transit system called in at the last minute to negotiate a new agreement with the union, the president of a football team called upon to work out a contract with the holdout superstar, the head of a major corporation leading a group to negotiate a new stock issue with the financial community. My study provides two quite different illustrations of the *negotiator* role:

> A meeting is held to negotiate the acquisition of a firm. Present are members of the firm to be acquired and the president and a number of vice-presidents of the firm making the offer. The president leads the contingent from his organization, opens the proceedings, and plays a central role in the negotiations.

> The chief executive and his deputy meet two members of a consulting firm currently serving the organization. The two groups are in conflict over certain expenses that have been charged. Eventually, the chief executive states his demands, and an agreement is reached.

Some writers on the management process have criticized the manager's participation in negotiation activity, suggesting that it is unnecessary and nonmanagerial. I believe negotiation is a vital part of the manager's job. The manager participates because as *figurehead* his presence adds credibility to the proceedings and as *spokesman* he represents his organization's information and value system to outsiders. But most important, as *resource allocator* the manager has the authority to commit organizational resources. Negotiation is resource trading in real-time. It requires the presence of someone with enough authority to commit the quantity of resources at stake, and do it quickly.

Hence, we often hear of examples of labor representatives stopping negotiations to demand the presence of senior management who, they know, must ratify the final proposal anyway. We see the participation of chief executives in certain kinds of negotiations in my study, and the same participation of lower-level managers in Sayles's study. To Sayles, negotiation is a most significant part of these managers' jobs, at the core of their horizontal relationships.

> Sophisticated managers place great stress on negotiations as a way of life. They negotiate with groups who are setting standards for their work, who are performing support activity for them, and to whom they wish to "sell" their services. However, negotiations primarily concern costs, specifications, and time (1964: 131).

This completes the discussion of the decisional roles. In closing, it is important to stress again the power that the manager of an organization has over the making of its strategy, power expressed by his ability to initiate and supervise improvement projects, by his handling of significant organizational disturbances, by his control over the allocation of organizational resources, and by his supervision of all major negotiations.

Table 2 contains a summary description of the ten managerial roles discussed in this chapter together with details on the managerial activities identifiable with each role and the treatment of each role in

Table 2. Summary of Ten Roles

Role	Description	Identifiable Activities from Study of Chief Executives (see Appendix C)	Recognition in the Literature
Interpersonal			
Figurehead	Symbolic head; obliged to perform a number of routine duties of a legal or social nature	Ceremony, status requests, solicitations	Sometimes recognized, but usually only at highest organizational levels
Leader	Responsible for the motivation and activation of subordinates; responsible for staffing, training, and associated duties	Virtually all managerial activities involving subordinates	Most widely recognized of all managerial roles
Liaison	Maintains self-developed network of outside contacts and informers who provide favors and information	Acknowledgments of mail; external board work; other activities involving outsiders	Largely ignored, except for particular empirical studies (Sayles on lower- and middle-level managers, Neustadt on U.S. Presidents, Whyte and Homans on informal leaders)
Informational			
Monitor	Seeks and receives wide variety of special information (much of it current) to develop thorough understanding of organization and environment; emerges as nerve center of internal and external information of the organization	Handling all mail and contacts categorized as concerned primarily with receiving information (e.g., periodical news, observational tours)	Recognized in the work of Sayles, Neustadt, Wrapp, and especially Aguilar
Disseminator	Transmits information received from outsiders or from other subordinates to members of the organization; some information factual, some involving interpretation and integration of diverse value positions of organizational influencers	Forwarding mail into organization for informational purposes, verbal contacts involving information flow to subordinates (e.g., review sessions, instant communication flows)	Unrecognized (except for Papandreou discussion of "peak coordinator" who integrates influencer preferences)

Spokesman	Transmits information to outsiders on organization's plans, policies, actions, results, etc.; serves as expert on organization's industry	Board meetings; handling mail and contacts involving transmission of information to outsiders	Generally acknowledged as managerial role
Decisional			
Entrepreneur	Searches organization and its environment for opportunities and initiates "improvement projects" to bring about change; supervises design of certain projects as well	Strategy and review sessions involving initiation or design of improvement projects	Implicitly acknowledged, but usually not analyzed except for economists (who were concerned largely with the establishment of new organizations) and Sayles, who probes into this role
Disturbance Handler	Responsible for corrective action when organization faces important, unexpected disturbances	Strategy and review sessions involving disturbances and crises	Discussed in abstract way by many writers (e.g., management by exception) but analyzed carefully only by Sayles
Resource Allocator	Responsible for the allocation of organizational resources of all kinds—in effect the making or approval of all significant organizational decisions	Scheduling; requests for authorization; any activity involving budgeting and the programming of subordinates' work	Little explicit recognition as a role, although implicitly recognized by the many who analyze organizational resource-allocation activities
Negotiator	Responsible for representing the organization at major negotiations	Negotiation	Largely unrecognized (or recognized but claimed to be nonmanagerial work) except for Sayles

the literature. In closing, one point should be noted. It has been claimed throughout this chapter that managers are essentially generalists in organizations of specialists. This is only partly true. Managers are generalists when considered in terms of the set of specialist functions performed by their organizations. But when compared with other kinds of work, managerial work is also specialized. Managers must perform ten roles that involve their own kinds of specialized behavior.

THE MANAGER'S BASIC PURPOSES

Having completed the description of managerial work in terms of the ten roles, it is now appropriate to go back to the beginning and ask why organizations need managers in the first place. Chester Barnard claims that "Executive work is not that *of* the organization, but the specialized work of *maintaining* the organization in operation" (1966: 215). And David Braybrooke takes one further step and suggests that managers are needed only because of imperfections in the organizational system.

> As one investigates, one seems to discover that an executive can be said to do something clearly identifiable only when he is doing something that in a larger or more perfect organization would be done by a subordinate, or, in other words, it would seem that the more specialized the role of leadership becomes, the more difficult it is to say what a leader does.
>
> For in a perfect organization, would not every specialized power be delegated to some specialized functionary? The man at the top would be left with nothing, or what seems to approach nothing, to do (1964: 534).

Katz and Kahn identify four reasons for leadership that relate to imperfections and unpredictabilities, both inside and outside the organization:

> The incompleteness of organizational design.
> Changing environmental conditions.
> The internal dynamics of organization.
> The nature of human membership in organizations (1966: 304–308).

Arguing in a similar vein, a number of writers claim that true managerial work involves only unprogrammed activity—dealing with the issues that are new and different (see, for example, Myers, 1967). And then we have the complementary view of the classical writers that managers focus primarily on those tasks that are removed from the day-to-day concerns of operating the system—such as planning or organizing.

Our evidence is that each of these views tells only a part of the story. Certainly managers must take the broad view; they must do unprogrammed work; and they must buttress the system where it is imperfect. But they must also involve themselves in certain regular operations (like negotiations); they have their share of ordinary work to do (as *figurehead* and *spokesman*); and they must make decisions that are fully expected (*resource allocation,* for example). Each organization requires a formal authority to, among other things, carry out a group of basic, regular duties.

Combining these regular duties with those related to change and imperfection in the system, we emerge with a statement of five basic reasons why organizations need managers:

1. The prime purpose of the manager is to ensure that his organization serves its basic purpose—the efficient production of specific goods or services. This gives rise to the next two purposes of the manager.

2. The manager must design and maintain the stability of his organization's operations. The manager must program the operations of his organization and monitor these programs to ensure a steady pattern of workflow. He must correct deviations when they occur and he must allocate new resources, as they become available, to ensure the smooth flow of operations. As *leader,* he must develop and sustain an atmosphere in which the necessary work will get done. Essentially, he must ensure that the organization functions as an integrated unit.

3. The manager must take charge of his organization's strategy-making system, and therein adapt his organization in a controlled way to its changing environment. As *monitor,* the manager must be familiar with environmental trends and as *entrepreneur* and *leader* he must provide direction for his organization and introduce change in such a way that the organization adapts to it without unnecessary disruption. The maintenance of a balance between stability and change is among the manager's most difficult tasks.

4. The manager must ensure that his organization serves the ends of those persons who control it. The manager must act as the focus for organizational values. Influencers exert pressures on him to have the organization serve their ends. The manager must interpret the values of each influencer, combine all these to determine the true power system, and then inform his subordinates of this in the form of organizational preferences to guide them in their decision-making. Should growth or profit or some other value be preeminent, the manager must ensure that these ends are achieved as a result of the decisions taken.

5. The manager must serve as the key informational link between his organization and its environment. Only the manager, because of his formal authority, is capable of creating that vital link between certain special sources of information and his organization. He must serve as nerve center for this kind of information. As *liaison* the manager creates the link, as *monitor* he receives the information, and as *disseminator* he transmits it to subordinates. In essence, the manager takes relatively ambiguous and unstructured data inputs from above and outside, sorts these out and gives order to them, and then transmits clear information down the line. Furthermore, the manager is obliged to create the link in the opposite direction, by sending organizational information to the environment in his *spokesman* and *negotiator* roles. In both cases, this work is not "long-run" or "big picture." Ths two-way flow of information is continuous, real-time, and specific in its detail.

6. *As formal authority, the manager is responsible for the operating of his organization's status system.* Although the work is often routine and programmed, the manager must nevertheless perform a number of duties to operate his organization's status system. Included here are activities associated particularly with the *figurehead* role, but also to some extent with the *spokesman* and *negotiator* roles.

PROPOSITIONS ABOUT MANAGERIAL ROLES

1. Managerial activities and managerial roles may be grouped in three categories—those concerned primarily with interpersonal relationships, those that deal primarily with information processing, and those that involve the making of significant decisions.
2. The work of managers of all types may be described in terms of ten observable roles: *figurehead, liaison,* and *leader* (interpersonal roles), *monitor, disseminator,* and *spokesman* (information roles), and *entrepreneur, disturbance handler, resource allocator,* and *negotiator* (decisional roles).
3. These ten roles form a *gestalt*—an integrated whole. The three interpersonal roles derive from the manager's formal authority and status; these give rise to the three informational roles; and these in turn enable the manager to perform the four decisional roles.
4. The simplest of managerial roles, that of *figurehead*, identifies the manager as a symbol, obliged to carry out a number of social, inspirational, legal, and ceremonial duties. In addition, the manager must be available to certain parties that demand to deal with him because of his status or authority.
5. The *leader* role identifies the manager's relationship with his subordinates. He defines the milieu in which they work, motivates them, probes into their activities to keep them alert, and takes responsibility for hiring, training, and promoting them. The manager attempts to bring subordinate and organizational needs into a common accord to promote efficient operations. The *leader* role pervades virtually all the manager's activities in which subordinates are involved, even those whose main pur-

pose is not interpersonal. The power of the manager is most clearly manifested in the *leader* role.

6. In the *liaison* role the manager develops a network of contacts outside of his organization, in which information and favors are traded for mutual benefit. Managers spend considerable amounts of time performing this role, first by making a series of commitments to establish these contacts, and then by carrying out various activities to maintain them.

7. Evidence suggests that the manager serves as "nerve center" of his organization's information. His unique access to all subordinates and to special outside contacts (many of them nerve centers of their own organizations) enables the manager to develop a powerful data base of external and internal information. In effect, the manager is his organization's generalist with the best store of nonroutine information.

8. As *monitor* the manager continually seeks and receives information from a variety of sources in order to develop a thorough understanding of the organization and its environment. Information arrives on internal operations, external events, ideas, and trends, and in the form of analyses and pressures.

9. A good part of the manager's information is current, tangible, and nondocumented. Hence the manager must take responsibility for the design of his own information system, which he does by building liaison contacts and by training subordinates to bypass their superiors in delivering information to him.

10. The manager uses his information to detect changes, to identify problems and opportunities, to build up a general understanding of his milieu for decision-making, to determine organizational values, and to inform outsiders and subordinates.

11. As *disseminator* the manager sends external information into his organization and internal information from one subordinate to another. This information may be of a factual or value nature.

12. The manager serves as the focal point for his organization's value system. Influencers direct their statements of preference to him; he, in turn, assimilates and combines these according to the power of the source, and disseminates information on overall organizational values to subordinates who use it as a guide in decision-making. The dissemination of values occurs in terms of specific statements on specific issues, not in terms of global preferences.

13. The manager faces a "dilemma of delegation." Only he has the information necessary to make a great many important decisions. But the information is in the wrong form—verbal and in memory rather than documented. Hence dissemination of it is time-consuming and difficult. The manager must overload himself with tasks or spend a great amount of time disseminating information, or delegate with the understanding that the job will be done with the use of less information than he has.

14. As *spokesman* the manager must transmit information to var-

ious external groups. He must act in a public relations capacity; lobby for his organization; keep key influencers (board of directors or boss) informed; inform the public about his organization's performance, plans, and policies; and send useful information to his *liaison* contacts.

15. As *spokesman,* furthermore, the manager must serve outsiders as an expert in the field in which his organization operates.

16. The manager must take full responsibility for his organization's strategy-making system, the system by which important decisions are made and interrelated. He has the necessary authority and information, and by having control over all important decisions he can integrate them.

17. As *entrepreneur* the manager initiates and designs much of the controlled change in his organization. He continually searches for problems and opportunities. When a situation requiring improvement is found, the manager initiates an "improvement project"—a series of related decisions and other activities, sequenced over a period of time, that leads to the actual improvement.

18. The manager may involve himself in an improvement project on one of three levels. He may delegate all responsibility to a subordinate, implicitly retaining the right to replace him; he may delegate responsibility for design but retain responsibility for choice via authorization; or he may supervise the design phase himself.

19. At any one time senior managers appear to maintain supervision over a large inventory of improvement projects. These vary widely in stage of development, with some under active development, some in limbo, and some nearing completion. Each is worked on periodically, with each step followed by a period of delay during which the manager waits for the feedback of information or the occurrence of an event. Occasionally, a project is completed or a new one added to inventory.

20. As his organization's generalist, the manager must take charge when his organization meets with an unexpected stimulus for which there is no clear programmed response. In effect, he assumes the role of *disturbance handler.* Disturbances may arise from conflicts between subordinates, conflicts between the manager's organization and another, and losses of resources or threats thereof. Disturbances arise both because "poor" managers are insensitive and because innovation by "good" managers inevitably leads to unanticipated consequences. Faced with a disturbance, the manager gives it priority and devotes his efforts to removing the stimulus—to buying time so that it can be dealt with leisurely by an improvement project.

21. In his *resource allocator* role the manager oversees the allocation of all forms of organizational resources (such as money, manpower, reputation). This involves three essentials—schedul-

ing his own time, programming the work of the organization, and authorizing actions.

22. In scheduling his own time the manager implicitly sets organizational priorities. What fails to reach him fails to get support. Thus, his time assumes a significant opportunity cost.

23. The manager takes responsibility for establishing the basic work system of his organization and programming the work of subordinates—deciding what will be done, who will do it, what structure will be used.

24. Basic continuing control over resource allocation is maintained by the manager by authorizing all significant decisions before implementation. This enables him to interrelate decisions. Some decisions are authorized within a regular budgeting process; most are authorized on an ad hoc basis. These are difficult choices—time is limited, yet the issues are complex and subordinates' proposals cannot be dismissed lightly. In some cases the manager decides on the proposer rather than the proposal.

25. To help in evaluating proposals, managers develop loose *models* and *plans* in their heads. The models describe a great variety of internal and external situations. The plans—in the form of improvement projects to be initiated—serve to provide a common basis against which to evaluate proposals. The plans are loose, flexible, and implicit, so that they can be updated with the arrival of new information.

26. As *negotiator* the manager takes charge when his organization must engage in important negotiation activity with other organizations. He participates as *figurehead,* as *spokesman,* and as *resource allocator.*

27. The ten roles suggest that managers, while generalists when viewed within their organizations, are in fact specialists required to perform a particular set of specialized roles.

28. Organizations require managers not only because of imperfections in the system and unexpected changes in the environment, but because a formal authority is required to carry out certain basic, regular duties. The ten roles suggest six basic purposes of the manager—to ensure the efficient production of the organization's goods and services, to design and maintain the stability of organizational operations, to adapt the organization in a controlled way to its changing environment, to ensure that the organization serves the ends of those persons who control it, to serve as the key information link between the organization and its environment, and to operate the organization's status system.

5
Variations in Managers' Work

Not chaos-like together crush'd and bruis'd
But, as the world, harmoniously confus'd:
Where order in variety we see,
And where, though all things differ, all agree.

from Windsor Forest
by Alexander Pope

In Chapter 1, the manager was defined as that person in charge of a formal organization or one of its subunits. He may be called vice president, foreman, prime minister, sergeant, archbishop, or any one of a great variety of other titles. He may come from a private or a public organization, an organization of any one of an infinite variety of sizes and rates of growth. His job may be found at any level of the organizational hierarchy (except the lowest) and he may supervise people in any one of a variety of organizational functions. He may have much or no experience in his job. He may find that its requirements vary according to the climate of the organization and the needs of the moment. In fact, there are an enormous number of variables that can influence the work that managers do. This chapter presents a framework for analyzing work variations and reviews the available evidence on the subject. At the end the findings are summarized by describing eight basic types of managerial jobs.

To develop the material of this chapter, the empirical studies of managerial jobs were surveyed in search of evidence on variations and their causes. The diary study by Rosemary Stewart (1967) of 160 managers in various environments was of considerable help, and it was possible to reach some conclusions by comparing the findings of different studies (for example, Sayles's study of lower- and middle-level managers versus my own study of chief executives). But for the most part the survey turned up a plethora of bits and pieces. Because of this, it should be made clear that what follows is a series of hypotheses, each of which requires further investigation.

A CONTINGENCY THEORY OF MANAGERIAL WORK

To begin, it should be stressed that the empirical studies of managerial work to date have produced more evidence of similarities than of differences in jobs. Two reviews of this literature point this out—one by Nealey and Fiedler (1968) and one by Campbell and his collaborators (1970). Each had hoped to isolate job differences and each reluctantly draws the conclusion that the similarities outweigh the differences. Yet both express confidence that better evidence will show that the differences are most significant. For example, Nealey and Fiedler found 32 "methodologically sound" empirical studies that presented data on managers from at least two levels of the hierarchy. They conclude:

> The literature on management attitudes and behavior by organizational level leads to the overall impression that the similarities outweigh the differences. Before this verdict is accepted, however, two points should be considered. First, information involving management behavior is very scarce. Second, the literature almost certainly contains data which are influenced by response bias and observer bias (1968: 318).

Using some rather questionable logic, these writers claim (1) that "response bias" derives from the lower manager's desire to move up the hierarchy and so to describe his job as more like that of higher managers, and (2) that "observer bias" stems from the stereotype that has largely ignored the possibility of variations in managers' jobs.

But perhaps, as suggested in the theory presented in Chapters 3 and 4, managers' jobs do indeed resemble each other markedly; perhaps there is something basic about the job of managing, no matter what the organization being managed. My own contention is that both the fundamental similarities and the individual differences in managers' jobs must be identified. We cannot accept the statement that "managers' jobs differ greatly from one to another in both substance and modes of operation" (Campbell et al., 1970: 93) any more than we can conclude that managers' jobs are all identical.

In this chapter, I shall endeavor to analyze work differences in terms of the fundamental similarities—the common characteristics and roles described in Chapters 3 and 4. I shall look for pronounced emphasis of certain roles or for additional roles in particular jobs, and for muted or highlighted characteristics. Is the *entrepreneur* role especially significant for chief executives? Are managers of staff groups subject to less interruption in their work than others are? Answers to questions such as these enable us to build some theoretical understanding of variations in managers' work.

The framework for a *contingency theory* of managerial work was developed by analyzing the differences in the work of the five men of my study (presented in Appendix C) and by considering the variables that were held constant in the study (such as type of managerial job and size of organization). According to this framework, shown schematically in Figure 11, the work of a particular manager at a particular point in time is determined by the influence that four "nested" sets of variables have on the basic role requirements and work characteristics. First, and most broadly, the manager's job is influenced by the organization, its industry, and other factors in the *environment*. Second, there are work variations caused by the job itself—its *level* in the organization and the *function* it oversees (such as marketing or production). Third, there are variations within a given job stemming from the *person* in that job—the effects of his personality and style. Finally, there are variations within a particular individual's job caused by the *situation* (seasonal variations or temporary threats, for example). The work any manager does at a certain point in time can be described as a function of these four sets of variables.[1] Each shall be dealt with in turn.

---

[1] Campbell et al. use a similar typology:

"First, [managerial jobs] are subject to time-determined changes; the things an executive does when preparing an annual budget differ from those he does when conducting labor contract negotiations. Second, there are person-determined changes; managers are typically given broad administrative assignments, but they are allowed great latitude in the means they use to accomplish them. Finally, managerial jobs are often subject to situation-determined changes; they may differ according to organizational level and function (for example, sales management versus research management), or they may differ from company to company, region to region, country to country, etc." (1970: 71).

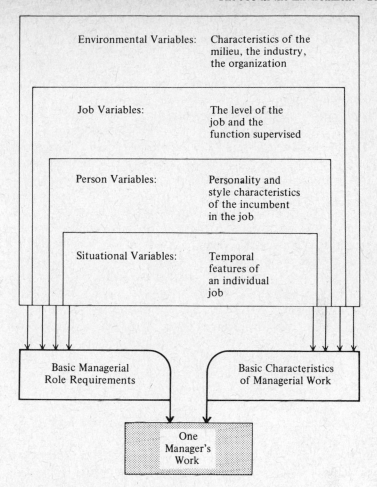

Figure 11. A Contingency View of Managerial Work

THE JOB IN THE ENVIRONMENT

A variety of environmental factors may influence the manager's work. These include the culture of the milieu; the nature of the industry; various dynamic factors such as competition, rate of change, and type of technology; and the characteristics of the organization itself, including its age and size. Unfortunately, we know very little about the influence of most of these factors on the manager's job.[2] We can find

[2] With regard to culture, for example, we have the finding of Stieglitz (1969) that non-U.S. chief executives ranked external relations as more important and planning as less important than American chief executives did. He suggests that this may be attributable to the American preoccupation with management science and professionalism, to an emphasis on growth, or, perhaps,

reasonable evidence for only two sets of variables—size of organization and industry.

Focus on Operations in Smaller Organizations

The size of the overall organization appears to have a considerable effect on what its senior managers do. Specifically, we find that chief executives of smaller organizations engage in fewer formal activities but are much more concerned with the operating work of their organizations. This can be explained by the lack of depth in their management and staff—they must keep closer watch on operations and must be prepared to fill in when the need arises.

A study by Irving Choran (1969) provides the best evidence of these phenomena. He used structured observation to study, for two days each, the work of the presidents of three small companies—a producer of industrial chemicals, a producer of consumer cosmetics, and an operator of restaurants. The study exactly parallels my study of five executives and provides data that are useful in comparing chief executives of organizations of different sizes. In his analysis Choran claims, by virtue of his evidence, that his subjects performed all the basic roles discussed in Chapter 4 and that their work exhibited the six sets of characteristics discussed in Chapter 3.

A number of interesting differences appear, however, as shown in Table 3. The managers of the small firms engaged in many more activities per day. For two of the three the number was particularly high (99 and 104), and their work showed pronounced characteristics of brevity and fragmentation. The three small-firm managers made greater use of the informal media, especially the telephone. They spent less time in scheduled meetings, and, interestingly, not one of these meetings had more than three participants (as against 43 percent for the five chief executives of the larger organizations). Their networks of external contacts were more restricted and specialized, with subordinates, suppliers, and associates taking up more of their time. The amount and type of mail they received indicated that these men had less well-developed formal communication networks. They also engaged in more organizational work and less ceremony, and two of the three spent substantially more time in observational tours (13

---

to the inability to plan in societies with unstable political climates. Inkson et al. (1970), in contrasting the work of senior managers in Midlands, England and Ohio, U.S.A., found that the latter appear to have a greater belief in the principles of scientific management. Curiously, however, the empirical studies of the actual work activities of managers appear to show no variations by country. Evidence from the diary studies of Carlson (1951) in Sweden, Stewart (1967) in Great Britain, and Dubin and Spray (1964) in America suggest that the basic characteristics of managerial work know no national boundaries.

Table 3. Selected Comparisons of the Work of Chief Executives
of Small and Large Organizations[a]

	Small Companies 3 presidents 6 days of observation Choran Study	Large Organizations 5 chief executives 25 days of observation Mintzberg Study
Number of activities per day	77	22
Desk Work Sessions		
Number per day	22	7
Proportion of time	35%	22%
Average duration	6 min	15 min
Telephone Calls		
Number per day	29	5
Proportion of time	17%	6%
Average duration	2 min	6 min
Scheduled Meetings		
Number per day	3	4
Proportion of time	21%	59%
Average duration	27 min	68 min
Unscheduled Meetings		
Number per day	19	4
Proportion of time	15%	10%
Average duration	3 min	12 min
Tours		
Number per day	5	1
Proportion of time	12%	3%
Average duration	9 min	11 min
Proportion of Activities Lasting Less Than 9 Min	90%	49%
Proportion Lasting More Than 60 Min	0.02%	10%
Number of Pieces of Mail Processed Per Day	17	36
Proportion of Mail From		
Subordinates	54%	39%
Peers	2%	16%
Suppliers and associates	24%	8%
Proportion of Time in Verbal Contact With		
Subordinates	56%	48%
Clients	7%	3%
Suppliers and associates	31%	17%
Peers and trade organizations	0.2%	11%
Directors and codirectors	0%	12%
Others	7%	8%

Table 3. *(Continued)*

Proportion of Scheduled Meetings With More Than 3 Participants	0%	43%
Proportion of Contact Time for Purposes of		
Organizational work	15%	2%
Ceremony	4%	12%

[a] Figure selected to show only differences between work of two groups.

and 10 percent compared with an average of 1 percent for the five chief executives of the larger organizations).

A clear picture emerges from this comparison. Apparently, in the smaller organizations there is a marked decrease in formality and a marked increase in the concern for internal operating issues. Lack of formality is indicated by the pronounced brevity of activity, by the frequency of telephone calls and unscheduled meetings, by the lack of scheduled meetings with more than three people, by only a trickle of formal correspondence, and by the small amount of time spent on ceremony. In Choran's view, the *figurehead* and *liaison* roles—while still performed by his managers—did not assume the same importance as they did for the five chief executives of the larger organizations.

Related to informality is the intensified concern for operations in the work of the heads of the smaller firms. This is shown best by the finding that almost all external interactions were with suppliers, associates, and clients—those people who fed, and were fed by, the firms' daily operations. Choran notes that these managers sought information on inventory levels, received copies of orders and invoices, signed checks, and purchased materials. They spent more time touring their firms, making its strategy, and doing its operating work. Choran concludes that the *leader* and *information processing* roles (*within* the firm) were more significant for these managers than for the chief executives of the larger firms.

Choran notes that the managers of his study spent one-eighth of their time in work that can be assigned to two new roles—*specialist* and *substitute operator*. The manager engages in the former role if he "deems that any one function is vital to the organization's well-being. . . ."

> Mr. [Cosmetics] implemented an inventory control system for his organization. He operated the system and felt that he was the most capable person in the organization to handle the position. As Mr. [Cosmetics] saw it, a well-run inventory control system was the heart of any business.

Mr. [Restaurant] . . . acted as the purchasing agent for his firm. Here again the manager felt he was the most capable person to handle the assignment (1969: 134).

The *substitute operator* role reflects the dearth of slack in small firms. As generalist, the manager must be prepared to step into a job when any one of a number of needs arise—an employee is absent, the plant is operating at full capacity and an extra hand is needed, and so on.[3]

Some of Choran's findings are supported by the evidence of other studies. Stieglitz (1970), who polled 48 chief executives from companies with less than 3,000 employees and 61 from firms with more than 10,000, also found that the heads of the small firms were more personally involved in short-term, more operational problems. Stieglitz concludes that they simply lacked the staff support of their counterparts in the larger firms. Another interesting Stieglitz finding is that almost all the heads of the larger firms saw themselves as "professional managers" while a sizable number of the presidents of the smaller firms thought of themselves as "entrepreneurs."

Rosemary Stewart (1967) provides some evidence of the greater formality in larger organizations. She found that in the larger companies more time was spent by functional heads in group communication, "probably because of a greater need for discussions to coordinate the work of the various departments" (p. 56). She designates one of her five job-profiles—the committeemen—as high on group discussion and found only in large organizations.

To conclude, we find that in smaller organizations, chief executives give more attention to operating problems; they are more inclined to do some of the staff work themselves and to step into non-managerial jobs in order to fill in when necessary; they see themselves more as entrepreneurs; and they are less involved in formal activities, particularly group discussions and duties related to the *figurehead* role.

The Influence of Industry

It may be assumed that managers in public organizations are called upon to work somewhat differently from the way those in business organizations work. Moreover, there are probably differences between managers in service and manufacturing firms, and between managers whose organizations operate in dynamic environments and those in more stable environments. Our evidence indicates the influence of some of these factors.

[3] The work of *substitute operator* can also be considered a part of the *disturbance handler* role. There may, however, be merit in clearly distinguishing this work where it assumes the special importance that it does for heads of small organizations.

My own study provides some evidence of the differences between business and public (or quasi-public) organizations. In the latter—which faced more complex coalitions of external forces—the chief executives spent more time in formal activity and more time meeting with outside groups, clients, and directors. Decisions taken in public organizations are more sensitive politically; hence there is a need to weigh more carefully the concerns of special interest groups and to be more careful about legitimizing the actions taken. The *liaison, spokesman,* and *negotiator* roles are presumably more important for the chief executives of public organizations.

The situation may be different at middle levels of management. André Costin (1970) mailed questionnaires to business and government managers in which he asked them to note the frequency with which they performed the ten roles (for example, the *disseminator* role—"passing on information from outside your organization to your subordinates"). In his analysis of 100 responses from each group, he found not only that both groups described their work as comprising all ten roles, but that there were no significant differences between the two groups in the ratings of the importance of nine of the ten roles:

> It may be concluded that the roles which managers are called to perform are qualitatively and quantitatively similar. . . . However, the activities of the two groups differ in one critical respect. . . . A significantly greater proportion of businessmen are involved in a more active search for new ways to involve their organizations and in improvements which they can bring to their organizations [*entrepreneur* role] (1970: 39).

We can conclude that because businesses face more competitive environments than public organizations, their middle managers tend to perceive the *entrepreneur* role as more significant in their work.

There is some specific evidence on the influence of the competitive and dynamic nature of the organization's environment. In my own study and that of Burns (1957), managers in the competitive organizations were found to spend more time in informal communication than others. Presumably, these managers must have more complete, more up-to-date information, in order to react to sudden moves by competitors. Rosemary Stewart also found that for managers in more dynamic environments (where there was faster change, greater pressure to produce, an expanding company) the work was more varied and fragmented; whereas "the two general managers who spent an above average amount of time alone worked for companies employing under 250 people, which, they said, were subject only to a moderate rate of change" (1967: 51). It may, in fact, be possible to sort managers into two groups along these dimensions—those in dynamic jobs where the common characteristics of pace, brevity, variety, fragmentation, and orientation to live action and verbal media are intensified; and those in relatively stable jobs, where these characteristics are less pronounced.

Of further interest are the variations that appear when we delve into more specific aspects of different industries. In my study I found the *liaison* role to be of special importance in the consulting industry, where contacts and contracts are paramount. Stieglitz (1969) complements this with his finding that chief executives of financial and service organizations more frequently ranked external relations as important than did those of manufacturing firms.

Unfortunately, there is little further evidence on the influence of these variables; hence we can only conclude that the environmental variables will be important ones in the eventual development of a full contingency theory of managerial work.

THE JOB ITSELF—LEVEL AND FUNCTION

The greater part of the evidence on differences in managerial jobs relates to features of the job itself—namely, the level in the hierarchy and the function supervised. Researchers have found that these two factors—particularly function—account for more variation than any other factors. Shartle, for example, found both that "differences among naval and among business organizations were more pronounced than differences between the naval and business groups," and that "one study of a number of job variables in a naval organization suggested that less than half of the performance could be ascribed to the man and a little over half to the demands of the particular job" (1956: 90 and 94).

A number of conclusions appear frequently in the literature. Moving down the hierarchy, the job becomes more structured, the "real-time" roles assume more importance, and some of the characteristics are more pronounced. Furthermore, there is considerable evidence of role specialization by function.

Workflow Orientation at Lower Levels

How do managerial jobs at the bottom of the hierarchy differ from those at the top? [4] We saw evidence in Chapter 3 of some remarkable similarities. For example, managers at all levels appear to divide their contact time in approximately equal proportions among superiors (on the order of 10 percent), subordinates, and peers (one-

[4] To a large extent, in this section we contrast managerial jobs near the top and bottom of the hierarchy. Middle-management jobs appear to be more strongly influenced by variables related to function. These are discussed in the next section.

third to one-half each). But what of their working roles? Are managerial jobs at lower levels different in kind from those at the top?

Katz and Kahn claim that they are. They introduce three types of leader behavior—"(1) the introduction of structural change, or policy formulation, (2) the interpolation of structure, i.e., piecing out the incompleteness of existing formal structure, or improvisation, and (3) the use of structure formally provided to keep the organization in motion and in effective operation, or administration" (1966: 308). Each, they contend, requires distinct knowledge and style, and each is associated with a distinct organizational level.

> Except in democratically constituted systems, only the top echelons of line and staff officers are really in a position to introduce changes in structure. The piecing out of structure is found most often in the intermediate levels of the organization. And the lowest supervisory level has open to it mainly the exercise of leadership by the skillful use of existing structure (Katz and Kahn, 1966: 311).

Katz and Kahn do not, however, provide evidence to support this contention, and there is evidence that directly contradicts it. Sayles (1964) talks specifically about the introduction of long-term structural change by the lower- and middle-level managers that he studied; Costin (1970) found "no significant positive correlation between managerial authority and the entrepreneurial consciousness of managers as predicted. It appears that management at lower levels are as opportunity-oriented as are higher-level managers" (p. 48).

This contradiction appears to reflect a different frame of reference. Katz and Kahn describe the manager's job in terms of the overall organization, whereas Sayles and Costin look at the man and his job directly. The conclusion reached in Chapter 4 was that every manager stands in the same basic relationship to his organizational unit and its environment. As a result, he is responsible for the introduction of structural change *in his own unit,* for interpolating that structure, and for using it to keep his unit going. Clearly, the production supervisor does not design the corporation's structure, but he is as concerned with structure in his shop as is the president with structure in his corporation.

Although I have found no support for the contention that managerial jobs at different levels differ in kind, there is considerable evidence that they differ in orientation. Specifically, managers at lower levels appear to be more concerned with the maintenance of work-flows, and this leads them to emphasize the "real-time" aspects of their jobs. In comparing my study of chief executives with Sayles's study of lower- and middle-level managers, for example, we find that the chief executives collected a wide variety of information to be used in strategy-making of a broad nature; the lower-level managers collected information to maintain the steady flow of work in their organizational units. Whereas our chief executives negotiated acquisitions, Sayles's managers negotiated delivery dates on orders.

Chapple and Sayles (1961) present further evidence—a job description for superintendents—developed from a study of actual activity patterns. A typical section reads:

> (a) Receives daily machine-load charts from each of his departments. Analyzes to see what machines were down and for how long. (b) If he was not notified by the foreman as to the reason on the preceding day, goes to him to find out the cause. (c) If he and foreman agree that faulty material caused the down time, gets a sample and takes it to the superintendent of the responsible department to request corrective action. (d) If the cause is mechanical, goes to chief mechanic to determine whether the fault is routine maintenance, operating, or machine construction (p. 49).

The roles most concerned with daily operating problems—the real-time roles, *disturbance handler* and *negotiator*—appear to be most significant in the work of these superintendents:

> The manager's basic function is maintaining or stabilizing several interrelated work flows. Job descriptions can be written describing these work flows clearly and further specifying the conditions or signals that tell him something needs to be done to avoid breakdowns or inefficiencies. Most of these "somethings" involve detecting deviations and having interaction with one or more people in the organization, started either by the manager or by one of his subordinates, superiors, or fellow supervisors (p. 67).

An analysis of Chapple and Sayles's full job description suggests that these superintendents performed activities associated with nine of the ten roles described in Chapter 4. The one exception is the *figurehead* role. In contrast, the studies of chief executives (Carlson, 1951; Stieglitz, 1969; and my study in Appendix C) suggest that social pressures and ceremonial work are a significant part of the senior manager's job. While no doubt there is some *figurehead* work in all managers' jobs—foremen escort visitors around their shops and attend the weddings of their subordinates—the amount of it probably decreases at lower levels of the hierarchy, together with all kinds of formality.

As the roles change in orientation, so do certain of the characteristics, again to reflect concern with the day-to-day problems of maintaining the workflow.[5] As noted in Chapter 3, the characteristics

---

[5] One characteristic that apparently changes for other reasons is that of working hours. Copeman (Copeman, Luijk, and Hanika, 1963) and Burns (1967) found that senior managers worked the longest hours, while Horne and Lupton (1965) felt that the middle managers they studied were not overworked. Perhaps

of brevity and fragmentation become more pronounced at lower hierarchical levels. Our chief executives averaged 22 minutes per activity, while Guest's foremen averaged 48 seconds.

There is evidence also that managers' jobs at lower levels are
more oriented toward issues that are current and specific, and are
more focused—concentrated on a narrower range of issues, which
span shorter periods of time. Martin's paper (1956) provides the firm-
est evidence of these phenomena.[6] He studied, by observation, interview, and examination of correspondence, the decision situations encountered at four levels—works manager, division superintendent,
department foreman, and shift foreman. At lower levels, decisions
were found to be more continuous, in the sense that they arose and
were completed in single quick sequences,

> whereas at higher levels they tend to display a discontinuous char-
> acter, with wide intervals of time separating the various component
> parts of the decision situation. Here in many instances a lapse of
> time occurs, say, between the phase of inquiry and the actual
> decision—the problem is, as it were, out of sight and out of mind.
> The executive frequently delegates the handling of a problem to a
> subordinate, to return to it at a later date (p. 252).

As shown in Table 4, decisions at lower levels involved shorter
time horizons. They were also more frequent and their time limits were
less elastic and ambiguous. Again we see the influence of the "real-
time" focus: "Thus the shift foreman must take action immediately if,
for example, a pipe breaks" (Martin, 1956: 253).

In concluding this section, it seems appropriate to address the
question of the amount of control managers have in their own jobs.
Are managers at lower levels less able to control their work than those
in senior positions? The general conclusion of Chapter 3 was as follows: Every manager faces an imposing array of pressures in his job.
As a result, he appears to *re*act far more than he acts of his own free
will. But closer examination discloses two important degrees of freedom—the latitude to develop certain long-term commitments (for example, to establish information channels or initiate projects), and the
right to turn obligations to his own advantage. In other words, *all*
managerial jobs are constraining; only the strong-willed managers
control their jobs, whether they be chief executives or foremen. There
may be some exceptions to this—particularly where the bureaucracy
is so rigid that certain jobs are designed to allow almost no freedom

---

this reflects the greater opportunity cost of the senior manager's time because
of his responsibility for more resources; perhaps natural selection simply ensures
that those at the highest levels are most committed to their work.

[6] Further evidence is provided by Thomason (1967), Dubin and Spray
(1965), and Marples (1967).

Table 4. Comparison of Time Perspectives of Decision Situations
at Four Levels of Management[a]

Time	Works Manager (Percent)	Division Superintendent (Percent)	Department Foreman (Percent)	Shift Foreman (Percent)
Short (0-2 weeks)	3.3	54.2	68.0	97.7
Moderate (2 weeks to year)	46.1	41.4	30.4	2.1
Distant	50.0	4.3	1.5	0.0
Total	99.4	99.9	99.9	99.8

[a]From Martin (1956: 251).

to the incumbent. The jobs of certain foremen and branch managers in certain large banking firms, for example, appear to fit this pattern. Unfortunately, we have little empirical evidence on this significant issue.[7] But it is my personal belief that managerial jobs are not inherently constrained or inherently open-ended simply because they are at a particular organizational level; managers at *any* level can exhibit a wide range of job control, depending on job design and their individual abilities to cope with the pressures.[8]

This section can be summarized with the claim that managers at all levels perform common roles, but with different emphasis. At lower levels the work is more focused, more short-term in outlook, and the characteristics of brevity and fragmentation are more pronounced. The *figurehead* role becomes less significant—a reflection of informality at lower levels—and the *disturbance handler* and *negotiator* roles increase in importance for the lower-level manager. He is concerned largely with the maintenance of workflow; as a result, he operates in real-time. But we cannot conclude that his job allows for less personal control. At all levels the pressures are great; in most jobs, no matter what the level, it is the incumbent himself who determines whether he will control the job or the job will control him.

[7] Wikstrom (1967) described one such situation—the foreman whose job is so eroded by specialists that he is left with little decision-making authority. He contrasts this with the foreman who is a "manager" because he has responsibility to coordinate the work of these specialists. (See Appendix A for more detail on Wikstrom's study.)

[8] An hypothesis presented by Thomason (1966 and 1967), if supported by subsequent evidence, would add considerable support to this conclusion. He suggests that managers at different levels specialize in the information they process, that communication constellations form at different levels in the organization to handle specialized information and problems. For example, we might find responsibility for production focused at a relatively low level in a particular firm, responsibility for marketing in a middle-management group, and responsibility for finance in the executive suite. Hence, managers at middle and lower levels can have considerable discretion about one specialized function, although they may be tightly controlled in other ways.

Role Specialization by Function

Considerable evidence has been found to indicate that the particular function that is supervised accounts in large part for the variations in managers' work. For example, Aguilar (1967) found that "executives in the same functional area appeared to exhibit notably more similar profiles [in the external information they identify as important] than do executives at the same level in the hierarchy" (p. 50).[9] As we shall see below, there is evidence that production, sales, and staff managers tend to concentrate their time on different sets of roles.

Line Production Managers. Rosemary Stewart (1967) was able to draw a number of conclusions about the characteristics of the work of line production managers. Relative to other managers, her "works managers" spent more time with subordinates, had less time alone, had more variety in their work, and experienced greater fragmentation of work (for example, many fleeting contacts). Most important, the five works managers in her study were found to spend one-quarter to one-third of their time on inspection even though

> These five varied considerably, both in the number of people that they controlled (from 100 to nearly 2,000) and in the kind of industries in which they worked. The high proportion of time that they spent on inspection may have been due in part to their conception of their job, but clearly it was due also to the kind of job that they had. The five had one thing in common: they were concerned only with running their plant efficiently (p. 42).

Miss Stewart titled one of her five job profiles, "the trouble shooters," and found that it contained most of the works managers, several factory managers, and "a few general managers of small companies or subsidiaries, who spent nearly all their time in their own company, and who were mainly concerned with works management" (p. 119).[10] She describes the "trouble shooters" as follows:

> [These] are the managers with the most fragmented work pattern. This was shown both by the frequency of their diary entries and by their large number of fleeting contacts. This fragmentation arose because they, far more than the managers in the first three groups,

[9] For further evidence, see Hemphill (1959 and 1960) who presents findings of a questionnaire study of 93 managers at three levels and in five functional areas. See also Chapple and Sayles (1961), who contrast the work of four middle managers in different functional areas.

[10] This similarity between production managers and chief executives of small firms—who must maintain workflow in the absence of staff groups and formal control systems—is also suggested when Choran's findings are compared with these.

had to cope with crises. Even though they may have planned carefully to avoid trouble, much of their time was spent dealing with problems which, when they arose, needed a speedy solution. The repercussions of a failure to solve problems were likely to be more rapid and dramatic than they would be in other departments of the business (p. 118).

These findings clearly complement those of Walker, Guest, and Turner (1956), who, in *The Foreman on the Assembly Line,* also emphasize the importance of crises. They conclude that these line production managers spend "much" of their time resolving unexpected difficulties. They cite a foreman who remarked that "emergencies are normal" (p. 76).[11] We can conclude that the decisional roles, particularly *disturbance handler* (and perhaps *negotiator*), appear to be most important in the job of the line production manager.

Line Sales Managers. The enduring conflict between sales and production managers is clearly reflected in their work. Although both hold basic line jobs, in their work they emerge almost as direct opposites. Whereas the production manager appears to be most involved with the *negotiator* and *disturbance handler* roles (production orientation), the sales manager demonstrates a major preoccupation with the three interpersonal roles (people orientation). External contacts *(liaison* and *figurehead* roles) are of great importance to him, and he appears also to spend considerable time training and developing his sales staff *(leader* role).

Rosemary Stewart found that sales managers spent more time than average outside the company, often in social activity and entertainment and often with customers.[12] Clearly important in this job are public relations and image-building activities. Miss Stewart's first job profile—the "emissaries"—describes the sales manager:

> The Emissary's work brought him in close touch with the world outside. He spent much of his time away from his company and in talking to people who were not its employees. He often spent several days away, visiting other companies, attending conferences or exhibitions. He worked longer hours than managers in any of the other groups, but this was mainly due to the time spent in travelling and in entertaining (p. 102).

[11] Further related evidence is provided by Guest (1956).

[12] This pattern reflects itself in staff jobs in these two functional areas as well. Landsberger (1962) concludes from his observational study:

> As might be expected, the sales liaison managers have the highest percentage of horizontal interactions, for their job is mediating between the field sales force and the factory. Production schedulers and stock controllers are likewise intermediaries, but their percentage of horizontal interaction units is lower since the points between which they mediate are far fewer than those of sales liaison (p. 314).

Davis's book, *The Performance and Development of Field Sales Managers* (1957), provides our best evidence on this job. He discusses a study made by one company of the activities of several hundred branch managers, in which customer contacts accounted for 10 percent of their time, public relations 3 percent, and promotional activity 7 percent, for a total of 20 percent. At least another 30 percent of their time was consumed in leadership activities—working at branches with agents, working in the office with salesmen, interviewing sales applicants, traveling to district offices and agencies in the field, and so on. In line with this, Davis discusses the activities of field sales managers under five headings. These are described below with the related roles in parentheses.

> Developing salesmen. Recruiting, selecting, coaching, and training the men (*leader*).
> Supervising salesmen. Assigning them to jobs and controlling performance; motivating them in these jobs (*resource allocator, monitor, leader*).
> Personal selling. Making joint calls with salesmen, for training purposes; personal handling of accounts (*leader, figurehead*).[13]
> Operating a field office. Includes customer service, record keeping and paper work, pricing and trade-ins, housekeeping chores, etc. (informational and decisional roles).
> Providing local title and prestige. Goodwill calls on customers, attendance at trade shows and conventions, participation in community affairs, trouble shooting, being "Mr. Company" (*figurehead, liaison, disturbance handler*).

We can conclude that the interpersonal roles—*figurehead, liaison, leader*—appear to be most important to the line sales manager. His orientation is interpersonal, his concern is for people and for contacts.

Managers of Staff Specialists. Staff managers—those who oversee units charged with speciality, technocratic functions—appear to form another distinct group. Here we include those who manage groups of accountants, planners, industrial engineers, personnel specialists, industrial relations people, researchers, social workers, and other staff experts. All the evidence suggests strongly that these managers spend more time alone ("solitary by comparison" is Rosemary Stewart's term), are more involved with paperwork, demonstrate the least amount of fragmentation and variety in their work, spend more

---

[13] Davis comments: "Regardless of the question of desirability, much of the time of many field sales managers is spent on personal accounts and must be included, therefore, in any inventory of management activities" (p. 35).

time advising people in peer and lateral relationships, and spend considerable time in the speciality functions of their units.[14]

In general, managers of staff groups appear to act both as managers and experts. They must manage organizational units, but they themselves must also serve in a staff capacity. Hence, they spend considerable time alone at their desks doing analytical work and in consultation with their units' "clients."

One must *be* an expert in order to *manage* experts. People in the environment expect the manager of specialists to represent the expertise of his organization, and the subordinates expect their leader to lead in a technical as well as managerial sense. Hence, the role of *expert,* discussed as a part of the *spokesman* role in Chapter 4, merits separate designation for the work of the manager of staff specialists. As Shartle (1956) notes:

> Professional consulting is an activity which may appear out of place in the list [of fifteen activities performed by executives]. However, many executives are professionally trained in a field such as law, cost accounting, teaching, engineering, or science. In their daily work they sometimes perform professionally. A line executive may be a trained cost accountant and may be called upon to give technical advice on cost accounting problems in his organization because of his special qualification. Because he performs the activity frequently it becomes an important part of his activity (p. 85).

In addition, we find that the information processing roles are particularly important for managers of staff groups. They must serve as sophisticated "nerve centers" for a specialized kind of information, and must disseminate this to subordinates and to others. Aguilar (1967), in his analysis of the manager's sources of external information, explains this orientation as follows:

> So far as technical and professional *specialists* are concerned, the relative reliance on horizontal rather than vertical transfers of external information can be explained in part by the smaller number of subordinates such specialists have in comparison with line managers. We can also speculate that these specialists tend to act more as screens for, than as procurers of, external information for top management (p. 74).

Hence, the *monitor* and *spokesman* roles, as well as the *expert* role, appear to be most important to the manager of staff specialists.

There is evidence as well that the roles related to external con-

---

[14] Evidence here comes from the studies of Stewart (1967), Stogdill, Shartle, and Associates (1956), Hemphill (1959 and 1960), Shartle (1956), Chapple and Sayles (1961), and others.

tacts—*liaison* and *negotiator*—are also of special concern. Rosemary Stewart (1967) notes that "jobs that provide a service for one's colleagues mean closer contact with them" (p. 62). She further comments:

> Staff posts often provide a wider range of contacts. Success in them may depend, to a large extent, on a man's ability to influence and persuade many different kinds of people (p. 68).

The *figurehead, leader, disturbance handler,* and *resource allocator* roles appear to be rather less important to staff managers as their formal authority usually does not extend beyond a small group of specialists. Rosemary Stewart points out, "It is managers in the works who need to carry bleeps, not those in finance or administration" (p. 83).

To summarize this section, clear variations appear in managers' jobs due to differences in level and function. The decisional roles are important to production managers, the interpersonal roles to sales managers, and the informational roles to managers of staff specialists.

THE PERSON IN THE JOB

In this section, we take the job environment and the job itself as given, and we look at the incumbent. The evidence shows that the incumbent's values, his personality, and his style, all contribute to the determination of the work he does.

Two brief studies carried out under the author's supervision provide some introductory comparisons. In one, the chief executive of a middle-sized real estate firm was found to prefer the external contact work, involving little operating detail. His activities were described as largely associated with the *liaison, figurehead,* and *spokesman* roles. He left to his subordinates—to one vice-president, in particular—many of the *leader* and *disturbance handler* activities. In another study of the executive team of a convalescent hospital, the chief executive was described as being firmly in command, but—perhaps because the environment was French-speaking and she was Italian—most of the external *liaison* and *spokesman* work was delegated to one of her assistants.

Similar patterns have been observed in many small firms with two partners—one concentrating on internal, production problems (the "inside man"), the other on external contacts and selling (the "outside man"). Shartle (1956) found that jobs among managers and their assistants reflected this same separation:

> When the work patterns of the seven heads were compared with the patterns of their principal assistants, the head who spent the most time in public relations had the assistant who spent the least of the

seven in this activity; and the head who spent the least in public relations had an assistant who spent the most time in this work (p. 88).

Further evidence of the effect of personal preference and style is found in the study of presidents of small firms made by Choran (1969). One man conducted his matters in a more formal way than the others—fewer informal contacts, longer formal ones. A second president focused much of his attention on getting information (the *monitor* role). The president of the restaurant chose to orient himself to the *liaison* and *entrepreneur* roles; because of his own preferred way of working, his activities were particularly brief and informal, many with clients.

These bits of evidence suggest that we may be able to learn much of interest by studying the effect that the personality and style of the incumbent have on the work performed. Unfortunately, little evidence has been produced so far. A great number of research studies have been carried out on managerial style; the vast majority of cases simply compared autocratic and participative styles. In most cases there was no attention to the influence of style on work performed; rather, many of the researchers attempted to link style directly with managerial effectiveness. In one area, however, there is some evidence on the influence of personality and style on work performed. We turn to that now.

Job Sharing in Executive Teams

We have already seen evidence of informal job sharing—a president deals largely with outside matters while his deputy handles internal matters. In governments, we frequently find the same relationship on a more formal basis, as between the minister and deputy minister in parliamentary government. Furthermore team management is becoming more prevalent. The Soviet troika and the corporation executive office are examples.

It appears to be quite common for job sharing to evolve informally in formal organizations, especially at top levels. In effect, one managerial job—the task of running a single organization—is split up among two or more managers. One gravitates to certain of the roles because of his personality and interests, leaving to others the rest of what is essentially a single managerial job. Hodgson, Levinson, and Zaleznik describe this type of situation, referring to the grouping of managers as an "executive role constellation":

> The executives' roles in the organization tended to become specialized around the performance of certain tasks and the expression of certain emotions. Role specialization was seen to have important roots in the executive's personality and important consequences for

his behavior in the organization. Several specialized roles were differentiated from one another in the top executive group, yet maintained a tightly integrated complementarity. They formed what we have called an *executive role constellation* (1965: 477).

Although the psychiatric hospital these researchers studied clearly had one chief executive, in actual fact, he specialized and shared his job with two of his subordinates. This job sharing was along both task and emotional dimensions. The superintendent related his organization to its environment *(liaison, figurehead, spokesman, negotiator* roles) and was both assertive and controlling. The clinical director operated internal clinical services *(disseminator, disturbance handler, resource allocator* roles) and was the supportive one *(leader* role); the assistant superintendent dealt with nonroutine innovation *(entrepreneur* role) and expressed friendship and equalitarian norms (another approach to the *leader* role). The researchers suggest that the triad is a most unstable role constellation, because the third party is always in between. They believe the diad to be more stable, both in a peer relationship (business partners) and in a superior-subordinate relationship.

Although the evidence has so far been largely concerned with the inside/outside role split, there is evidence also for the task/people split suggested above.

> Bales concludes that the group elevates to leadership positions two complementary leaders: a "task specialist" and a "social-emotional specialist." The task specialist is selected because he is seen as having the best ideas and as doing the most to guide the discussion. He concentrates on the task of the group, playing an aggressive role in moving the group toward a solution. He thus tends to incur hostility and is disliked. Concurrently, a second man emerges as a leader. Chosen as highly liked, he is the "social-emotional specialist" who concerns himself with solving the social-emotional problems of the group, resolving tensions and conflicts within the group to preserve group unity (Krech, Crutchfield, and Ballachey, 1962: 433).

In a recent article entitled "The Co-Manager Concept," John Senger (1971) gives evidence that shows how common this arrangement may be: "A survey of naval officers who had served in 312 separate commands during their careers revealed that in 60 percent of the cases the task and social functions were divided between the commanding officer and the second in command" (p. 79).

Stieglitz (1969) deals with the issue of job sharing in a pragmatic vein. He describes four variations of "a twosome at the top" arrangement, as detailed in Figure 12 below.

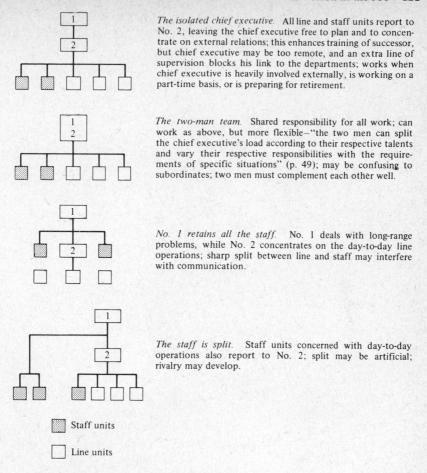

The isolated chief executive. All line and staff units report to No. 2, leaving the chief executive free to plan and to concentrate on external relations; this enhances training of successor, but chief executive may be too remote, and an extra line of supervision blocks his link to the departments; works when chief executive is heavily involved externally, is working on a part-time basis, or is preparing for retirement.

The two-man team. Shared responsibility for all work; can work as above, but more flexible—"the two men can split the chief executive's load according to their respective talents and vary their respective responsibilities with the requirements of specific situations" (p. 49); may be confusing to subordinates; two men must complement each other well.

No. 1 retains all the staff. No. 1 deals with long-range problems, while No. 2 concentrates on the day-to-day line operations; sharp split between line and staff may interfere with communication.

The staff is split. Staff units concerned with day-to-day operations also report to No. 2; split may be artificial; rivalry may develop.

Figure 12. **Four Job Sharing Structures**

Stieglitz also discusses the "chief executive office," a formalization of the management committee or "inner cabinet." In one model, a committee of "associate chief executives" is made up of the chief executive and a few of his key subordinates who maintain their positions as managers of line or staff groups. A second model divorces these managers from individual responsibilities, leaving the "office" in charge of the organization. Such arrangements, in the view of Stieglitz, show recognition of the difficulties of the single individual charged with administering a complex business, but they can also lead to confusion and ambiguity. But he believes there are times when they may be justified—when new general managers must be trained, or when organizations face complex environments or demanding external relationships.

In closing this section of executive teams and job sharing, it should be remembered that in Chapter 4 the point was emphasized that the ten managerial roles form a *gestalt*. Formal authority allows the manager to play the *liaison* and *leader* roles, and these bring the crucial nerve-center information required for effective execution of the informational and decisional roles. Hence, the job can be shared effectively only if information can be shared effectively. But with so much of it verbal, and with the severe time constraints faced by the manager, it is often difficult to do so. Hence, it must be concluded that job sharing is a most difficult thing to do, since its success is largely dependent on the ability of the participants to share information. (I shall return to this point in Chapter 7.)

To sum up, the evidence on job sharing is helpful in developing an understanding of how style and personality variables influence the work done. But more direct evidence on these variables is needed.[15]

THE JOB OVER TIME

A given person in a given job in a given environment does not continually engage in the same work. His job varies according to many situational factors such as annual budgeting requirements, periodic expansion programs, or major periods of crisis. In addition, as managers gain experience in their jobs, they change their working behaviors, and as times and social norms change, so must the work of the manager. The variety of time-related factors influencing the manager's work will be discussed under five headings—periodic patterns, the change–stability cycle, the period of threat, the new job pattern, and societal shifts.

Periodic Patterns

In Chapter 3 it was noted that an analysis of the activities of the chief executives of my study revealed no important short-term

[15] To make real progress on the study of the effectiveness of various managerial styles (and it is hoped that, in the future, styles will be described in more than one-dimensional terms, viz., autocratic/participative), we may have to treat behaviors as intermediate variables. One study that does this is reported by Ponder (1958). He used structured observation to compare the work of effective and ineffective foremen. The former "engaged in significantly fewer different activities and contacts" (200 versus 270); they spent half as much time on production issues, and twice as much on personnel administration; they spent more time with people in general (56% vs. 45%) and especially with staff and service personnel (32% vs. 20%); they spent more average time in each contact; they spent less time seeking information, more time answering requests for it, and more time in two-way communication. (No data are offered to support these last four conclusions.)

patterns in their work. Mornings appeared no different from after-noons, nor did certain days of the week from others. One example of an annual pattern did, however, show up. The year-end work of the school superintendent was characterized by a high incidence of social functions—that is, *figurehead* activities—and little incoming mail.

Rosemary Stewart (1967), who collected much more data in this regard (although not enough, in her view, to detect certain impor-tant cyclical patterns), presents complementary findings:

> Most jobs have some element of repetition. Some, such as journal-ism, have a definite time cycle. Few management jobs have a daily cycle, although there may be recurrent daily activities such as in-spection. More have a monthly or seasonal cycle. Managers in such jobs will spend their time in different ways at different periods of the cycle (p. 99).

Miss Stewart's work contains a number of examples of man-agers with periodic variations in their work. She cites the manager of an accounting group that produced a monthly report. His marked monthly work cycle reflected "a burst of team activity in the last week [before the report was due] and time to work on his own in the first week" (p. 42). Another manager in a small company visited salesmen and customers every six weeks and otherwise worked alone; the man-ager of a brewery experienced more work fragmentation in the sum-mer months when output peaked, pressure was great, and changes occurred hourly. Clearly, some managers emphasize different roles at different times of the month or year.

The Change–Stability Cycle

In his book, *Managerial Behavior,* Leonard Sayles points out that managers need to balance change and stability in their organiza-tions. Presumably, this can be done in two ways—by changing a few things at a time while holding all others constant, or by alternating periods of intense change with periods of consolidation and stability. The latter approach, of course, leads to cyclical variations in the man-ager's job. In one chief executive's work, at the time of observation he was leading his organization in a major acquisition program. He was, as a result, busily involved in those activities associated with the *entrepreneur* and *negotiator* roles; he spent almost half his contact time with suppliers and associates. One can speculate that when the program was completed, this chief executive began to spend more time in the *leader* and *disturbance handler* roles as he and his subordi-nates attempted to bring the new acquisitions under control.

It is likely that this cyclical pattern of change and stability—periods of entrepreneurship followed by periods of leadership—is found in the jobs of managers at all levels, even when the change is initiated at the top of the hierarchy. Katz and Kahn cite Mann who suggests that the results of change at the top move

> like a wave through the organization, beginning at the top and spreading rapidly downward as the top executives formulate major objectives and policy changes and then expect the next echelon to make the complementary changes which will create a new organizational state of equilibrium (1966: 331).

One other aspect of the change–stability cycle in manager's jobs can be seen as the organization emerges from its formative stage. Filley and House (1969), among others, discuss the stages of organizational growth, distinguishing the entrepreneurial stage, in which growth is rapid and consequential decisions are taken easily, from the administrative stage in which "professional" managers move in a more calculated and careful manner. The entrepreneur who creates an enterprise begins with no established patterns—much of what he does is innovation. But as he takes each decision, he reduces his organization's flexibility, until the stage emerges in which established patterns prevail. Where the *entrepreneur* and *negotiator* roles dominated before, now the *leader* and *disturbance handler* roles assume greater importance.

The Period of Threat

Many organizational disturbances are minor, and although they may necessitate some rescheduling, they can be dealt with quickly without major disruption in the normal pattern of work. But in some instances the organization faces a major threat, and the manager must alter his behavior for a substantial period of time. In his experimental study, Hamblin (1958) found that people were prepared to allow their leaders to have more influence over them in times of crisis. One clear example of this might be found in the military. In peacetime an army general has time for leisurely *figurehead, spokesman,* and *entrepreneur* activities—reviewing the troops, making speeches, improving the overall system. In wartime, his time horizon likely shortens considerably, and the roles of *disturbance handler* and *leader* no doubt emerge as the crucial ones.

Following a period of intensive threat, one should expect to find one of replenishment. Environmental linkages are renewed *(liaison* and *spokesman* roles); resources are replaced *(resource allocator* role).

The New Job Pattern

One factor that has an interesting effect on the manager's work is experience. There is evidence that managers in new jobs adopt behavior patterns that change as they gain experience. For one thing, the new incumbent lacks the contacts and the information that would enable him to play the *spokesman* and *disseminator* roles effectively. One would therefore expect him to spend a good deal of his time developing these contacts and collecting information *(liaison* and *monitor* roles). Rosemary Stewart found that "managers who had recently taken up a new post generally spent longer with their boss" (1967: 60). Aguilar, who specifically compared the monitoring habits of new managers with those of experienced ones, found that the former relied more for their external information on publications and on outsiders who sent information for their own benefit (as opposed to the benefit of the new managers).

> Thus, we may conclude that one reason inexperienced managers obtain so high a portion of unsolicited information not designed to benefit the receiver lies in the shortcomings of their personal communication networks. . . . Typically, the inexperienced manager has not yet fully developed an effective network of communication, and so information designed to benefit the source continues prominent in what he receives (Aguilar, 1967: 111–112).

As information and contacts develop, but while the manager is still quite new in his job, attention probably shifts to the *entrepreneur* role; as a newcomer, he is sensitive to what should be improved and desirous of putting his personal stamp on his organization. Once this is done he may settle down to the more balanced work of carrying out the ten roles. We may then call him "experienced" in the job.

A related issue, which can be called the "new manager syndrome," merits brief attention at this point. In my experience (no empirical evidence was found) certain people who assume managerial duties for the first time express an initial dislike for the job. This appears to be especially common among those who come from jobs involving concentration on single issues, such as that of university professor or staff specialist in a firm. They dislike the new work characteristics of variety, discontinuity, and brevity; they resent the frequent interruptions; they find it difficult to adjust to the pace of work; and they are unused to dealing primarily with current and specific issues. They long for more time to read and to delve into issues, and they resent having to make decisions with superficial understanding. Decisions pile up on their desks while they attempt to make each one carefully. Eventually the organization slows down, and pressure mounts on the new manager to make some decisions. Either he learns to act with superficial knowledge so as to keep things going, or he returns to his former job.

Societal Shifts

The final set of factors affects the job of all managers, in a slow but permanent way. This is the shifting of values in society. As norms change, managers must change behavior. Two trends seem evident. First, organizations are becoming more democratized internally. Managers are likely to find increasing pressures to become more sensitive to the personal needs of their subordinates (until, presumably, the word "subordinate" will cease to be used). The effect of this will be to enhance the significance of the *leader* role. In an autocratic environment leadership is relatively unimportant—one merely gives orders. As autocracy becomes less acceptable, more attention must be given to interpersonal contacts with subordinates for reasons other than the direct production of outputs.

A second trend is the increasing size and complexity of the power system that controls organizations. Where once trustees controlled hospitals and universities, and owners controlled businesses, today we see employees, students, governments, unions, and other special pressure groups demanding power in policy decisions. The chief executive, at the interface between external environment and organization, must deal with this complex coalition of interests.[16] He must be prepared to spend more time with these groups, with the result that the *figurehead, liaison, spokesman,* and *negotiator* roles become more and more important in his work.

Situational or time-related factors are many and varied, and they influence managers' jobs in a great number of different ways. All that it has been possible to do here is to cite a number of examples to illustrate the effect of these factors.

EIGHT MANAGERIAL JOB TYPES

This chapter has presented a rather diverse array of findings about variations in managers' jobs. However, it may be that there are natural groupings among these variations such that a small number of managerial job types encompass most of the variations. Eight types are suggested by our analysis. They are presented below in the belief that studying such natural groupings may be the best way to develop manageable theory in this area. Three of these types bear close resemblance to three of the five job profiles of Rosemary Stewart (1967; see also Appendix A), arrived at through a cluster analysis of her data on work characteristics.

The eight managerial job types are described here, with indication of their most important roles, as shown in Table 5.

The Contact Man. Some managers spend much of their time outside their organizations, dealing with people who can help them by

---

[16] Cyert and March (1963) and Lindblom (1965) present theories about the ways in which he does this.

Table 5. Eight Managerial Job Types

Managerial Job Type	Key Roles
Contact man	Liaison, figurehead
Political manager	Spokesman, negotiator
Entrepreneur	Entrepreneur, negotiator
Insider	Resource allocator
Real-time manager	Disturbance handler
Team manager	Leader
Expert manager	Monitor, spokesman
New manager	Liaison, monitor

doing them favors, giving them sales orders, providing privileged information, and so on. In addition, this type of manager expends much effort developing his reputation and that of his organization by giving speeches or doing favors himself. We may call him the "contact man," noting the similarity to Rosemary Stewart's "emissaries." His two primary roles are *liaison* and *figurehead*. Many sales managers fit this description, as do many ex-military chiefs who hold executive positions in defense-contracting firms. Some chief executives as well, particularly in service industries, tend to fit this description.[17]

The Political Manager. Another type of manager also spends a good part of his time with outsiders, but for different purposes. He is caught in a complex managerial position where he is required to reconcile a great many diverse political forces acting on his organization. This manager must spend a good part of his time in formal activities, meeting regularly with directors or the boss, receiving and negotiating with pressure groups, and explaining the actions of his organization to special interest parties. His key roles are *spokesman* and *negotiator.* This description is probably typical of managers at the top of most governments and institutions, including hospitals and universities, where the political pressures from below are as great as those from outside. The widening coalition of all organizations (as evidenced, for example, by Ralph Nader's attacks on various business firms) suggests that there will be more of the political manager in all chief executives of the future, whether they work in the private or in the public sector. In addition, we may find something akin to the political manager in the middle levels of some large organizations. Such managers may be required to spend considerable time on orga-

---

[17] We might also mention another type, the "figurehead." These individuals serve somewhat the same purposes, but only in the sense of extending the reputation of their organizations through *figurehead* duties. The monarch or formal head of state in many republics is such a person. Despite their titles, these people are not managers in that they are not charged with responsibility for any part of the organization.

nizational politics when the duties of their units are vague (so that no one can be sure how effectively they are performing), when there is enough slack in the system to allow for such political activity, and when the organizational climate promotes it.

The Entrepreneur. A third type of manager spends a good part of his time seeking opportunities and implementing changes in his organization. His key role is *entrepreneur,* but he must also spend considerable time in the *negotiator* role to implement his proposed changes. The entrepreneur is commonly found at the helm of a small, young business organization, where innovation is the key to survival. He may also be found at the head of, or within, a large organization that is changing rapidly. But his tenure here is probably short-lived. A large organization can tolerate extensive change only for a short time before a period of consolidation must set in. When it does, the entrepreneur is likely to become an insider, as described below.

The Insider. Many managers are concerned chiefly with the maintenance of smooth-running internal operations. They spend their time building up structure, developing and training their subordinates, and overseeing the operations they develop. They work primarily through the *resource allocator* role and, to a lesser extent, the *leader* role. The typical middle- and senior-level production or operations manager is probably an insider in that he is trying to build up and maintain a stable production system. Another insider is the number two man in the managerial diad, since the number one man tends to be a contact man. We can also include here the manager who is attempting to rebuild his organization after a major crisis or settle it after a period of disruptive change.

The Real-Time Manager. Akin to the insider is another type whose primary concern is also with the maintenance of internal operations, but whose time scale and problems are different. We can use the term *real-time manager* (Rosemary Stewart uses the term "trouble shooter") to describe that person who operates primarily in the present, devoting his efforts to ensuring that the day-to-day work of his organization continues without interruption. Hence primacy is given to the *disturbance handler* role. The work of the real-time manager exhibits all the regular characteristics in the extreme—it is highly fragmented; contacts are very many and very brief; there is little time given to mail or reports. This manager always appears to be exceedingly busy; he has his "finger in every pie"; he is prepared to substitute for any employee, and do any necessary job himself. The real-time manager is usually found in the basic line-production job (foreman), as the head of a small, one-manager business, at the helm of an organization faced with a severe crisis, and, in general, in any organization (or organizational unit) in a dynamic, competitive, high-pressure environment.

The Team Manager. There is another type of manager who is oriented to the inside, but he has a special concern. He is preoccupied with the creation of a team that will operate as a cohesive whole and will function effectively. The "team manager" is found where the organizational tasks require difficult coordination among highly skilled experts. Obvious examples of team managers are hockey coaches and heads of research and development groups charged with complex projects. The team manager is primarily concerned with the *leader* role.

The Expert Manager. In some situations a manager must perform an expert role in addition to his regular managerial roles. As head of a specialist staff group this manager must serve as a center of specialized information in the larger organization. He advises other managers and is consulted on specialized problems. His key roles are *monitor* and *spokesman,* his related duties, the collection and dissemination outward of specialized information. Because much of his work is associated with his speciality function, the usual managerial work characteristics appear less pronounced for him (although present, nevertheless). He does more desk work, is alone more of the time, does more reading and writing, experiences less fragmentation and variety in his activities, encounters less pressure. He spends more time in non-line relationships—advising others, for example. Rosemary Stewart calls members of this group "the writers"; here they are called the "expert managers."

The New Manager. Our last type of manager is the one in a new job. Lacking contacts and information at the beginning, the "new manager" concentrates on the *liaison* and *monitor* roles in an attempt to build up a web of contacts and a data base. The decisional roles cannot become fully operative until he has more information. When he does, he is likely to stress the *entrepreneur* role for a time, as he attempts to put his distinct stamp on his organization. Then he may settle down to being one of the other managerial types—contact man, insider, or some other type.

PROPOSITIONS ABOUT VARIATIONS IN MANAGERS' WORK

1. Variations in the content and characteristics of managers' work can be explained by a contingency theory comprising four sets of variables—environmental variables, including characteristics

of the milieu, the industry, and the organization; job variables, including the level in the organization and the function supervised; person variables, including the personality and style of the incumbent; and situational variables, including a host of time-related factors.

2. The level of the job and the function supervised appear to account for more of the variation in managers' work than any other variables.

3. The more dynamic his organization's environment (competition, rate of change, growth, pressure to produce), the more time the manager spends in informal communication, the more varied and fragmented his work, and the greater his orientation to live action and to verbal media.

4. Top managers of public organizations and institutions spend more time in formal activity (such as scheduled, clocked meetings) and more time meeting directors and outside groups than do managers of private organizations. Top managers of service organizations spend more time in the *liaison* role than do those of product organizations.

5. The larger the overall organization, the more time the top manager spends in formal communication (memos, scheduled meetings), the less brief and fragmented his activities, the greater his range of external contacts, the more developed his formal communications network (especially mail), the greater his involvement with external work (ceremony, external board work), the less his involvement with internal operations, and the less time he spends substituting for subordinates. Managers of small firms spend more time on the roles of *specialist* and *substitute operator*.

6. The higher the level of the manager in the hierarchy, the more unstructured, unspecialized, and long-range the job, the more complex, intertwined, and extended in time the issues handled, the less focused the work.

7. The lower the level, the more informal the job and the less time spent in the *figurehead* role.

8. Managers at lower levels are oriented more directly toward maintaining a steady workflow than those at higher levels; hence the former spend more time in the real-time roles— *disturbance handler* and *negotiator*.

9. The lower the level, the more pronounced the characteristics of brevity and fragmentation and the greater the focus on the current and specific issues.

10. Senior managers work longer hours than others, both on the job and in their off-hours.

11. Managers at given levels specialize in the information they process and spend much of their contact time with a related "clique" of people.

12. Line production managers are more oriented toward·operating problems, and experience greater fragmentation in their work;

they spend more time in the decisional roles, especially *disturbance handler* and *negotiator*.

13. Line sales managers focus on external relationships and the development of subordinates; they spend more time in the interpersonal roles—*figurehead, leader, liaison.*

14. Managers of staff specialists spend more time alone, are more involved with paperwork, demonstrate the least amount of fragmentation and variety in their work, spend more time advising outsiders in peer and lateral relationships, and spend considerable time in their speciality functions; they serve as experts as well as managers; and they spend more time in the informational roles, *monitor, spokesman, disseminator.*

15. In some organizations top managers informally create executive teams of two (diads) or three (triads) that share responsibility for the performance of the ten roles of a single managerial job; these team arrangements succeed to the extent that nerve-center information can be shared efficiently.

16. Most common is the diad in which the chief executive concentrates on the external roles (*figurehead, liaison, spokesman, negotiator*), leaving much of the responsibility for the internal roles (*leader, disseminator, resource allocator, disturbance handler*) to his second in command.

17. Time-related variations in managerial jobs suggest annual and perhaps monthly patterns but few weekly or daily patterns.

18. Managerial jobs tend to reflect a change–stability cycle in which periods of concentration on change (more time in *entrepreneur* and *negotiator* roles in particular) are followed by periods in which the changes are consolidated (more time in *leader* and *disturbance handler* roles).

19. Periods of intensive threat require the manager to spend a great proportion of his time in the *disturbance handler* role; these are followed by periods of replenishment of contacts and of resources—*liaison, spokesman,* and *resource allocator* roles.

20. Managers in new jobs tend to spend a greater proportion of time than others developing contacts and collecting information (*liaison* and monitor roles); later they go through a period of innovation (*entrepreneur* role); finally, they settle into the regular working patterns.

21. Societal shifts toward greater organizational democracy and extension of the organization's coalition will require that managers of the future spend more time on the *leader* role and the external roles, *figurehead, liaison, spokesman,* and *negotiator.*

22. Managerial jobs may be grouped into eight basic types: contact man (for whom the *liaison* and *figurehead* roles are most important); political manager (stressing the *spokesman* and *negotiator* roles); entrepreneur (*entrepreneur* and *negotiator* roles); insider (*resource allocator* role); real-time manager (*disturbance handler* role); team manager (*leader* role); expert manager (*monitor, spokesman* roles); new manager (*liaison, monitor* roles).

6
Science and the Manager's Job

The centipede was happy quite
   Until a toad in fun
Said, "Pray, which leg goes after which?"
That worked her mind to such a pitch,
She lay distracted in a ditch
   Considering how to run.

Mrs. Edward Craster [1]

The evidence of the preceding three chapters indicates that there is as yet no science in managerial work. That is to say, managers do not work according to procedures that have been prescribed by scientific analysis. Indeed, except for his use of the telephone, the airplane, and the dictating machine, it would appear that the manager of today is indistinguishable from his historical counterparts. He may seek different information, but he gets much of it in the same way—by word of mouth. He may make decisions dealing with modern technology, but he uses the same intuitive (that is, non-explicit) procedures in making them. Even the computer, which has had such

[1] *Cassell's Weekly,* Pinafore Poems (1871).

a great impact on other kinds of organizational work, has apparently done little to alter the working methods of the general manager.

Thus the management scientist, despite his accomplishments in the fields of production and data processing, has done virtually nothing to help the manager manage. The reason is simple. Analytical procedures cannot be brought to bear on work processes that are not well understood. And we have understood little about managerial work. Hence management scientists have concentrated their efforts elsewhere in the organization, where procedures were amenable to quantification and change.

In this chapter I shall discuss the two necessary components for a science of managing—precise description of managerial work and systematic improvement of it. The first section takes up, in a general way, the issue of describing the manager's work in terms of programs, and the second section reviews some specific attempts to do this. Later sections examine a number of possible ways in which the management scientist might help analyze these programs and improve managerial work.

PROGRAMMING THE MANAGER'S WORK

The history of science is, in one sense, the history of man's endeavor to describe his world in ever more precise terms and then to improve it in a systematic way. In *The Naked Ape* Desmond Morris describes this innate propensity of man to explore and experiment:

> [Man's play rules] can be stated as follows: (1) you shall investigate the unfamiliar until it has become familiar; (2) you shall impose rhythmic repetition on the familiar; (3) you shall vary this repetition in as many ways as possible; (4) you shall select the most satisfying and develop these at the expense of others; (5) you shall combine and recombine these variations one with another; and (6) you shall do all this for its own sake, as an end in itself.
>
> These principles apply from one end of the scale to the other, whether you are considering an infant playing in the sand, or a composer working on a symphony (1967: 121).

Frederick W. Taylor, the father of "scientific management," provided us with a first explicit expression of this process in the field of management. Writing early in this century (1911) about the analysis of factory work, Taylor outlined a five-step procedure:

> *First.* Find, say, 10 or 15 different men (preferably in as many separate establishments and different parts of the country) who are especially skilful in doing the particular work to be analyzed.
>
> *Second.* Study the exact series of elementary operations or mo-

tions which each of these men use in doing the work which is being investigated, as well as the implements each man uses.

Third. Study with a stop-watch the time required to make each of these elementary movements and then select the quickest way of doing each element of the work.

Fourth. Eliminate all false movements, slow movements, and useless movements.

Fifth. After doing away with all unnecessary movements, collect into one series the quickest and best movements as well as the best implements (1947: 117–118).

In other words, Taylor first described precisely the procedures (or programs) actually used by these men and then he "reprogrammed" the procedures—that is, systematically redesigned them. Once these new procedures were made explicit, a necessary first step had been taken toward automating them.

The thrust of management science during this century has been toward the describing and reprogramming of more and more sophisticated forms of work in the organization. Taylor began the process at the turn of the century with his famous attempts to improve the work of laborers—the handling of pig iron, the shoveling of coal. Industrial engineers later used time- and methods-study techniques to carry this effort to all parts of the factory and to the clerical jobs of the office. When the computer appeared, the field of operations research developed quickly, with the basic purpose of reprogramming the more sophisticated information-processing jobs found in the middle of the hierarchy. Programs were developed to balance assembly lines, schedule production, and control inventories, among other things. Today much of the routine work of what is called *middle management*—and here we refer to the work of specialists, not managers, at the middle levels [2]—is, or can be, programmed for execution by the computer.

This is essentially where the forward thrust of management science has reached. But there is good reason to believe that the next item on the management scientist's agenda is the work of senior management. From production work to clerical work to the complex information-processing activities of the specialist, the power of management science has been demonstrated. As he achieves more and more success in reprogramming the complex tasks of the specialist, it is inevitable that the management scientist will turn his attention to the job of the senior manager, the last and greatest of his challenges.

Where do we stand now on the development of a science of

[2] The term *middle management* is often used for managers as well as specialists, all working at middle levels of the organizational hierarchy. Elsewhere in this book the term "middle manager" is restricted to the *managers* working at this level.

managing? It was clear in my study of five chief executives that almost nothing senior managers do is explicitly programmed—that is, formally recorded as a series of steps to be carried out in a systematic sequence. The manager's decision is "unprogrammed." But, in a strict sense, there is no such thing as an unprogrammed decision. The brain must use some procedure—some higher order program—to react to any stimulus. Cognitive psychologists have had some success with attempts to program complex thought processes, such as chess playing.[3] For management there is the well-known study by Clarkson (1962), who established that a seemingly complex decision-making process— the trust officer's choice of an investment portfolio—could be so described by a researcher that it could be accurately simulated on the computer. Hence there is now good reason to believe that it is possible, in theory at least, to program all the decision-making behavior of the manager.

To develop a science of managing, we shall first have to determine what programs managers use. Our categorization of managerial activities and roles suggests a number of basic programs, such as scheduling time and negotiating agreements. The second step will be to describe the content of each program—the stimuli that evoke the program, the information used in its execution, the sequence of steps that are executed (including the heuristics, or decision rules used), and the outputs of the program. The third step will be the linking together of these programs to develop a full-scale simulation of managerial work. The prescriptive part of the work will necessitate detailed study of programs, with the objective of modifying (and perhaps automating) them to improve the effectiveness of the work.

By all indications managerial work is so complex that this will constitute an enormous undertaking. Few of the manager's programs will be easy to describe, and many may prove to be extremely complex. It is likely that programs associated with the *leader* role will be the most difficult to understand. Programs associated with the *figurehead, spokesman,* and *disseminator* roles may be the simplest. And those associated with the *liaison* role, the *monitor* role, and the four decisional roles will probably fall somewhere in between.[4] In any event it will be a long time indeed before we develop a reasonable simulation of managerial work. Nevertheless, some important programs are certainly amenable to description, and these are likely to be the first to draw the attention of the management scientist.

The remainder of this chapter is devoted, first, to a description

---

[3] See Feigenbaum and Feldman (1963), Simon (1965), and Newell and Simon (1972).

[4] Note that a role is merely a categorization of *what* the manager does; each program is, in effect, a description of *how* one specific aspect of a role is carried out.

of some of the preliminary attempts to describe managerial work in terms of programs and, second, to an assessment of those areas in which the management scientist can have some influence on the manager's work.

STUDIES OF THE MANAGER'S PROGRAMS

Let us examine two views of managerial work as a programmed system, and the results of two other research studies that delved into specific programs that managers appear to use. Klahr and Leavitt suggest one interesting approach to the programming of the work of the manager. They draw an analogy between organizational work and computer programs. Describing the complex computer program as a set of closed routines tied together by an "executive program," they outline managerial work in terms of this executive program.

1. [Executive programs, or executives] look *outside* the program [organization], receiving information from the environment in one form and transmitting it back to the environment in another form. They observe what kind of work has piled up, what needs to be done next, etc.
2. They look *inside* the program [organization] and they maintain control over its subprograms.
   a. They *detect,* checking what is done and what still needs to be done.
   b. They *interrupt.* They command one subprogram to stop and another to start.
   c. They *monitor,* making sure that no errors or intolerable conditions have occurred or are imminent.
   d. They *allocate* resources, assigning computer time, space, and computational facilities [money, space, personnel, etc.] to the appropriate routines [departments], and they assign processes to problems.
   e. They *coordinate.* They make sure that when subparts of the activity are completed, the results are properly fed to the next stage of the process. They schedule things in appropriate sequences and make sure the subparts are gradually put together into a meaningful entity.
   f. They do *housekeeping.* They inspect and clean up their own over-all working areas. They clean out unused areas and make them available for new information. The housekeeping routines initialize and finalize the loose ends that the subprograms may have neglected. They keep the total program [organization] in fighting trim (1967: 114–115).

What is interesting about this approach is that it ties the description of the manager's work to a set of programs that have already been specified. Should the analogy that Klahr and Leavitt present prove to be reasonably valid, then it will be possible to treat the computer's executive routine as a preliminary simulation of the manager as a system of programs.

Liong Wong (1970) used a more direct approach to describe managerial work as a programmed system. His method coupled my form of structured observation (see Appendix C) with the methods of studying thought processes that were used by Clarkson (1962) and by others. Wong studied three middle managers—a city manager of a middle-sized municipality, an assistant vice-president of a transportation company, and a university professor acting in an administrative capacity. While observing them he collected data on mail and verbal contacts, and he tape-recorded their "protocols"—verbalizations of their activities during execution. Using these data Wong described in flow-chart form a number of programs that these men appeared to use in their work.[5]

Wong's study focuses on the informational and decisional roles described in Chapter 4. In essence, he describes the manager's work processes (as shown in Figure 13) in four interrelated parts—information scanning, information storage, decision-making, and information disseminating. Through scanning (or monitoring) activity, the manager receives new information from his environment. Some of this is stored, perhaps to be disseminated later or to be used in the making of decisions. Some evokes immediate decision-making activity. Once a decision is made, its results as well as other related information are disseminated to the environment by the manager.

Two of the programs described by Wong are shown in modified form in Figures 14 and 15. Wong's information-storage program is evoked by new information that the manager receives. He must decide what to discard, what to store for later use, and what to disseminate immediately. Three basic storage modes may be delineated. *Natural memory* contains concepts, ideas, information on values, models of the real world. *Fingertip storage* refers to things like loose documents, diary, memo pads that managers keep within easy reach. *Official storage* comprises the various files of the organization, information on magnetic tape and disk, and so on. The program shown in Figure 14 is a simple one and suggests that managers use simple rules in making decisions on the storage of information.

Figure 15 shows an adapted version of Wong's conception of the negotiation process. He describes negotiation as the coupling of two

[5] It should be noted that, although Wong's descriptions were arrived at by induction from data that was collected systematically, the validity of the programs he described was not formally tested.

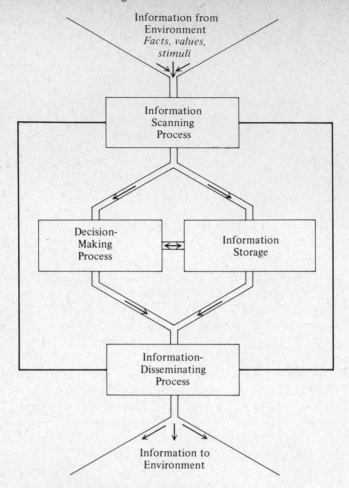

Figure 13. Four Managerial Work Processes

Source: Wong, 1970: 13.

independent decision-making programs, where the final choice must be common to both. These two decision-making programs are shown on either side of the top half of the diagram and comprise four basic subroutines shown as circles—identifying the decision, developing objectives and constraints and searching for alternatives (carried out in parallel), and evaluating alternatives. The arrows feeding back from the evaluation subroutine suggest that if an alternative proves unacceptable, the decision-maker searches for new alternatives or reviews his objectives and constraints.

In this specific illustration, the two decision-makers are the manager and a prospective employee. Each first executes his own decision-making program. The candidate finds the organization and

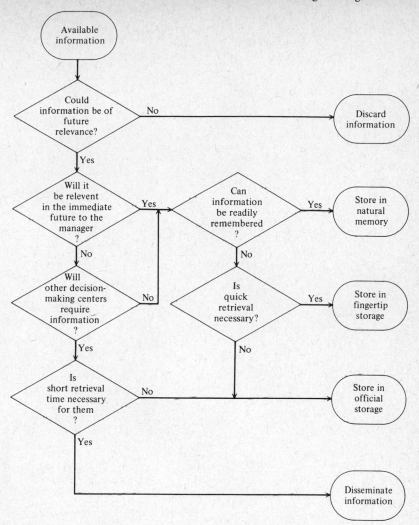

Figure 14. Information Storage Program

Source: Adapted from Wong, 1970: 52.

expresses interest; the organization finds the candidate and makes an offer. In the negotiating process (shown in the lower half of the diagram), they test for agreement on terms. If none is found, the two simultaneously review constraints, develop new offers, and negotiate again. This continues until agreement is reached or until one of the parties decides to search for a different alternative.

One version of the scanning (or monitoring) program that Wong includes in his repertoire is presented by Aguilar (1967), who questioned 137 managers from 41 companies to determine how they

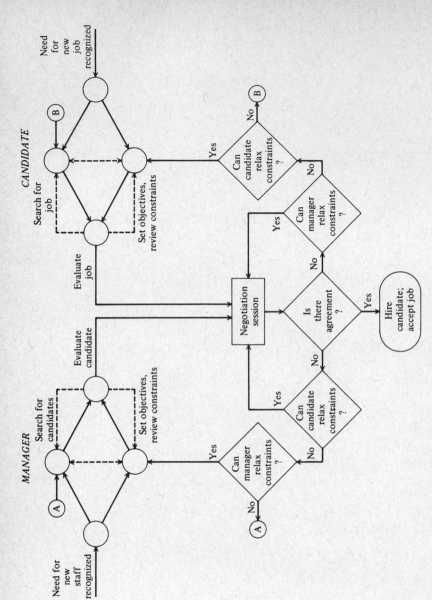

Figure 15. Negotiation Between Manager and Candidate

Source: Adapted from Wong, 1970: 108.

found information. Aguilar's scanning and mode-assignment rules are shown in Figure 16. A manager faced with an issue (point 2) first decides whether he needs more information (point 3). If he does not, he makes a decision on the issue (point 16). If he does, he assigns one of three modes to his subsequent search procedures(points 4–13) as follows. He passively exposes himself to a more or less clearly identified type of information ("conditioned viewing," point 6); he searches in an informal and limited way for information for a specific purpose ("informal search," point 10); or he deliberately and systematically searches for information related to a specific issue ("formal search," point 13). If further information shows the issue to be irrelevant, the manager returns to a fourth mode, "undirected viewing" (point 1), which Aguilar defines as "general exposure to information where the viewer has no specific purpose in mind with the possible exception of exploration" (1967: 19). If search is unsuccessful or if there is no appropriate search procedure available, the manager goes to a subroutine where he can change his scanning rules.

The manager uses one specific program to link his activities together. The "scheduling program" is evoked to determine priorities among tasks and which task to execute at a given time. It deals with relatively structured inputs (specific tasks; clearly defined blocks of time) and is probably a relatively easy one to simulate accurately.

In what is probably the most significant research of this type to date, John Radomsky (1967) studied the scheduling behavior of three middle managers of a large corporation. In his research, which he titles "The Problem of Choosing a Problem," Radomsky employed a most interesting research method. While the managers worked at their desks making decisions, they were asked to verbalize their thoughts. Radomsky recorded both the image and the protocols on videotape; he reviewed these with the managers on the following day. He found that this method stimulated their recall considerably (see Appendix B), and he was able to extract significant information about their scheduling rules.

Radomsky first analyzes the general organization of the manager's workday, noting the existence of preliminary agendas and the tendency to start the day

> by cleaning up odds and ends and doing short jobs before proceeding with a series of scheduled items. As new information comes to the manager's attention, this sequence is evaluated and the agenda is modified as required. . . . Thus, we are dealing with a dynamic process, making decisions based on the conditions of the moment (1967: 27–29).

Turning to the process by which managers decide on their next task, Radomsky notes the processes of scanning new information, switching

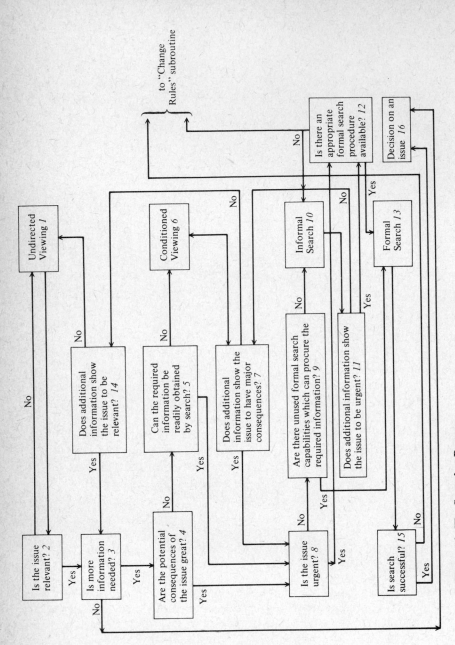

Figure 16. The Scanning Program

Source: Aguilar, 1967: 28.

some of it to other people (together with responsibility for execution of certain tasks), and sequencing remaining tasks. Sequencing of the manager's inventory of known problems is a complex process; according to Radomsky it involves the following implicit rules:

1. Locate the jobs with negative or zero slack or imminent start dates. Arrange in order of lateness penalty sequence.
2. Compare time available to time required for completion. If conflict exists, move obstruction if it has slack. If obstruction has no slack and has high visibility, resolve by assigning completion of project in hand or obstruction to a subordinate.
3. If no higher class jobs exist, consider completing any partially completed jobs ahead of a new job with slack.
4. Schedule jobs with slack according to priority value. Do not rearrange the fixed obstructions, but choose highest value jobs that will fit the span available.
5. Use short operation tasks as fillers for open spots, to break pace, and to start the day.
6. Whenever working on projects with slack, review new input immediately on a first come—first served basis (1967: 52–53).

Radomsky's depiction of this program is shown in Figure 17.

These four descriptions of various aspects of the manager's programs are no more than exploratory. Nevertheless, they are of considerable worth. Taken together they suggest that the manager has a repertoire of general programs, to be combined and sequenced for use in particular situations, and one special-purpose program—the scheduling program—to choose and sequence his tasks.[6] In addition the manager may use a number of other specific programs for specific purposes (like hiring a subordinate). To describe managerial work as a programmed system—to predict the manager's behavior accurately —it will be necessary to have full understanding of these general and specific programs and of the heuristics and other memory that the manager uses in his work.

THE ROLE OF THE MANAGEMENT SCIENTIST AT THE POLICY LEVEL

In Chapter 3 we examined various characteristics of managerial work. The manager is severely time constrained; he cannot devote long periods of uninterrupted time to single issues, no matter how complex

---

[6] We can probably add a "control program," which determines what programs and information will be used in executing a particular task. As in a time-shared computer, the scheduling program deals with event-selection and is time oriented, the control program deals with mode selection and is logic oriented.

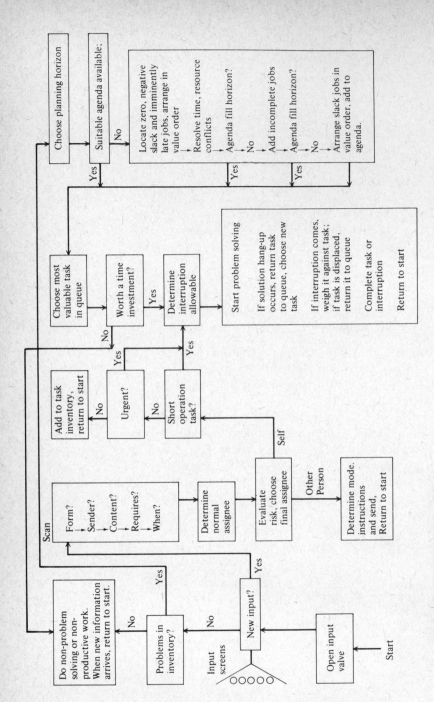

Figure 17. The Scheduling Program

Source: Radomsky, 1967: 60.

they are. He gravitates toward the current and concrete aspects of issues, even those that require investigation in a theoretical and historical way. The manager is led to prefer verbal contacts, although often there is a need for intensive examination of documents. These characteristics make it clear that there is a role for the management scientist to play in providing analytical back-up for the senior manager.

The term "management scientist" (and "analyst"), as used here, includes all those staff persons—operations researcher, planner, systems analyst, information systems designer, and others—whose job is to bring the findings of research and the techniques of analysis to bear on work processes in the organization. The management scientists are able to complement the manager. They have the time, the habit of concentrating on issues, the experience of developing knowledge from the study of formal documents, and the training in the application of analysis and theory. Clearly, those managers who can afford the cost —senior managers in large organizations—stand to benefit from the application of the management scientist's skills.

This need has been increasingly recognized in recent years. In indicative ways, management scientists have begun to turn their attention to the manager's job and to the policy problems found at the top of the hierarchy. The strategic planner in business has concentrated his efforts on the strategy-making process; the systems analyst in government has used cost-benefit analysis to deal with major decisions on resource allocation; the information systems designer has used the computer to feed the manager with information. But progress has been slow, for two reasons.

First, the management scientist has, along with the rest of us, lacked formal knowledge of the manager's working processes. These are complex; they cannot be subjected to analysis until they are clearly described. Second, the management scientist has been implicitly denied access to much of the manager's information. The manager is the nerve center of his organization, with unique access to a wide variety of internal and external contacts that provide privileged information. But most of this information is not documented, and much of it is unsubstantiated and nonquantitative. As a result, the manager lacks a systematic method for passing it on to the management scientist, and most of it never reaches him. Without an understanding of the manager's information, how can the analyst design an effective information system for him, and how can the planner make useful strategic plans?

The management scientist, therefore, has a great need to end what amounts to the manager's monopoly on undocumented information. This is the information that drives the organization, yet the analyst has limited access to it. A concentrated effort will be required by both manager and analyst if the latter is to attain the level of knowledge necessary to contribute to the solution of policy problems in organizations.

Properly informed, analysts would be able, in the tradition of Frederick Taylor, to "reprogram" some of the manager's work—to analyze the steps in the programs he uses, test alternative steps, and suggest modifications. Of all the activities that managers perform, many cannot easily be reprogrammed simply because they require flexible human responses. A manager must motivate his subordinates; he must engage in ceremonial activity; he must develop liaison contacts with peers. On the other hand, a second group of activities, probably a very small group, can be largely reprogrammed and automated. Certain information sorting and scheduling activities may fit into this category.

What is probably the largest group, however, comprises those activities that lend themselves to partial reprogramming. The manager would perform them with the support of the analyst (or perhaps the computer, in a man–machine system). The manager would contribute his special information and understanding of the dynamics of the environment, while the analyst (or computer) would contribute analytical capabilities and the time needed for analysis. Many of the important information-processing and decision-making activities of the manager probably fit into this group.

We now turn our attention to those areas where attention by management scientists will probably have the highest payoff—scheduling, information processing, and strategy-making. The views expressed here are speculative, but they suggest a number of directions in which management science can go.

REPROGRAMMING SCHEDULING ACTIVITY

As noted previously, the manager's time assumes an enormous opportunity cost. Lacking time, he can inhibit organizational development by postponing requests for authorization, by delaying improvement projects, by reducing the amount of information he disseminates, and so on. It appears, therefore, that management scientists can usefully turn their attention to the manager's scheduling activity. By bringing more consistency to the manager's schedule, by relieving him of much of the need to schedule his own work, and by using systematic analysis to design his schedule in accordance with his needs and those of his organization, the management scientist can achieve considerable gains in efficiency. In fact, it is surprising that there has been so little analytical effort in this area, considering the extent to which the activities of other workers in the organization have been studied.

A scheduling program would involve (1) determining the manager's time constraints, (2) defining and categorizing the demands for his time, and (3) developing a set of adaptable scheduling rules to control time allocation. Step one can easily be achieved by having the manager specify such things as his working hours and his attitude toward evening and lunchtime work. Likewise, it would be a simple matter to categorize the various demands for a manager's time. This has been done in a preliminary way in Appendix C—time for ceremonial functions, for bargaining and authority requests, for working on improvement projects, for touring, and so on.

A set of scheduling guidelines for a senior manager might be established as follows:

1. Certain periods of time would be regularly blocked out. Managers now tie very little of their activity regularly to the clock; as a result they are required to spend large amounts of time coordinating and scheduling their efforts with others. The rules might call for (a) a certain time each day for mail processing, (b) regularly-scheduled sessions each week with subordinates, (c) various monthly sessions to review certain functions, (d) a particular half-day each week to review progress of improvement projects in active inventory, and (e) a fixed time for touring and other investigational work.

2. Certain other times would be blocked out to satisfy ad hoc requests for the manager's time. Various priorities could be established—that requests for authorization would receive first preference, for example. Other rules might insure that on the average a certain proportion of time would be spent on personal contacts, figurehead duties, information processing, and other activities.

3. A system of master control over improvement projects would be established. Since each project develops as a sequence of episodes subject to various delays, the master control would monitor each, determine when each episode should be scheduled, and set aside the appropriate time. (This point will be discussed further under strategy-making.)

4. One rule would insure that scheduled activities be so staggered that numerous blocks of time would be left free throughout each day. These would allow the manager to adapt to dynamic conditions —to receive "instant communication" from subordinates, to work on crises, to return telephone calls.

5. The day would be designed with regard to working efficiency. Depending on the manager's preferences, successive activities could be scheduled to ensure either variety or consistency. For example, a taxing activity could be followed by ceremony or by mail processing. Rest periods—a scheduled activity for every worker in the organization except its manager—could be designed to increase efficiency. If the manager is most effective in the mornings, then information-processing and resource-allocation activity would be scheduled for the morning, ceremony and the like for the afternoon.

Such a system, although ostensibly similar to that now used by some managers in major positions, probably differs in at least three respects:

1. To the extent that he can make his scheduling heuristics explicit and allow them to be established as standard rules, the manager need not concern himself with scheduling activity. Some of his time is therefore freed for other activities. An assistant (perhaps, some day, a computer) can do this job for him.

2. The manager tends to schedule activities at the request of others, thereby leaving to chance much important work—monitoring, developing improvement projects, touring, disseminating information. As Carlson (1951) notes in the section quoted in full in Chapter 3, managers become "slaves to their appointment diaries," carrying out only the specific activities that find their way into specific time slots in their diaries. Simon has suggested that there exists a Gresham-type law of managerial work, that programmed activity tends to drive out nonprogrammed activity (1965: 67). Two corollaries of that law might be that scheduled work tends to drive out unscheduled work and that unimportant work tends to drive out important work. By explicitly scheduling certain less demanding, but important, activities —those related to information processing and strategy-making—the manager would give them the attention they might not otherwise receive.

3. With a set of explicit rules—a scheduling model, in effect— and the data generated by using it, various analyses could be undertaken. Specifically, the allocation of time to basic activities—like information processing, project development, and figurehead tasks—could be varied, and the effects on the organization could be assessed. The analyst could ask if the manager should spend more time collecting information, or would he be better advised to spend more time disseminating the information he has? Should he supervise more or fewer improvement projects? Can he spend less time in figurehead duties, more time in leadership duties, or in liaison duties? Answers to these questions would lead to a better balance in the manager's schedule.

REPROGRAMMING THE INFORMATION SYSTEM

There are three essential elements in the manager's information-processing system—monitoring, storing, and disseminating. The possibilities for reprogramming each will be discussed below.

The Monitoring System

In Chapters 3 and 4 we saw that the manager's information tends to conform to a number of distinct characteristics, including the following:

1. Current information. Getting information *rapidly* appears to be more important to the manager than getting it absolutely *right*. Hence gossip, hearsay, and speculation constitute a large share of his information diet. Rumor takes time to become substantiated fact, and it takes even longer for that fact to find its way into a quantitative report.

2. Trigger information. The manager clearly prefers to have his information in the form of concrete stimuli or triggers, not general aggregations. In Neustadt's words, the manager needs "tangible detail" not "bland amalgams" (1960: 153). He wishes to hear of specific events, ideas, and problems.

3. Verbal information. Because of the information he seeks, the manager must rely largely on verbal media. The mail contains little that can be acted on, whereas meetings and telephone calls bring him the current, trigger information he requires.

These characteristics put the manager in direct conflict with most formal information systems. He seeks trigger, speculative, current information, but the formal system gives him largely aggregated, precise, historical information. Furthermore, the manager demonstrates a thirst for external information, whereas formal systems provide largely internal information. The formal system deals with information for control and regulation (production schedules, sales reports, standard costs) that is useful primarily to the specialist in middle and lower echelons. It excludes much of the intelligence information that senior managers need for their unprogrammed decisions.

As a result the manager must often ignore the formal information system. Instead he designs his own system, which provides him with the information that he believes he needs. He develops external contacts, subscribes to periodicals, joins trade organizations, and encourages subordinates to circumvent the established lines of communication to bring him information.

But must the manager design his own monitoring system, and must he do his own filtering? Although it gives the manager what he needs, such a monitoring system is a crude and inconsistent one. It is subject to his time constraints, which are severe, and because it is largely verbal, the system provides inadequate coverage. The manager simply lacks the time to disseminate by word of mouth all the information that his subordinates need. He can keep only a few, close subordinates properly informed; the system breaks down when information must reach those who are not within his routine verbal reach.

The information analyst has the available time and the knowledge of information theory to help design, and to partially operate, a monitoring system that could be more effective than the manager's own. The analyst might begin by finding out what information a particular manager needs, not by asking him, but by studying what he seeks, what he receives, and what he uses.[7] Does he disseminate much external information to his subordinates? Does he spend much time touring to find problems? Does he attend many trade conferences? Are technological reports of great interest to him? Does he use these periodicals to seek information on trends in the industry? What kind of trade gossip interests him, and how does he get it? The analyst will no doubt conclude that many sources of information will remain open only to the manager—he has the status necessary to tap them. But in a number of areas—information on technology, market trends, internal operations—the analyst can be of help. He can undertake a comprehensive search for other sources of this information, and he can put together a carefully designed monitoring system in these areas, one that not only covers more channels, but does much of the manager's scanning and filtering for him. The analyst can then present the manager with the relevant facts—the ideas, the problems, the bits of gossip, the events.

A Data Bank in Official Storage

Today the manager is the real data bank for an important class of organizational information. Unfortunately, he is a walking and a talking data bank, but not a writing one. Herein lies the problem. When he is busy, information ceases to flow. When he departs, so does the data bank.

The manager's information must be made more accessible to members of his organization. Some of it is documented and can easily be made available. Much of it, however, exists only in the manager's natural memory and can be disseminated only by word of mouth. It appears to be desirable, however, that the manager make a determined effort to document much of his hitherto undocumented information and transfer it to the official storage of the organization where it can be more readily available to his subordinates. (In practical terms, this probably means a weekly debriefing session where the important information of the week can be recorded and later transcribed into reports.) By putting such information into official storage, and combining it with the information that analysts can collect in a repro-

---

[7] One hears frequently about the frustrated information analyst who cannot understand why managers do not want to use the information the analyst thinks they should have. Also not uncommon is the analyst who has tried to solve the problem by asking the manager what information he needs and has learned nothing. There is some evidence (presented in Appendix A) that managers have difficulty describing their work at a level of abstraction useful for the analyst. Furthermore, managers have no reason to believe that the man with the computer wants to hear about their speculative, current, trigger information. To learn about the managerial informational needs, the analyst will have to go out and study the manager's actual use of information.

grammed monitoring system, there can emerge an explicit data bank of key information necessary for strategy-making.[8]

The Disseminating System

A data bank in official storage would allow for the development of a systematic information-disseminating system. The specific informational needs of different members of the organization would be determined, and information from the data bank could be disseminated to them accordingly.

Such a disseminating system, based on an explicit data base, would eliminate many of the weaknesses of a system operated strictly by the manager. The amount of information disseminated would not be a function of the free time the manager has available. Furthermore, those who work at a distance from the manager, where verbal communication is difficult (overseas, for example), need not be at a disadvantage relative to their colleagues at the head office who have verbal access to the manager. An explicit data base would also stay in place when the manager leaves the organization, so that the necessary information would continue to be available to those who need it.

There has been much speculation about the role of the computer at senior-management levels.[9] Our evidence suggests that its use in a reprogrammed information system would be marginal. Much of the information would be qualitative and imprecise, and much would require only simple transfer—a transcript of a meeting forwarded from one manager to another, for example. The costs of doing computer analysis with data inputs of this type would probably be prohibitive in most situations. Furthermore, the number of executives involved in a typical system of this kind would not likely be very large. The costs of coding the information would be high relative to the savings effected from computer sorting and printing. In other words, it simply may not be economical to pass this kind of information through a computer.[10]

[8] One obvious question about such a data bank is the threat it poses to security. This threat must, however, be weighed against the benefits of having better-informed subordinates. (This issue is discussed in more detail in Chapter 7.)

[9] For a variety of views on the use of the computer at the chief executive level, see Myers (1967).

[10] If one wishes to speculate about sophisticated uses of information-processing hardware, one may visualize the organization of the future with consoles in the office of each senior executive. Then, true to the manager's information needs, the transmission of "instant communication" would be automated. An executive with fresh information would simply decide which managers were to receive this current bit of news; he would then key in the code to open the proper channels, and the message would appear simultaneously in the appropriate offices. Perhaps, as in a newspaper office, the urgency of the news item would be signaled by the use of one, two, or three rings of a bell!

Today, one finds two information systems in large organizations —the formal system built into the computer, and the informal system designed by managers. Organizations are greatly in need of "in-between" systems, formal management information systems that would systematically process the information the computer does not now handle but that the manager now needs. Such in-between systems would be operated in part by analysts but would probably not be automated.[11]

REPROGRAMMING THE STRATEGY-MAKING SYSTEM

The most complex, although the most lucrative, job facing the management scientist today is the reprogramming of the system by which important organizational decisions are made and interrelated, that is, strategy-making. This section begins with a comparison of two approaches to strategy-making described in the literature. In one, strategy is said to evolve as the manager reacts to environmental pressures; in the other, strategy is to be created through formal analysis by planners. These two points of view are captured in what may be called the "planning dilemma," in which managers have the authority and information, while planners have the time and techniques. We shall

---

[11] It has been popular among management theorists to debate the centralizing vs. decentralizing effects of the computer on the organization structure. (See, for example, Leavitt and Whistler, 1958.) From the above discussion, it would appear that any system (computerized or not) that makes the manager's information more accessible to his subordinates will have a *de*centralizing effect on the organizational structure. Today, every manager keeps much of the information important to his organization in his head; he is unable to disseminate a good part of it, and then only to a few people. He thus maintains centralized control over the major decisions of his own organization by virtue of his more comprehensive knowledge. Given an efficient means of disseminating information, the manager will be encouraged to share responsibility for these decisions, since his subordinates will share a larger common data base. Hence, authority for decision-making will be transferred down the line and there will be a general decentralizing effect.

This argument makes one major assumption, however—that the information system will be reprogrammed, but not the strategy-making system. This may be true in the short run, because the information system is simpler and easier to reprogram. In the long run, however, the management scientist may be able to reprogram strategy-making. One day, perhaps, with powerful planning programs and access to the necessary information, the planning department may be able to *re*centralize the organizational structure by making better decisions than can be made by a group of informed, individual managers. (Galbraith, 1967, in *The New Industrial State,* suggests this has already happened. Our findings of Chapters 3 and 4 suggest that he is premature in this assessment.) Thus, it appears that we shall have decentralization to the extent that we design effective information systems, centralization to the extent that we design effective strategic planning systems.

examine this dilemma and then look at seven areas in which managers and planners might be able to cooperate to reprogram the strategy-making system.

The Planning Dilemma

A fundamental debate has developed in the literature of strategy-making between those who describe an adaptive or incremental approach and those who propose a grand planning process.[12] In Chapter 2, under the decision theory school, the works of the "incrementalists" were reviewed.[13] The evidence from Chapter 4, where the manager's decisional roles were examined, tends to support their description of strategy-making as a complex, adaptive process. Strategy appears to evolve over time as managers make a wide variety of resource allocation decisions. Managers tend to break their improvement projects into series of sequential decisions because of their need for feedback and timing. Neither their search for, nor their evaluation of, alternatives appears to be conducted according to any systematic design, and organizational values are applied to decisions in some manner that remains mysterious. The strategy-making process appears to be integrated only in the sense that the manager, by virtue of his great store of information and the loose plans he develops in his head, can interrelate the decisions he makes. Thus, current strategy-making practice cannot be characterized as "grand planning." Although the incrementalists play down the role of entrepreneurship, and underestimate the power of the manager and the ability of the organization to impose major change on itself, there is little doubt that they present the better description of current strategy-making behavior.

But must strategy-making remain a judgmental process carried on solely by the manager? There are at least three good reasons why it should not.

1. The manager is under time constraints while his team of planners is not. What is a part-time job for the manager can be a full-time job for the planner. A U.S. senator has commented:

> You know the typical week in the life of a Cabinet officer—seven formal speeches, seven informal speeches, seven hearings on the Hill, seven official cocktail parties, seven command dinner engagements. It is a schedule which leaves no time for the kind of reflection essential for creative planning. What they can do, should do, must do—and all that they should be asked to do—is to pass judgment on sharply defined policy issues. . . .
> . . . I am convinced that we never will get the kind of policy planning we need if we expect the top-level officers to participate

[12] See Mintzberg (1967).
[13] See, in particular, the works of Cyert and March (1963) and Braybrooke and Lindblom (1963).

actively in the planning process. They simply do not have the time, and in any event they rarely have the out-look or the talents of the good planner. They cannot explore issues deeply and systematically. They cannot argue the advantages and disadvantages at length in the kind of give-and-take essential if one is to reach a solid understanding with others on points of agreement and disagreement (quoted by Anthony, 1965: 46–47).

2. As organizations grow larger and their decisions become more complex, the relative cost of analysis decreases, while the intuitive methods of the manager, which can improve only slowly, become less acceptable. Furthermore, as it becomes economically feasible to document more and more of the information, the formal approach gains in advantage. Charles J. Hitch has written:

> Almost never do we find one person who has an intuitive grasp of all the fields of knowledge that are relevant to a major defense problem. We may be able to assemble a group of experts, each of whom has a good intuitive grasp of the factors relevant for answering one of the many subquestions and after discussion emerge with a fairly unequivocal answer. But in general, and especially when the choice is not between two but among many alternatives, systematic analysis is essential.
>   . . . And wherever the relevant factors are diverse and complex, as they usually are in defense problems, unaided intuition is incapable of weighing them and reaching a sound decision (1965: 56).

3. It is difficult to interrelate decisions that are made incrementally in an adaptive process. An explicitly planned strategy can more easily be integrated.

Proponents of the planning approach envisage the use of analytical programs to develop bold, integrated strategies. Typical of this group are H. Igor Ansoff (1965) and George A. Steiner (1969) who, in their books on planning, present detailed procedures for designing organizational strategies; and Hitch and McKean (1960) who, in *The Economics of Defense in the Nuclear Age,* outline the planning-programming-budgeting system first adopted by Robert McNamara in the U.S. Department of Defense. These analytical approaches derive from the economist's view of "rational" decision-making. As generally described in the literature, the strategic planning process begins with the study of the values and objectives of top management, the strengths and weaknesses of the organization, and the opportunities and problems facing it. Strategic plans are then designed to solve the problems and exploit the opportunities, building on the strengths and attending to the objectives. A number of projects and long- and short-range budgets are then specified as operating manifestations of the plan.

The critics of this "rational" approach to strategy-making suggest that it is an overly simple and somewhat sterile approach when viewed in the light of the complexity faced by the strategy-maker. Lindblom argues in *A Strategy of Decision* (with Braybrooke, 1963) that the "synoptic" approach must fail because it is not suited to man's limited capacity to solve problems, the inadequacy of information, the analyst's inability to specific operational goals, the manager's need to sequence his moves, and the general complexity and openness of the strategy situation faced by the manager. Lindblom notes further that analysis is costly. Although he is addressing the issues in the public sector, most of Lindblom's arguments apply to business planning as well. For small firms planning is costly. For large corporations the strategy environment is complex.

Hence, we find a "planning dilemma." [14] The manager, who has the information and the flexibility to operate in a dynamic environment, lacks the time to focus intensively on complex issues. The planner, who has the time and skill to do systematic analysis, lacks the required flexibility and information. The manager understands the need to adapt to what is going on; the planner is prepared to integrate what will go on. A purely incremental approach, with the manager chasing opportunities when he is not being chased by crises, with improvement projects being considered independently and intermittently, and with plans existing only in the manager's mind, is increasingly inadequate. But the dynamic and ambiguous nature of the environment renders formal planning an oversimplified, sterile procedure and encourages the use of an adaptive approach to strategy-making. Clearly there is a need to couple the capabilities of the manager with the skills of the analyst.

Seven Areas of Manager–Analyst Cooperation

A successful reprogramming of the strategy-making system would draw on the manager's access to information and his ability to react to unanticipated problems and chance opportunities, while the analyst would contribute his analytical capabilities. It would recognize both the manager's responsibility for making final decisions and the need for these decisions to be systematically integrated. It would reflect the fact that the manager is severely time constrained whereas the analyst has time to delve deeply into strategic issues.

There appear to be a variety of areas where managers and analysts might be able to cooperate. Seven possible areas will be discussed below, with speculations on a number of different joint arrangements to reprogram the strategy-making process. The areas discussed include finding problems and opportunities, evaluating the costs and benefits of proposed projects, building models, planning for contingent

[14] For a more extensive treatment of this issue, see Hekimian and Mintzberg (1968).

events, analyzing in "real-time," monitoring improvement projects, and developing adaptive plans.

Opportunity and Problem Finding. In his role of *entrepreneur,* the manager searches for opportunities and for problems that require action. The analyst can do some of this work. He has more time, and given some guidelines he can identify certain types of problems and opportunities for the manager. He can analyze organizational strengths and gaps in activities, conduct market research studies, and carry out forecasting studies.[15] Analysts now do some of these things; it is proposed that they do them not because a manager has asked for a specific study, but because they are charged with searching in the broadest sense for situations calling for decisions. The analyst's role here should not be to feed data on trends and changes to the manager, but to infer the problems and opportunities these suggest.

Cost-Benefit Analysis. The making of strategic choices is the prerogative of the manager. He best understands the organization's power system and its values, and he is responsible for its commitments. Although economists have written much about utility and preference functions, and management theorists have called repeatedly for the setting of explicit goals in organizations, there is still considerable question as to whether this can be done in a useful way. As Lindblom suggests, the value systems of many organizations may simply be too dynamic and complex to allow goals to be stated in other than the most general (and nonoperational) terms. In the absence of explicit, operational goals, the manager must retain full responsibility for choices; the analyst's role must be to enhance the manager's ability to make them.

Cost-benefit analysis (or return-on-investment analysis)— whereby the analyst carefully and systematically assesses costs and benefits associated with alternative solutions to a problem—is one method by which he can improve decision-making. By taking the time to extract and order the data that the manager needs for making choices, the analyst can improve the quality of the manager's decisions. He can study and diagnose a situation, develop alternative solutions, and systematically analyze the consequences of each for the manager.

Despite the rise and fall of cost-benefit analysis in Robert McNamara's Department of Defense, we shall probably see a steady growth in the use of this important approach to policy issues. The

---

[15] In forecasting, the analyst working at the policy level would be likely to spend most of his time predicting contingent events (e.g., trade legislation, technological breakthroughs) and social changes (e.g., consumer taste, governmental orientation), as opposed to projecting economic and other quantitative parameters.

initial concept of operations research—in which an interdisciplinary team of clever analysts tackled a problem in depth—was a most powerful one. It is unfortunate that the recent focus of this field has been on the application of specific sophisticated techniques. For policy analysis there is a need to return to this basic approach.

Model Building. In addition to providing the manager with the results of specific analyses, the management scientist can also develop for him the analytical capability to make better decisions in general. In Chapter 4 it was suggested that managers build implicit models for themselves to help them in making choices. Analysts can formalize this process, with the aim of developing better models for the manager.

Analysts may be able to develop certain computer models to simulate explicitly some situations managers must face. For example, industrial dynamics models could be designed to simulate the production and fund-flow system of the organization (Forrester, 1961); input/output grids could be designed to describe trading relationships between industries. Computer models could be designed for special situations—for example, a manager entering labor negotiations might find use for one that would calculate the cost of wage proposals in real-time. Despite the obvious appeal of such an approach, however, there may be few policy areas for which effective computer models can as yet be built. The requirements that they be both accurate enough and sufficiently flexible to adapt to new information as easily as the manager can are difficult to meet at the present time.

A second approach to model building is less ambitious but probably more relevant. Managers collect and piece together various scraps of information; gradually, patterns appear in their minds, and these combine into models that describe various aspects of the environment. Such models are, in essence, simple conceptions of reality. Sometimes they are very powerful and lead to effective decisions; at other times they are crude and lead to gross errors. For example, the validity of the model that a U.S. President has of enemy behavior or of the operations of his own economy will determine to a large extent the effectiveness of his military or economic decisions. We have seen enough examples of decisions at this level based on oversimplified models to appreciate the value of good models.

One way to improve the manager's models is to expose him systematically to the best available conceptual understanding of the situations he faces. A key role of the management scientist could be to put good models into the manager's head, to expose him to simple but powerful descriptions of complex phenomena—how his organization's consumers behave, how his competitors react to events, how his organization's markets are influenced by changes in technology, how funds flow through his organization. Some of these descriptions may be found in the contemporary or theoretical literature, some may have to be developed by the management scientist. The main point is that the manager will develop models of these things anyway; by explicit focus on them, the management scientist can help ensure that the models are the best ones possible.

Contingency Planning. Every manager must deal from time to time with a major disruptive event that he knew in advance had some probability, albeit a low one, of occurring. The bank calls in a loan, a major supplier misses a delivery date, a facility is destroyed by fire, a key subordinate leaves.

Managers often cannot take the time to anticipate all these events; they must simply react to many of them as crises. The management scientist, however, has the time to study both their probability of occurrence and their possible effect on the organization. Where the contingency poses a considerable threat to the organization, the analyst may be able to convince the manager to act in advance to prevent the problem. In other cases, the analyst can draw up a contingency plan (or sets of alternative ones) so that should the events occur and the pressures become intense, the manager will have immediately available a course of action worked out under calmer circumstances.

Real-Time Analysis. Despite the best contingency planning, unanticipated events will occur. Sometimes sudden opportunities will present themselves; at other times crises will arise. In part, crises simply reflect the unanticipated consequences of innovation; it is difficult to imagine a healthy organization that can eliminate all crises. Rather than condemning "management by crisis" as the management scientist has been prone to do, he would be better advised to develop methods by which the manager faced with a crisis can call upon his services.

The management scientist of today is often not prepared to work on a "real-time" decision. His methods tend to have large startup costs and to consume much time. He has been trained in the economist's tradition of "rational" choice. He prefers to search comprehensively for alternatives and their consequences and to quantify costs and benefits whenever he can. Furthermore, he is oriented toward using elegant techniques, often involving sophisticated mathematics. These approaches are time-consuming, often so much so that the analyst must be excluded from participating in real-time decision-making. The analyst must develop the ability to perform "analysis in real-time"—to give answers to the manager while the problem is current.

With a thorough understanding of the manager's environment and the ability to act quickly, the analyst would be able to apply his analytical approach to help the manager under pressure. He would be prepared to forecast with simple mathematics, to conduct brief market-research studies without concern for statistical validation, and to perform quick cost-benefit calculations using only a few alternatives and rough estimates.

> In part, the planner has done what the manager might do if he had the time. But he has done it more thoroughly and with far less time pressure. The manager has continued to manage as he must, giving attention to the mail and callers, while the planner gives attention to the problem. The key to this system is leverage. The manager may spend one hour defining the issue to the planner and one hour listening to the planner's recommendations one week later. During that one week, the planner and his staff of eight may be able to put in two man-months working on the problem (Hekimian and Mintzberg, 1968: 16).

This "quick and dirty" analysis might not be elegant, but it would greatly improve the manager's ability to deal with pressure.

Project Monitoring. The manager takes personal responsibility for the design of many of his organization's most important improvement projects, and he works on these intermittently. The typical senior manager may supervise fifty or more of these projects at one time, each at a different stage of development. To maintain control of these is a difficult task, especially for the manager who has many other things to think about. One obvious role for the analyst is to monitor these projects, keeping track of the progress of each and scheduling its sequence of episodes. (One can imagine the analyst working in a large war room surrounded by walls covered with PERT or Gantt Charts.) Under this system, the manager continues to supervise his projects, but he is relieved of the difficult job of keeping track of their progress.

Adaptive Planning. A formal strategic plan is, in an operational sense, simply an explicit statement of a proposed set of improvement projects, integrated for mutual complementarity. The development of such a plan may, however, prove to be an enormously difficult undertaking. The organization must be able to bring an immense quantity of reliable material together at one point in time, and then be able to understand it sufficiently well so that it can be integrated into one sensible document. When most of the important information is available in documented form, when the environment is sufficiently predictable and stable so that plans made today will have some meaning tomorrow, and when the organization is large enough to afford the costs of what could be an expensive exercise, then it may make sense for it to undertake comprehensive strategic planning.

Typically, a plan is presented as a set of determinate decisions to be implemented, as is. But managers—even those in stable environments—need plans that they can implement flexibly. They need the option of choosing *when* to implement particular projects, and in some cases they need to be able to decide *how*—to be able to choose from among different alternatives. Uncertain events and uncertain timing must be accounted for in the plans, if they are to be useful. For example, a manager may wish to have the option of waiting to finalize an expansion project until he has been able to assess the mood of the government with respect to monetary policy; or he may prefer the option of delaying a choice from among a number of possible new organizational structures until after he has seen the results of pending personnel changes.

In effect, managers need adaptive plans, ones that will allow them to operate as they must in their dynamic environments. The planner must work out alternative plans and consider timing factors; he must produce plans in decision-tree form. In the words of one writer, the plans should resemble the "Lewis-and-Clark" rather than the "Cook's-Tour" approach to probing the unknown, as illustrated in Figure 18. [16]

This completes some thoughts on seven areas in which the management scientist can play a role at the policy level. To conclude, let me return to the words of Frederick Taylor, who wrote over fifty years ago:

> It is true that whenever intelligent and educated men find that the responsibility for making progress in any of the mechanic arts rests with them, instead of upon the workmen who are actually laboring at the trade, that they almost invariably start on the road which leads to the development of a science where, in the past, has existed mere traditional or rule-of-thumb knowledge. When men, whose education has given them the habit of generalizing and everywhere looking for laws, find themselves confronted with a multitude of problems, such as exist in every trade and which have a general similarity one to another, it is inevitable that they should try to gather these problems into certain logical groups, and then search for some general laws or rules to guide them in their solution. . . . The workman's whole time is each day taken in actually doing the work with his hands, so that, even if he had the necessary education and habits of generalizing in his thought, he lacks the time and the opportunity for developing these laws (1947: 103–104).

Today, managing remains an art, not a profession grounded in scientific discipline. This is so even though all managers appear to perform the same basic roles. To perform these roles, managers deal with

---

[16] James R. Schlesinger, "Organizational Structures and Planning," *The RAND Corporation p-3316* (February 25, 1966).

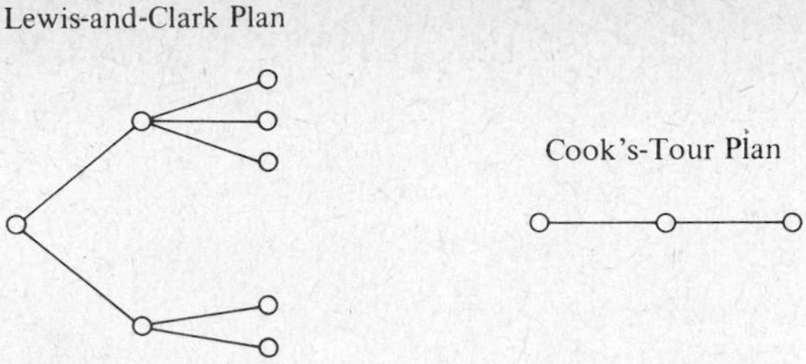

Lewis-and-Clark Plan

Cook's-Tour Plan

Figure 18. Lewis-and-Clark versus Cook's-Tour Plans

nondocumented information that is difficult to transmit, and they use intuitive methods that are difficult to understand. For these reasons managers receive little help from management scientists. As a result, certain important information-processing and strategy-making tends to be centralized in the hands of the one man in each organization who heads it.

There is every indication that the management scientist can begin to perform effectively at the policy level, just as he did at the operations level more than fifty years ago. The prerequisites for doing this are clear—description of the programs managers use, documentation of the information they carry in their heads, and a return to flexible analysis with a focus on basic problem-solving rather than the use of elegant techniques.

Modern organizations are expanding very rapidly, both in size and in complexity, due in large part to better production technology. Developments in the social sciences, especially in management science, must keep pace. Particularly in the public sector, the decisions of modern organizations are becoming too momentous for us to allow the traditional methods of managing to suffice.

PROPOSITIONS ABOUT A SCIENCE OF MANAGING

1. There is as yet no science in managerial work. Managers do not work according to procedures that have been prescribed by scientific analysis, and the management scientist has had no impact on how the manager works. In essence, managers work today as they always have.
2. A science of managing will require that managerial programs be identified, that the contents of the programs be specified, that they be linked together into a simulation of managerial work, and that specific programs be systematically analyzed and improved (reprogrammed) by the management scientist.
3. Although almost none of the manager's work is explicitly programmed, research suggests that all managerial decision-making behavior can be described in terms of high-order programs.

4. The manager has in his repertoire a number of general programs, which can be applied to a great variety of situations. He combines and sequences these programs according to the needs of a particular situation. Among the general programs that can be identified are information scanning, information disseminating, and negotiating. In addition, other programs exist, such as a group of leadership programs, which are more difficult to isolate.

5. The manager uses one specific program—the scheduling program—to control all his activities, to determine the sequence of tasks and when and for how long each will be executed. In addition, he probably uses a great number of other specific programs for specific purposes (to hire a subordinate, for example).

6. Despite recent interest in the use of management science at the policy level, progress has been slow and will continue to be so until there is developed a clearer understanding of the manager's working processes and until the management scientist can gain access to the manager's hitherto undocumented information.

7. A few managerial programs (perhaps scheduling) may be amenable to full automation. Many others (such as those associated with leadership) require flexible human responses and will be difficult to reprogram. Probably the largest group of programs will lend themselves to partial reprogramming, so that the manager will operate them in man–machine or manager–analyst systems.

8. On the least sophisticated level, a team of informed analysts can play a useful role by reprogramming the scheduling activity of the manager. The manager provides some of the scheduling rules; analysis of his work habits provides the others. Once these rules are made explicit, they can be applied to requests for the manager's time, and can be used in the development of a more productive workday.

9. Traditional information systems were not designed for the manager. They provide internal, historical, precise information of an aggregated and reference nature, whereas he seeks in large part external, current, speculative information of a trigger nature. Hence the manager is forced to rely on his own monitoring system, which is necessarily crude. By coming to understand the manager's actual use of information, the analyst can help design and operate a more effective monitoring system. His would be an "in-between" monitoring system—formal but probably not computerized—which would provide the manager with much of the information he seeks.

10. By putting the manager's information in official storage—through regular debriefing sessions held by him and through the collection and documentation of some of his information by the analyst—a formal data bank of some of the organiza-

tion's most important information would be created. This data bank would form the basis for an improved information-disseminating system. It would also have the advantage of staying in place when the manager left the organization. Such an explicit data bank is a necessary condition for the effective reprogramming of strategy-making.

11. The most difficult (but lucrative) job facing the management scientist is the reprogramming of strategy-making. Current practice, largely in accord with the "incremental" view of strategy-making presented in the literature, is becoming more and more inadequate because of the time constraints of the manager, the increasing complexity of organizational decisions, and the difficulty of integrating decisions made incrementally. Unfortunately, formal strategic planning as generally presented in the literature is an overly simple procedure that cannot cope with the complexity of the policy environment.

12. The "planning dilemma" suggests that managers have the information and the understanding of the dynamics of the environment, analysts have the time and the inclination to do the systematic analysis that complex strategic decisions require. There are at least seven areas (outlined below) in which managers and analysts may be able to cooperate to reprogram strategy-making.

13. The analyst can undertake systematic *search for opportunities and problems* that require action. His job would entail, not the feeding of data on trends and changes to the manager, but the inferring of the problems and opportunities these suggest.

14. The analyst can conduct *cost-benefit analysis* as a means of clarifying the policy issues that managers face. There is likely to be a steady growth in the use of this important approach, which requires clever, interdisciplinary problem-solving rather than elegant technique.

15. The manager needs powerful but simple models to help him make choices. Analysts can undertake formal *model building* in those areas where the data are available and where the computer model can be made sufficiently flexible to present the manager with a current and accurate simulation. But what may turn out to be more useful may be the analyst's efforts to expose the manager systematically to powerful descriptions of the complex phenomena he faces so that the models in his head can be based on the best conceptual understanding available.

16. The analyst can take the time to forecast contingent events that may have disruptive effects on the organization and then undertake *contingency planning* to prevent some of the problems or to have a plan available should a particular event occur.

17. When opportunities and crises do occur unexpectedly, the informed analyst who is prepared to forego elegance in his techniques can undertake *real-time analysis*. Analysts with a

thorough understanding of the manager's environment, able to act quickly, and ready to drop time-consuming, exhaustive techniques in favor of "quick-and-dirty" ones should prove to be of enormous help to the manager faced with a high-pressure situation.

18. The analyst can assume responsibility for *project monitoring*. Senior managers generally surpervise a great number of improvement projects, each one at a different stage of development. The analyst can monitor these, keep track of their progress, and sequence and schedule the steps of each for development by the manager.

19. In some situations formal comprehensive planning may be warranted—in relatively stable and predictable environments, where the data are documented and reliable, and where the organization can afford the cost. But the plans should be designed to allow the manager to be flexible in implementing them. The planner can undertake *adaptive planning*. This would allow the manager to adjust to his environment and make the prearranged decisions only when he feels the timing is right; in certain cases it would give him the option of choosing from among a number of alternative courses of action.

7

The Future
of Managerial
Work

Now this is not the end.
It is not even the beginning
of the end. But it is,
perhaps, the end of the
beginning.

Winston Churchill

This final chapter begins with an integrated review of the basic findings presented in Chapters 3 through 6. But whereas those findings were derived in four separate analyses of the available empirical data, here their order of presentation is reversed to show the logical interrelationships among them. From a definition of the manager and a statement of his basic purposes, we see the derivation of ten working roles. These roles indicate the manager's considerable responsibility in his organization; this responsibility in turn gives rise to a number of basic characteristics of the job of managing. It is because of these characteristics that a science of managing has not yet emerged. The second section of this chapter describes the manager in a "loop."

This descriptive summary is followed by four sections that present some normative implications of these findings. The third section is addressed to the manager himself, and contains a list of self-study questions as well as ten basic points the manager might consider to improve his effectiveness. In the fourth section the implications of the findings for the teacher of managers are considered, particularly in the area of skill development, and in the fifth section the implications for the management scientist are reviewed briefly. The final section contains some suggestions for further research. These four sections are organized to suggest the order in which change will come to the manager's job. Today's managers can make immediate changes in the way they work, while the teacher of managers will influence the next generation of managers. The management scientist can help the manager in a number of areas today, but it will take considerable time to develop a true science of managing. Finally, to the researcher will fall the task of developing the thorough understanding of the manager's job that all participants—managers, teachers, management scientists —will eventually require if they are to make truly profound changes in the work of managing.

A COMPREHENSIVE DESCRIPTION
OF MANAGERIAL WORK

I present below a summary of the basic propositions about managerial work developed in Chapters 3 to 6. It should be noted that these are supported by differing amounts of evidence—some are simply hypotheses while others have considerable empirical support. For details on each the reader can turn to the appropriate sections of the previous chapters. These propositions are presented here in an integrated description to show the interrelationships among the manager's purposes, roles, and characteristics, and the influence these have on the development of a science of managing.

Definition and Basic Purposes. The manager is that person in charge of a formal organization or one of its subunits. He is vested with formal authority over his organizational unit, and this leads to his two basic purposes. First, the manager must ensure that his organization produces its specific goods or services efficiently. He must design, and maintain the stability of, its basic operations, and he must adapt it in a controlled way to its changing environment. Second, the manager must ensure that his organization serves the ends of those persons who control it (the "influencers"). He must interpret their particular preferences and combine these to produce statements of organizational preference that can guide its decision-making. Because of his formal authority the manager must serve two other basic purposes as well. He must act as the key communication link between his organization and its environment, and he must assume responsibility for the operation of his organization's status system.

Ten Working Roles. These basic purposes are operationalized through ten interrelated roles, performed by all managers. The roles fall into three groupings—three *interpersonal* roles, which derive from the manager's authority and status, three *informational* roles, which derive from the interpersonal roles and the access they provide to information, and four *decisional* roles, which derive from the manager's authority and information.

As *figurehead,* the simplest of managerial roles, the manager is a symbol, required because of his status to carry out a number of social, inspirational, legal, and ceremonial duties. In addition, the manager must be available to certain parties who demand to deal with him because of his status and authority. The *figurehead* role is most significant at the highest levels of the organizational hierarchy.

The *leader* role defines the manager's interpersonal relationships with his subordinates. He must bring together their needs and those of the organization to create a milieu in which they will work effectively. The manager motivates his subordinates, probes into their activities to keep them alert, and takes responsibility for the hiring, training, and promoting of those closest to him. The societal shift toward greater organizational democracy will cause managers to spend more time in the *leader* role.

The *liaison* role focuses on the manager's dealings with people outside his own organizational unit. He develops a network of contacts in which information and favors are traded for mutual benefit. The manager spends a considerable amount of time performing this role, first by making a series of commitments to establish these contacts, and then by engaging in various activities to maintain them. For some managers this role is paramount. In the managerial diad, for example, the chief executive generally focuses on outside work and the second in command concentrates on internal operations (notably the *leader* and the decisional roles). Line sales managers, because their orientation is external and interpersonal, give special attention to this role, and to the other two interpersonal roles as well.

Through the *leader* and *liaison* roles, the manager gains access to privileged information and he emerges as the "nerve center" of his organization. He alone has formal access to every subordinate in his own organization, and he has unique access to a variety of outsiders, many of whom are nerve centers of their own organizations. Thus the manager is his organization's information generalist, that person best informed about its operations and environment.

As *monitor* the manager continually seeks and receives internal and external information from a variety of sources to develop a thorough knowledge of his milieu. Because a good part of this information is current and nondocumented, the manager must take prime responsibility for the design of his own information system, which is necessarily informal. Managers in new jobs, particularly, spend considerable time on the *monitor* and *liaison* roles in order to build up their information systems and bring themselves up to the level of knowledge needed for effective strategy-making.

As *disseminator* the manager transmits some of his internal and external information to subordinates. In this way, he maintains their only access to certain privileged information. Some of this information is of a factual nature; some relates to the values of the organization's influencers.

As *spokesman* the manager transmits information to individuals outside his organizational unit. He acts in a public relations capacity, lobbies for his organization, informs key influencers, tells the public about the organization's performance, and sends useful information to his liaison contacts. Furthermore, the manager must serve outsiders as an expert in the industry or function in which his organization operates. Managers of staff groups, because their subunits are highly specialized and oriented to analysis, spend considerable time in this expert capacity as well as giving relatively more attention to the other informational roles.

Because of his formal authority and special information, the manager must take responsibility for his organization's strategy-making system—the means by which decisions important to his organizational unit are made and interrelated. Strategy is made through four decisional roles.

As *entrepreneur* the manager is responsible for the initiation and design of much of the controlled change in his organization. He continually searches for new opportunities and problems and he initiates improvement projects to deal with these. Once started, an improvement project may involve the manager in one of three ways. He may delegate all responsibility to a subordinate, implicitly retaining the right to replace him; he may delegate responsibility for the design work but retain responsibility for authorizing the project before implementation; or he may supervise the design work himself. Senior managers appear to maintain supervision at any one time over a large inventory of these projects. Each is worked on periodically, with each step followed by a period of delay during which the senior manager waits for the feedback of information or the occurrence of an event.

As *disturbance handler* the manager is required to take charge when his organization faces a major disturbance. Since each subordinate is charged with a specialized function, only the manager is able to intervene when the organization faces a novel stimulus that is unrelated to any particular function and for which it has no programmed response. In effect, the manager again acts as his organization's generalist—the problem-solver who can deal with any kind of stimulus. Disturbances may reflect an insensitivity to problems, but they may also result from the unanticipated consequences of bold innovation. Hence we may expect to find many disturbances in the work of managers of both innovative and insensitive organizations. One can also expect to find the *disturbance handler* role emphasized following a period of intense innovation; a period of major change must be followed by a period in which the change is consolidated. Furthermore, managers of small companies and those in line production jobs, especially at lower levels in the hierarchy are likely to give the greatest attention to the *disturbance handler* role (and to the other decisional roles) because they tend to be most involved with the day-to-day maintenance of the workflow.

As *resource allocator* the manager oversees the allocation of all his organization's resources and thereby maintains control of its strategy-making process. He does this in three ways. First, by scheduling his own time the manager implicitly sets organizational priorities. Issues that fail to reach him fail to get support. Second, the manager designs the basic work system of his organization and programs the work of subordinates. He decides what will be done, who will do it, and what structure will be used. Third, the manager maintains ultimate control by authorizing, before implementation, all major decisions made by his organization. The authorization decisions are difficult ones to make; the issues are complex, but the time that can be devoted to them is short. The manager can ease the difficulty by choosing the person rather than the proposal. But when he must decide on the proposal, the manager makes use of loose models and plans that he develops implicitly from his nerve-center information. The models describe in a conceptual way a great variety of the internal and external situations that the manager faces. The plans—in the form of anticipated improvement projects—exist as his flexible vision of where the organization might go. Such plans serve as the common frame of reference against which he can evaluate, and hence interrelate, all proposals.

Finally, as *negotiator* the manager takes charge when his organization must have important negotiations with another organization. As *figurehead* he represents his organization, as *spokesman* he speaks for it, and as *resource allocator* he trades resources in real-time with the opposite party.

To summarize, the manager must design the work of his organization, monitor its internal and external environment, initiate change when desirable, and renew stability when faced with a disturbance. The manager must lead his subordinates to work effectively for the organization, and he must provide them with special information, some of which he gains through the network of contacts that he develops. In addition, the manager must perform a number of "housekeeping" duties, including informing outsiders, serving as *figurehead,* and leading major negotiations.

Thus, the popular view of the manager as the one who must take the broad view, do the unprogrammed work, and buttress the system where it is imperfect is only partly correct. Managers must also do their share of regular work and must involve themselves in certain ongoing organizational activities.

Basic Job Characteristics. It has been noted that the manager must take responsibility for the operation of his organization's strategy-making system, that he alone must find and process a significant amount of its important information, and that he must also perform a number of "housekeeping" duties. Added to all this is the open-ended nature of his job. There are no clear mileposts in the job of managing, never an indication that nothing more need be done for the moment, always the nagging thought that something could be improved if only the time could be found. Hence the manager's burden of responsibility is inherently great.

His problem is further compounded. The current and speculative nature of so much of the manager's information means that it is verbal. But the dissemination of verbal information is time-consuming. Hence the manager faces a "dilemma of delegation." He has unique access to much important information, but he lacks a formal and efficient means of disseminating it. The result is that the manager finds it difficult to delegate certain tasks with confidence, since he has neither the time nor the means to send along all the necessary information.

The net effect of all this is that the manager's time assumes a great opportunity cost. He carries this great burden of responsibility, yet he cannot easily delegate his tasks. As organizations become increasingly large and complex, this burden increases, particularly for senior managers. Unfortunately, these men cannot significantly increase their available time or significantly improve their abilities to manage. Hence the leaders of large complex bureaucracies face the real danger of becoming major obstructions in the flow of decisions and information.

These points explain a number of distinctive characteristics that can be observed in managerial work. The manager feels compelled to perform a great quantity of work and the pace he assumes is unrelenting. The manager seems to have little free time during the workday and he takes few breaks. Senior managers appear unable to escape from their work after hours because of what they take home and because their minds are constantly tuned to their jobs.

The manager's activities are characterized by brevity, variety, and fragmentation. The vast majority are of brief duration, on the order of seconds for foremen and minutes for chief executives. A great variety of activities are performed, but with no obvious patterns. The trivial are interspersed with the consequential so that the manager must shift moods quickly and frequently. There is great fragmentation of work, and interruptions are commonplace. The characteristics of brevity and fragmentation, apparently present in virtually all managers' jobs, are most pronounced for those who are closest to the "action"—top managers of small organizations, managers at lower levels in the hierarchy, particularly in production jobs, and managers working in the most dynamic environments.

Interestingly, the manager shows signs of preference for brevity and interruption in his work. No doubt, he becomes conditioned by his workload. He develops an appreciation for the opportunity costs of his own time and he lives with the awareness that, no matter what he is doing, there are other, perhaps more important, things that he might do and that he must do. A tendency toward superficiality becomes the prime occupational hazard of the manager.

In choosing activities the manager gravitates where possible to the more active elements in his work—the current, the well-defined, the nonroutine. Very current information—gossip, hearsay, speculation—is favored; routine reports are not. Time scheduling reflects a focus on the definite and the concrete, and activities tend to deal with specific rather than general issues. These characteristics are clearly found in the activities of chief executives and most become even more pronounced at lower levels of the hierarchy. The manager's job is not one that breeds reflective planners; rather, it produces adaptive information manipulators who favor a stimulus-response milieu.

The manager's work is essentially that of communication and his tools are the five basic media—mail, telephone, unscheduled meetings, scheduled meetings, and tours. Managers clearly favor the three verbal media, many spending on the order of 80 percent of their time in verbal contact. Some managers, such as those of staff groups, spend relatively more time alone. But the greatest share of the time of almost all managers is spent in verbal communication. The verbal media are favored because they are the action media, providing current information and rapid feedback. The mail, which moves slowly and contains little "live action" material, receives cursory treatment. Mail processing tends to be treated as a burden.

The informal media—the telephone and the unscheduled meeting—are generally used for brief contacts when the parties are well known to each other and when information or requests must be transmitted quickly. In contrast, scheduled meetings allow for more formal contacts, of longer duration, with large groups of people, and away from the organization. Of special interest is the flow of incidental, but often important, information at the beginning and end of scheduled meetings. Scheduled meetings are used for the special purposes of ceremony, strategy-making, and negotiation. Managers in large organizations and top managers of public organizations spend more time in scheduled meetings and other formal activities, while the work of lower-level managers and managers in dynamic environments tends to exhibit less formality.

Tours provide the manager with the opportunity to observe activity informally. Yet, managers apparently spend little time in this medium, perhaps because it involves nonspecific activity that is non-action oriented.

An analysis of the characteristics of the manager's interactions with other people shows that he stands between his own organizational unit and an extensive network of contacts. These can include his unit's clients, suppliers, and associates, his peers and colleagues, and their superiors and subordinates. Nonline relationships are a significant component of every manager's job, generally consuming one-third to one-half of his contact time. Managers in large organizations appear to have greater ranges of these contacts and better communication patterns. Much of their horizontal communication, however, appears to be with small cliques of colleagues that serve as centers for specialized information. Subordinates consume about one-third to one-half of the manager's time. He interacts with a wide variety of subordinates, freely bypassing formal channels of authority to get the information he desires. Finally, the evidence suggests that managers spend relatively little time with their superiors, only about one-tenth of their contact hours.

It has been implied in a number of the above conclusions that the burden of his work results in the manager's being carried along by his job to a large extent. The evidence concerning who initiates the manager's contacts and what types of contacts he engages in would appear to bear this out. Nevertheless, the strong incumbent (in any but the most highly structured jobs) can control his own work in subtle ways. In the first place, he is responsible for many of his initial commitments which later lock him into a set of ingoing activities. In the second place, the strong manager can turn to his own advantage those activities in which he must engage; he can extract information, lobby for his causes, or implement changes.

An analysis of the roles further suggests a blend of duties and rights. The duties come with the roles of *figurehead, spokesman, disturbance handler,* and *negotiator.* But in the roles of *leader, entrepreneur,* and *resource allocator,* the manager has the opportunity to put his stamp on his organizational unit and set its course.

Science in the Job. The evidence suggests that there is no science in managerial work. That is to say, managers do not work according to procedures that have been prescribed by scientific analysis. Indeed, the modern manager appears to be basically indistinguishable from his historical counterparts. He may seek different information, but he gets most of it in the same old way, by word of mouth. He may make decisions dealing with modern technology, but he uses the same intuitive (that is, nonexplicit) procedures or "programs" in making them.

Managers use a whole repertoire of general-purpose programs in their work. Faced with a particular task, the manager chooses, combines, and sequences a set of programs to deal with it. We can identify a number of general-purpose programs—such as information dissemination, alternative selection, and negotiation. There are other general-purpose programs that are more difficult to isolate, such as those associated with the *leader* role. In addition, the manager has some special purpose programs. He uses one—the scheduling program—to control his activities and determine the sequence of tasks to be executed.

The current reality is that all these programs are locked in the manager's brain, not yet described by the management researcher. There can be no science of managing until these programs are demarcated, their contents specified, the set of them linked into a simulation of managerial work, and particular ones subjected to systematic analysis and improvement.

THE MANAGER IN A "LOOP"

To sum up, we find that the manager, particularly at senior levels, is overburdened with work. With the increasing complexity of modern organizations and their problems, he is destined to become more so. He is driven to brevity, fragmentation, and superficiality in his tasks, yet he cannot easily delegate them because of the nature of his information. And he can do little to increase his available time or significantly enhance his power to manage. Furthermore, he is driven to focus on that which is current and tangible in his work, even though the complex problems facing many organizations call for reflection and a far-sighted perspective.

It is these very characteristics of the work that impede attempts to improve it. The researcher has had immense difficulty trying to describe work of this nature. The features of brevity, fragmentation, and verbal communication, adopted by the manager in order to deal with the pressures and complexities of the job, stand in the way of the researcher who attempts to understand it. Hence, we have learned almost nothing about how managers perform their roles—about what programs they use and the contents of these programs.

The evidence from the professions is that the analyst must take a major responsibility for bringing science to bear on the performance of work. The practitioner is busy; his job is to do the work, not to analyze it. The management scientist has so far effected little change in the job of managing. Unable to understand the manager's work and describe his programs and unable to gain access to his information, the management scientist has concentrated his efforts elsewhere in the organization, where activities are explicit, structured, and routine, amenable to analysis.

Hence the manager continues to manage as he always has, receiving little help from the management scientist. But as organizational problems have become more complex, particularly in the public sector, work characteristics—like fragmentation and emphasis on concrete activities and verbal media—have become more pronounced. Such characteristics in turn render the manager less able to cope with difficult problems and further reduce the management scientist's ability to help. In effect, the manager is caught in a "loop"—work pressures lead to pronounced job characteristics that lead to increased work pressures—and he has been able to do little about it. Society loses, because it looks to its senior managers for solutions to its major problems.

Somehow this vicious circle must be broken. First, managers must better understand the nature of their work and its problems, and they must alter their working habits to deal with them. Second, the classroom must be used to teach the skills of managing and to develop insights into the job and better means of coping with its complexity. Third, the management scientist must help by devoting his energies to those areas where science can be brought to bear on the manager's job. And, finally, the researcher must develop a sufficiently precise understanding of the manager's job to allow the manager, teacher, and management scientist to make significant improvements in the execution of it.

IMPLICATIONS FOR THE MANAGER

Today managing is an art, not a science. Most of the methods managers use are not properly understood; hence they are not taught or analyzed in any formal sense. This means that it will be some time before managers face the dangers of technological obsolescence, in a specific sense. Managing requires first and foremost a set of innate skills. Up to now management science has done very little to supplement these.

The lack of a scientific base for managing has imposed severe pressures on the manager. Basically, he is charged with design of his own information system and operation of his organization's strategy-making system. As organizations grow larger and more complex, the pressures increase. But without any systematic means to disseminate information, the burden of work increases. The manager faces the real danger of becoming a major obstruction in the flow of decisions and information.

The manager can alleviate these problems in a number of ways. First, he can study his own job and come to know the impact he has on his organization. Posed below are a number of self-study questions to aid in such an analysis. Second, the manager can make changes in the way he manages. We shall look at ten points for effective managing that are suggested by our findings.

Self—Study

Above all, our study suggests that the way in which the manager works and the specific things he chooses to do have a profound impact on his organization. The more he understands about his job and himself, the more sensitive the manager will be to the needs of his organization and the better will be his performance.

This understanding can come from studying the results of research—material such as that presented in Chapters 3 and 4. But more important, the manager can study his own particular job, either formally or informally. A formal study implies engaging a researcher or staff person to observe the manager to work, record details of his mail and activities, analyze the results, and feed them back to him. (Seven methods for researching the manager's job are described in Appendix B.) Informal analysis can be undertaken by the manager himself (perhaps with the aid of his secretary). He would focus consciously on his own actions, trying to develop an understanding of specifically what he does and why. Perhaps he might collect data systematically, using the diary method described in Appendix B.

To stimulate managers to analyze their own work, and to aid in this self-study process, the following 15 groups of guideline questions are presented:

1. Where do I get my information and how? Can I make greater use of my contacts to get information? Can other people do some of my scanning for me? In what areas is my knowledge weakest and how can I get others to provide me with the information I need? Do I have powerful enough mental models of those things within the organization and in its environment that I must understand? How can I develop more effective models?

2. What information do I disseminate into my organization? How important is it that my subordinates get my information? Do I keep too much information to myself because dissemination of it is

time-consuming or inconvenient? How can I get more information to others so they can make better decisions?

3. Do I balance information-collecting with action-taking? Do I tend to act prematurely before enough information is in? Or do I wait so long for "all" the information that opportunities pass me by and I become a bottleneck in my organization?

4. What rate of change am I asking my organization to tolerate? Is this change balanced so that our operations are neither excessively static nor overly disrupted? Have we sufficiently analyzed the impact of this change on the future of our organization?

5. Am I sufficiently well informed to pass judgment on the proposals made by my subordinates? Is it possible to leave final authorization for some of them with subordinates? Do we have problems of coordination because subordinates in fact now make too many of these decisions independently?

6. What is my vision of direction for this organization? Are these "plans" primarily in my own mind in loose form? Should they be made explicit in order to better guide the decisions of others in the organization? Or do I need flexibility to change them at will?

7. Are we experiencing too many disturbances in this organization? Would they be fewer if we slowed down the rate of change? Do disturbances reflect a delayed reaction to problems? Do we experience infrequent disturbance because we are stagnant? How do I deal with disturbances? Can we anticipate some and develop contingency plans for them?

8. What kind of a leader am I? How do subordinates react to my managerial style? How well do I understand their work? Am I sufficiently sensitive to their reactions to my actions? Do I find an appropriate balance between encouragement and pressure? Do I stifle their initiative?

9. What kind of external relationships do I maintain and how? Are there certain types of people that I should get to know better? Do I spend too much of my time maintaining these relationships?

10. Is there any system to my time scheduling or am I just reacting to the pressures of the moment? Do I find the appropriate mix of activities, or do I tend to concentrate on one particular function or one type of problem just because I find it interesting? Am I more efficient with particular kinds of work at special times of the day or week and does my schedule reflect this? Can someone else (in addition to my secretary) take responsibility for much of my scheduling, and do it more systematically?

11. Do I overwork? What effect does my workload have on my efficiency? Should I force myself to take breaks or to reduce the pace of my activity?

12. Am I too superficial in what I do? Can I really shift moods

as quickly and frequently as my work patterns require? Should I attempt to decrease the amount of fragmentation and interruption in my work?

13. Do I orient myself too much toward current, tangible activities? Am I a slave to the action and excitement of my work, so that I am no longer able to concentrate on issues? Do key problems receive the attention they deserve? Should I spend more time reading and probing deeply into certain issues? Could I be more reflective?

14. Do I use the different media appropriately? Do I know how to make the most of written communication? Do I rely excessively on face-to-face communication, thereby putting all but a few of my subordinates at an informational disadvantage? Do I schedule enough of my meetings on a regular basis? Do I spend enough time touring my organization to observe activity at first hand? Am I too detached from the heart of our activities, seeing things only in an abstract way?

15. How do I blend my rights and duties? Do my obligations consume all my time? How can I free myself sufficiently from obligations to ensure that I am taking this organization where I want it to go? How can I turn my obligations to my advantage?

Some of these questions may sound rhetorical. None is meant to be. There are no simple solutions to the complex problems of managerial work. This book can perhaps ask some of the right questions; but if the manager is to improve his work today, he must provide his own answers. For this reason it is crucial that the manager develop a better understanding of his own work.

Ten Points for More Effective Managing

Our study suggests that there are a number of areas in which managers can concentrate their attention in order to improve effectiveness. Ten such areas are reviewed below. They are presented in the belief that managers must become sensitive to the key difficulties in their jobs and explicitly seek their own means of dealing with each.

Sharing Information. The manager is exposed to a significant amount of privileged information. His status gives him access to special contacts outside his own organizational unit who provide favored information. His position at the pinnacle of his own organizational unit leads to a unique knowledge of internal matters as well. But because so much of his important information is verbal, the manager lacks a convenient means of disseminating it. The result is a reluctance to disseminate information widely (which may seem like a desire to hoard it). Only a few subordinates within convenient verbal reach of the manager get any significant quantity of his information.

The manager must, therefore, give conscious attention to the dissemination of information to his subordinates. He must realize that they cannot tap many of the informational sources to which he has easy access, that they depend on him for much important information and cannot make effective decisions without it.

Subordinates need much of the manager's regular verbal information—the new idea from a customer or the gossip of a supplier. They also need two types of special information from him. First, they rely on the manager to specify organizational values or goals. He must establish the key trade-offs between profit, growth, protection of environment, and employee welfare. Second, subordinates look to the manager for a sense of direction, a plan. If the manager is not prepared to provide explicit and consistent guidelines as to goals and plans, then he must accept the fact that he will be unable to delegate responsibility for any major decision for fear that the result will not comply with the goals and plans he has kept to himself.

As long as the manager's key information remains only in his natural memory, dissemination of it will be difficult. He must make a concentrated effort to document his information so that it can be disseminated efficiently, even to those who are not in convenient verbal reach (overseas for example). Through regular debriefing sessions the manager can create a formal data bank of his important information, which will then be available to those who need it.

Two points might be raised in objection to such a free flow of information. First, some information is confidential, and documenting it might expose it to the wrong people. Second, information means power; sharing information means dissipating power. The second point merits only brief comment. The manager who hoards information is trading off effectiveness for power. This attitude is destined to cause him difficulties in the long run. The question of confidentiality involves a more significant trade-off—the effective management that derives from a free flow of information versus the risks of exposure. This trade-off may too often be made in favor of confidentiality. No doubt some information must remain private and nondocumented. But the risk of disseminating as much information as possible must be weighed against the significant advantages of having well-informed subordinates who can make effective and compatible decisions.

Dealing Consciously with Superficiality. Superficiality is a prime occupational hazard of the manager. The work is disjointed and fragmented; activities are characterized by variety and brevity; major decisions are taken in incremental steps. It is too easy in this job to operate continuously on a superficial level, so that all issues are dealt with quickly, as if none needs much attention.

The manager must deal consciously with the pressures driving him to be superficial. A balance must be found whereby certain issues receive the concentration and depth of understanding they require, and those that require marginal involvement receive just that. Issues may be treated in three ways.

First, a great number must be delegated, even though the manager knows that, given the time, he could deal with many of them more effectively than anyone else. The fact is that he is not given the time. When an issue is unimportant, when a specialized subordinate is better equipped to handle it, when the necessary information can be disseminated, the manager must delegate.

Second, the manager must deal with some other issues himself, but in a marginal way. That is, he must be involved only to authorize the final proposal. He must do so to ensure that the proposal is compatible with other changes taking place in the organization and to ensure that he is prepared to take responsibility for the commitment of resources. But in these cases the manager has to realize that he may understand the issue only superficially, that despite his general knowledge he may know far less than a subordinate about its specific details. The final decision on the issue must reflect both the manager's knowledge of the general situation and the subordinate's knowledge of the specific. Above all, the manager must recognize that a hasty *no* on a proposal he does not fully understand may discourage an otherwise enthusiastic subordinate.

A third group of issues require special attention by the manager. These are the most important, and often the most complex and sensitive ones—reorganizing structure, expanding the organization, dealing with a major conflict. Nevertheless, the nature of his job is such that the manager cannot give any one issue much time at an uninterrupted stretch. Hence each complex issue must be dealt with intermittently over a long period of time. But to make progress on an issue in incremental steps is to run the risk of veering off course without realizing it. The manager may become so involved with the latest increment that he may forget about the broad issue in all of its complexity. There are no panacean solutions to this difficulty, although the manager who is conscious of it should be better able to deal with it. One thing managers can do is to make better use of specialists who can feed them with reports that focus on issues in their broadest contexts. The management scientist has probably not been used sufficiently to do systems analyses of policy issues. The unbiased opinion of an analyst, who has the time and inclination to analyze policy issues in basic terms, can remind the manager of the broad perspective.

Sharing the Job If Information Can Be Shared. One way to overcome the heavy managerial workload, particularly at top levels of large organizations, is to share the job. A dyad or triad is created, perhaps called a "management team" or "chief executive office," in which two or three managers share a single managerial job. This method has two obvious advantages—it reduces the burden of work on one man and it allows individuals to specialize in certain roles. Particularly common is the diad arrangement whereby one manager concentrates on the external roles (*liaison, figurehead, spokesman, negotiator*) and the other deals with the inside work of leadership and decision-making. When it works, job-sharing is probably the most sensible answer to the pressures of managerial work. But when it fails, it aggravates the pressures.

It was claimed in Chapter 4 that the ten managerial roles form a *gestalt*—an integrated whole. Authority and status give access to information, and it is his information that enables the manager to perform the decision-making roles. Information is the key linking element in the different work the manager does. Hence the effectiveness of job sharing hinges on the abilities of the managers to share information. The *monitor* role cannot be divided—each member of the team must have full information. In the common dyad, for example, if the outside man cannot share his external information with the inside man, the latter cannot make effective decisions. Similarly, if the outside man cannot find out about internal matters, he cannot be an effective *spokesman, liaison,* or *negotiator* for his organization.

The main disadvantage of job sharing is that considerable time can be consumed simply in transmitting the information that must be shared. The members of the team may have to spend so much time communicating with each other that they lack the time necessary for other duties, and it may be more efficient to return to the single manager concept.

Other factors enter into the success of job sharing. Management teams must be composed of individuals who complement each other—who are prepared to do different types of work so that all the managerial roles will be performed. But this complementarity must be coupled with a certain compatibility. In particular, the managers must be able to communicate easily and efficiently, and they must share a vision of the direction in which they wish to take their organization. If they cannot agree with reasonable precision on these "plans," then they will pull in different directions and the team (or the organization) will break down.

Hence, we must conclude that job sharing is difficult to do effectively, but it is worthy of a careful try in the most demanding of managerial jobs.

Making the Most of Obligations. The manager must spend so much of his time discharging obligations that if he were to view them as just that, he would have too little time to make his mark on his organization. To an important extent, therefore, he succeeds—not because he has full freedom to do as he wishes, but because he can turn to his own advantage those things that he is obliged to do.

The unsuccessful manager tends to blame failure on his obligations. If not for the crises, the callers, and the ceremonial duties, he would have done better. But, what is an obligation to one is an opportunity to another. In fact, every obligation presents the shrewd manager with a chance to accomplish his own purposes. A crisis may simply be solved, or its resulting chaos may present an opportunity to make some desirable changes. A ceremonial duty may be a waste of time, or it may be an opportunity to lobby for a cause. The need to meet someone in a *figurehead* capacity may present the chance to tap a new source of information. The obligation to be present at a briefing session may give the manager a chance to exert some leadership. In everything he does the manager has a chance to extract information; every time he interacts with a subordinate he has a chance to influence him as his *leader*. Whether or not he turns obligation to advantage determines in large part whether or not he will succeed.

It should also be noted that many of the manager's obligations derive in fact from initial commitments he himself makes early in the job. It is he who sets up many of the liaison contacts that serve later as his information channels; he joins institutions and societies that later require his efforts; he is responsible for initiating many of the improvement projects that subsequently consume much of his time. A number of these early commitments are perhaps made inadvertently or at least without the full realization of their eventual effect. Managers must recognize the importance of these early commitments and make them accordingly.

Freeing Self from Obligations. Making the most of obligations is a necessary but not sufficient condition if the manager is to gain control of his job. He must be able to free himself so that some of his time is devoted to those issues that he (perhaps no one else) feels *should* be attended to.

The manager must seek a balance between change and stability in his organization. He is responsible for ensuring both that his organization produces today's goods and services efficiently and that it adapt to tomorrow's new environment. But the pressures of today's production may leave no time to think of tomorrow's changes. Between the mail, the callers, and the crises, not to mention the ever hovering subordinate waiting for a free moment, the passive manager will find no free time to address the major, but not pressing, issues.

"Free" time is made, not found, in the manager's job. The manager must force it into his schedule. As noted earlier, many managers suffer from a "diary complex"—what does not get scheduled does not get done. Trying to keep some time open for contemplation or for general "planning" will not work. The manager is not a planner in a reflective sense, and no amount of admonition in the literature will make him so. His milieu is one of stimulus-response. The manager must schedule those specific things he wants to do. Then he will be obliged to do them. If he wishes to innovate, he must initiate a project and involve others who will report back to him; if he wishes to tour facilities, he must commit himself so that others expect him to do so. He will then serve his own organization's broader ends while continuing to manage as he must.

Emphasizing the Role that Fits the Situation. Although required to perform all of the basic managerial roles, most managers must give special attention to certain roles in certain situations. A variety of factors determine what roles particular managers must emphasize. These factors include among others, the industry, the size of the organization, the level in the hierarchy, the function supervised, the situation of the moment, and the manager's experience.[1]

The job itself as well as the environment may suggest some obvious needs. Managers of governmental organizations may have to spend extra time on the *liaison* and *spokesman* roles to satisfy outside pressure groups; production managers may need to concentrate on the *disturbance handler* role to maintain the workflow; managers of competitive organizations may be required to emphasize the *entrepreneur* role in order to keep ahead of the competition. Clearly, the manager must study the needs of his job and tailor his work accordingly.

The choice of which roles to emphasize must also reflect the current situation. The manager's job is a dynamic one, requiring continual adjustment to meet the needs of the moment. In every managerial job (to paraphrase Ecclesiastes) there is a time to concentrate on change, and a time to seek stability; a time to stress leadership, and a time to build a data base; a time to handle disturbances, and a time to replenish resources.

Our study suggests certain patterns. As he begins a new job, the manager is likely to find that he lacks the external contacts and the information necessary to make and implement effective decisions. Clearly, the manager must devote considerable time at the start of a new job to developing liaison contacts, to building his own information channels, to collecting information about his new organization and its environment. Later, when he feels more secure in his knowledge, he may gradually shift emphasis to the *entrepreneur* role in an attempt to mold his organization to his own wishes.

The need to balance stability and change also may influence

[1] See Chapter 5 for an analysis of these factors.

the manager's attention to roles. Managers may find it effective under certain circumstances to alternate periods of extensive change with those of consolidation of change, rather than to adopt a pattern of slow, steady change. In other words, the manager emphasizes the *entrepreneur* role for a period, making what he considers the necessary changes, all at one time. Thus the organization undergoes all the disruption at once. When no more change can be tolerated, the manager then consolidates the gains and brings back stability—emphasizing the *leader* and *disturbance handler* roles. Later, when all is normal, a new cycle can start.

Seeing a Comprehensive Picture in Terms of Its Details. The manager faces the difficulty of the person putting together a jigsaw puzzle. Though always working with small pieces, he must never forget the whole picture. The manager must inform himself by piecing together tangible details. He needs specific information in order to develop an understanding of his environment and to find specific opportunities and problems.

Thus, effective managing means building channels that bring certain information in relatively raw form. Direct observation (touring) and personal discussion with as many people as possible are powerful means of gaining this information.

The danger is, however, that in his search for tangible details, the manager may be unable to see the broad issues. He must know how to step back from his data so that he can see when necessary, not the welter of detail but a set of broad, powerful models (conceptual descriptions) that provide simple but accurate pictures of various aspects of his reality. For it is the power of his mental models that determines to a great extent the effectiveness of his decisions. The manager whose model of the factory worker's behavior is based on the premise that he is motivated by money will make poor leadership decisions if the worker is in fact motivated only by the quality of his work. Similarly, the government leader who believes that inflation can be arrested by tight monetary policy may be in trouble if the economy does not in fact work according to this model.

Although his models are built largely from data he collects himself, the manager must be able to recognize the value of other people's models—of other conceptual descriptions of the situations he faces. Economists write books that contain models of the economy; marketing researchers develop models of the behavior of consumers, and psychologists describe worker motivation; operations researchers formulate computer models of production processes. The manager must expose himself to these and other models, compare them with his own, and retain in his mind the most effective models of the situations he faces.

Recognizing Own Influence in the Organization. The subordinate is most sensitive to the actions of his manager. He reacts to his priorities, his decisions, his attitudes, his moods. In the small organization, the influence of the top man is apparent to everyone. But even in the large organization with many levels in the hierarchy, the influence of the chief executive can be powerful indeed, perhaps often far greater than he imagines. Strange things filter down the hierarchy. What is trivial to the manager—a hasty comment, an idea dismissed quickly, a bit of careless information—can have a profound effect on the organization. Managers must act with conscious recognition of this fact.

A special word should be written about priorities. By the way in which he schedules his own time—by the determination of what he does—the manager exerts a significant influence on his organization. Should he favor one function—marketing or production, for example —subordinates will adjust accordingly and cater to this interest. If the choice of favored area is not made in accordance with real needs, the organization may suffer an imbalance. Managers should consciously allocate their own time as if they are setting the priorities of their organizations—for they are.

Dealing with a Growing Coalition. Any organizational unit exists because certain people ("influencers") created it and others are prepared to support it. To the manager falls the difficult task of keeping this coalition of influencers together. He must ensure that the benefits for each are balanced in accordance with their influence, and he must be able to convince them to forego benefits in times of crisis.

This juggling act has been relatively easy for those managers who faced simple coalitions. The company president who answered only to a homogenous board of directors or the middle manager who was dominated by one boss had little difficulty with questions of power. But today we see two major changes in society that will significantly alter the coalition and profoundly affect every manager's job.

First, Western society is broadening its view of democracy. No longer content to define freedom simply as the right to vote periodically for political leaders, people are increasingly seeking greater freedom in, and control of, their workplaces. Sometimes they do so at the expense of production efficiency (notwithstanding the claims of those organizational behaviorists who see an inevitable correlation between worker satisfaction and productivity). But people in a democratic society, particularly an affluent one, have every right to make this trade-off. Many workers in Yugoslavia now elect their managers, and in Western Europe workers are demanding greater influence in policy issues. In America, the enthusiasm for productivity has so far kept labor unions out of most policy issues; they have chosen to fight their battles in terms of wages and fringe benefits. But the pressures to democratize organizations are growing even in the United States, particularly among middle-level staff specialists.

Hence, the manager will have to face a new set of influencers, this time from below. The coalition will be broadened, with some power given to the employees who work for him. They will request work that is inherently more satisfying and demand some control over the actions of their leader—perhaps even over the choice of the leader.

Some managers may abhor these changes, but they would do well to understand them, for they will significantly affect their work. When power is represented by level in the hierarchy, as in the authoritarian form of organization, the *leader* role is a simple one. The manager simply issues orders down the line according to the dictates of efficiency. As the *leader* role changes to adjust to the new power structure, it will become significantly more complex. The manager will have to learn to accommodate to demands of employees who will be increasingly sensitive to the influence he has over them.

The coalition is being attacked from the outside as well. Where once businessmen could seek to satisfy only shareholders, and university presidents could answer primarily to trustees, today they must react to a diverse array of influencers. Indeed, the top managers of large corporations are becoming more and more like political leaders, engaged in balancing acts among pressure groups of every conceivable kind. It will not help the manager to question the legitimacy of these pressures. They are real, and they reflect the fact that an affluent society demands more from its organizations than efficiency. Social issues come to the forefront—pollution, treatment of minority groups, attitudes toward consumers. Where power is concentrated, as it is in the large corporation, there is a natural tendency for people to analyze its use and to expect it to be applied explicitly for the public good.

The influence of this trend on the top manager's job will be profound. He will be forced to give more attention to the external roles, *liaison, spokesman,* and *figurehead,* in order to maintain rapport with various pressure groups, and to the *negotiator* role in order to deal with their conflicting demands. In turn, he will have to delegate down the line more of the work associated with internal operations.

Using the Management Scientist. The trend in large organizations has been to use the skills of the management scientist to help deal with increasingly complex problems. Clearly, the complexity of the problems that senior managers face will require that they turn more and more to the management scientist for help. But for such cooperative efforts to succeed, managers and management scientists will have to learn to work together. The management scientist must learn to work in a dynamic system, and he must develop methods which, although less elegant than those he now uses, will be better suited to the problems of policy-making. His methods must be adaptive and they must operate in "real-time"—while issues are current.

The manager must learn to work effectively with the analyst, who deals in comprehensive investigation. Up to now the characteristics of managerial work have been such that there was little room for analysis. But if the manager will help the analyst to understand his work and his problems, and if he will allow the analyst access to his data base of verbal information, then the manager can expect significant support from him.

One can envision the development of sophisticated time-scheduling systems, with the manager defining his priorities and the analyst developing the system that will do the scheduling in an efficient and systematic manner. Furthermore, there is reason to believe that the analyst can do much of the monitoring of information for the manager (scanning periodicals, analyzing reports) and can filter and document much of what is received.

In the area of strategy-making, the management scientist will likely prove most helpful. Strategy issues are complex, yet the manager has limited time to analyze them. The management scientist can help the manager in his search for opportunities, in the analysis of costs and benefits of alternatives, in the development of better models for choice-making. He can design contingency plans to anticipate crises and carry out "quick and dirty" analysis for the manager faced with a high-pressure situation. He can monitor the projects that the manager must supervise. And he can develop explicit but flexible strategic plans for the organization.[2]

The analyst's participation in strategy-making hinges on the solution of what I have called the "planning dilemma." Managers have the information, and authority; analysts have the time and the technology. Somehow, the information must be transmitted to the analyst so that he can make his time and skills useful.

Hence, we close this section where we began. To take advantage of the help possible from management scientists, the manager must somehow share his information with them. The result could be the estabishment of entirely new and more effective ways of managing.

IMPLICATIONS FOR TEACHERS OF MANAGERS

We might well begin this section by asking whether management is indeed a profession and whether it can in fact be taught. A profession may be distinguished by two criteria—a common set of roles and programs in the performance of work, and "knowledge of some depart-

---

[2] See Chapter 6 for a detailed treatment of this material.

ment of learning or science" (Random House Dictionary). There is clear evidence that all managerial jobs require the incumbent to perform a common set of roles, but there is remarkably little evidence of the requirement for formal learning in the performance of any of these roles. What student of management is taught how to develop liaison contacts, handle the disturbances that inevitably arise, negotiate with other organizations, innovate in his organization? Some notions of leadership are usually taught, but the fact is that in general we know very little about teaching the managerial roles.

Our schools of administration and management have designed their curricula to do other things. At one time most concentrated on teaching by the case-study method, presumably in the belief that managers-to-be would benefit from practice in unstructured decision-making. (I should say choice-making, since both the problems and the data were provided, not found.) But our study gives us reason to believe that this kind of instruction does not develop the wide array of talents managers need.

The case study method probably came into wide use because management schools tacitly recognized that they were not able to teach explicitly the specific managerial talents. They could hope only to accelerate the learning that might otherwise take place on the job. Thus the classroom became a place for the simulation of practice.

In the 1960s many schools of management turned away from the case-study philosophy, devoting their attention instead to the teaching of theory. It is interesting to note that much of this theory deals, not with the job of managing per se, but with the underlying disciplines—economics, psychology, and mathematics. These schools teach applied theory also, but again little of it relates directly to the process of managing. It is theory of the specialist functions of the organization—marketing research, operations research, investment analysis, and so on. All of this knowledge will be useful to the manager-to-be, but almost none of it relates directly to those things he will be called upon to do in the job of manager. Regardless of its objectives, therefore, the management school has been more effective at training technocrats to deal with structured problems than managers to deal with unstructured ones. The one course that might have dealt with the management process—the course in policy—has either been conspicuously absent from the curriculum of the modern management school or it has more often than not been taught solely by the case-study method.

To conclude, we must recognize that although the management school gives students M.B.A. and M.P.A. degrees, it does not in fact teach them how to manage. Hence these degrees can hardly be considered prerequisites for managing, and the world is full of highly competent managers who have never spent one day in a management course.

Skill Development

The management school will significantly influence management practice only when it becomes capable of teaching a specific set of "skills" associated with the job of managing. Just as the medical student must learn diagnosis and the engineering student must learn design, so also must the student of management learn leadership, negotiation, disturbance handling, and other managerial skills.

Skills may be learned in three ways. In *cognitive* learning, the student is exposed to the current knowledge by reading about a skill or listening to a lecture on it. *Learning by simulation* involves practicing the skill in an artificial situation with feedback on performance (role playing, for example). And in *on-the-job* learning the student performs the skill as a natural component of his work; he then benefits from conscious introspection and the feedback of others.

Cognitive study is useful but generally sterile. Learning is most effective when the student actually performs the skill in as realistic a situation as possible and then analyzes his performance explicitly. One cannot learn to swim by reading about it. One must get into the water, splash around, and practice various techniques with advice from someone who knows what skills swimming requires. Eventually, with sufficient feedback, he learns to swim. The same holds true for many management skills. The student must be immersed in the milieu; he must practice the skill; and he must receive constructive feedback on his performance from someone who understands the skill.

The literature is beginning to reflect some recognition of the need to teach management skills. Livingston (1971), in a recent *Harvard Business Review* article entitled "Myth of the Well-Educated Manager," claims that "men who get to the top in management have developed skills that are not taught in formal management education programs and may be difficult for many highly educated men to learn on the job." He calls for the teaching of skills, for replacing "second-handedness" in education with teaching that helps students to learn from their own firsthand experiences.

Radosevitch and Ullrich, in their analysis of graduate professional education, call for "providing opportunities for students to practice newly learned skills," and they add:

> Graduates of professional programs must be "doers" as well as thinkers. Unlike other academic disciplines, professional education requires that the learning situation produce both intellectual and behavioral outcomes. . . . Standard lectures on McGregor's Theory

Y, for example, develop neither the empathy nor the skills which are necessary for the successful application of Theory Y to a work situation (1971: 23–24).[3]

One way to determine what skills managers need is to analyze the roles they perform. A study of the ten roles presented in Chapter 4 suggested eight basic sets of managerial skills that might be taught. These are discussed in turn below.

Peer Skills. The peer skills deal with the manager's ability to enter into and effectively maintain peer relationships. A number of skills can be included here. The manager must know how to develop implicit contacts with other parties to serve mutual needs. He must know how to build up and maintain an extensive network of contacts to bring him favors and information, and he must know how to communicate with equals on a formal and an informal basis. One specific peer skill is negotiation–the ability to trade resources in real-time. Also important, especially to managers of staff groups, is the consulting skill—the ability to manage an expert-client relationship. Finally, there are a whole host of "political" skills associated with the conflict and infighting in large bureaucracies.

Social psychologists provide us with some insight into the peer skills. Contracting relationships have been studied and the T-group concept has been developed, perhaps the one specific method we now have to develop peer skills in a simulated (should we say real?) environment. Empirical study of the negotiating behavior of managers should lead to the descriptions of methods or programs that can be taught. Game theory and "confrontation cases" may be other useful vehicles for the teaching of peer skills.

Peer skills lend themselves well to teaching by experience. In organizational development courses managers can easily draw on their peer experiences, and students in the university are certainly exposed to numerous peer situations. In both cases opportunities exist for systematic inspection of real-life situations.

Leadership Skills. The leadership skills focus on the manager's ability to deal with his subordinates—to motivate and train them,

[3] In his public policy course at the Kennedy School of Government, Richard Neustadt provides the students with a series of short memoranda in which he discusses several specific staff skills (e.g., briefing, motivating). Although claiming that skills are acquired on the job and not in the classroom, Neustadt introduces certain skill exercises in his course to give students a "nodding acquaintance" with the skills they may need in the staff jobs they are likely to hold in the early years of their careers. (From the outline for "Public Policy 240: Political Analysis," John Fitzgerald Kennedy School of Government, Harvard University.)

provide help, deal with problems of authority and dependence, and so on. We have considerable literature on the leadership skills, although much of it treats only the question of autocratic versus participative styles of managing. We have also a number of training programs in leadership skills, such as the Managerial Grid developed by Blake and Mouton (1964).

The leadership skills, perhaps more than any others, require participative training. Leadership, like swimming, cannot be learned by reading about it. Leadership skills are so closely related to innate personality, however, that it may be difficult to effect really significant behavioral change in the classroom.

Conflict-Resolution Skills. Included here are the interpersonal skill of mediating between conflicting individuals and the decisional skill of handling disturbances. In using both these skills, the manager must work under stress. Just as the body can be developed to tolerate physiological stress, so presumably can the mind be trained to tolerate psychological stress. Role-playing techniques may be useful to simulate conflict in the classroom and thereby to train managers in the conflict-resolution skills. Furthermore, we have some understanding of the skills of mediation; this understanding should prove useful in management training programs.

Information-Processing Skills. Management students should learn how to build informal information networks, find sources of information and extract what they need, validate information, assimilate it and build effective mental models. Furthermore, they should learn how to disseminate information, express their ideas effectively, and speak formally as representatives of organizations.

We spend some time on these things in university programs today. Operations research classes cover formal model building, and many of the functional area courses teach the students where to find specialized data (national income statistics in economics courses, cost information in accounting courses). Some schools expose students to readings on research methodology and, by requiring various projects or a thesis, provide them with practice in the skill of extracting field data and validating it. Library assignments develop the information-collecting skills. The case-study method enhances the student's ability to communicate his thoughts, and the incident-case approach, in which the student is given a short case and allowed to seek further data, is a more specific method for developing his data-collection skills.

Every Master's program in administration does some of these things. What is often missing, however, is the means to instruct the student in extracting the unstructured, undocumented information managers most often seek. We need to pay special attention in our management development programs to the development of verbal skills. In fact, we should develop methods to train management students in the use of all the managerial media. The telephone, the scheduled and unscheduled meetings, the tour, and the mail are the manager's prime tools. We should train the student systematically in their use.

Skills in Decision-Making Under Ambiguity. Most characteristic of top manager decision-making is the unstructured situation. The manager must first decide when a decision must be made; he must then diagnose the situation and plan an approach to it; he must search for solutions and evaluate their consequences; finally, he must select an alternative. This of course is only the tip of the iceberg, for as we have seen, a "decision" is in fact a series of nested smaller decisions. Furthermore, the manager does not handle decisions one at a time; he juggles a host of them, dealing with each intermittently, all the while attempting to develop some integration among them.

Management schools are presently devoting considerable attention to the teaching of decision-making skills. But the prescriptions provided for the students are rather elementary when viewed in the light of the complex ambiguity senior managers face. The case-study method offers the issue and the data in one neat printed package, asking the student to do some analysis and debate various alternatives. The business game provides a neat, structured situation in which a fixed set of decisions are required each period.

From management science come a variety of techniques to be taught—Bayesian analysis, linear programming, queueing theory, and investment analysis, to name but a few. But these techniques, while of some help in the selection of courses of action from given alternatives with given consequences, cannot deal with the open-ended, dynamic characteristics of the manager's decision. It is not the decision-making under *certainty, risk,* or even *uncertainty* of the textbook that the manager faces, but decision-making under *ambiguity.* Very little information is given to the manager faced with a strategic issue, and almost none of that is structured. The techniques of strategic or long-range planning, ostensibly designed to deal with interrelated strategic decisions, tend to be no more sophisticated. The state of the science of formal planning, when contrasted with managerial strategy-making practice, appears primitive indeed.

Management science has tended to serve the functional specialists of the organization who must make relatively routine decisions with structured inputs. Hence, to teach management science is to inform the student of the processes used by technocrats, not managers. This, of course, is worthwhile knowledge for any manager-to-be. Since the route to management is increasingly through the technostructure, schools of management can prepare students to follow it.

Furthermore, practice in management science probably improves skill in decision-making, even if the decisions dealt with in the manager's job are different. The student learns to structure problems, to think out solutions, and to seek hard data. Whatever truth there is in these arguments should not, however, stop our search for better means to simulate in the classroom the reality of decision-making under ambiguity, and to teach prescriptions which match the complexity of this reality. The management student should learn the skills necessary for finding problems and opportunities, diagnosing unstructured problems, searching for solutions, managing the dynamics of decision-making, and juggling parallel decisions and integrating them into plans.

Resource-Allocation Skills. Managers are required to choose among competing resource demands; they must decide how to allocate their own time, determine what work their subordinates must do and in what formal structure they must work, and pass judgments, sometimes very quickly, on projects that require organizational resources.

Except for what is taught of the theory of organization design (valid cognitive material for any manager), little is done in schools of administration to develop the resource-allocation skills. This is not quite true for management development programs, which sometimes give attention to the issue of time allocation. Courses that deal with this issue in a meaningful way are probably valuable, and merit further development. In addition, an effort should be made to simulate situations in the classroom in which the student must juggle and make decisions concerning a mixture of complex issues. The "in-basket" technique, whereby the student is required to process a mixture of documents, suggests the kind of thing that can be done in the classroom.

Entrepreneurial Skills. This set of decisional skills involve the search for problems and opportunities and the controlled implementation of change in organizations. With the exception of the "change agent" skills discussed in the literature of organizational behavior, there is a question as to how much can formally be taught in this area. But, in the very nature of our management schools and the philosophy underlying their program designs, it is possible to create a climate that encourages the use of entrepreneurial skills. Clearly, the management school can consciously promote entrepreneurship in its student body. Sensible risk-taking and innovation can be rewarded, and a high value can be placed on creativity, Clearly, inflexible program structure, passivity, and regurgitation should be discouraged. If these things are not done, there is the real risk of creating an academic environment that frightens away the very people who should receive formal managerial training.

Skills of Introspection. The manager should thoroughly understand his job; he should be sensitive to his own impact on his organization; he should be able to learn by introspection. It is presumably the role of the professor who teaches the policy course to inform the student about the essentials of managerial work—about the nature and characteristics of the job itself, the formulation of organizational goals, the nature of the strategy-making process, and the role of the planner. Most important, students should be encouraged to develop the skills of introspection needed to continue to learn by themselves on the job. Organizations can perhaps enhance this learning by providing their managers with vehicles for self-study and by encouraging sessions wherein managers can give each other honest (and confidential) feedback on their behavior. But no other learning environment—classroom, executive development program, peer feedback session—can surpass the job itself, provided the manager knows how to learn from his own experiences.

As has been emphasized, management schools have so far given little attention to the development of basic managerial skills; hence they have really done little to train managers. There are now signs that management schools are joining the executive development people in their recognition of the need to teach skills. Skill training will probably be—and should be—the next revolution in management education.

A Note on Selection

The efficiency of managerial training and development programs is significantly influenced by the selection of students. The right training for the wrong people is clearly wasteful. Formal education cannot make managers. All one can hope to do is to enhance the basic skills that students bring to the classroom and provide them with knowledge. If the student has the potential to lead, training will help him to lead more effectively; if he has not, nothing done in the classroom will make him into an effective manager. Hence the greatest successes will be scored by those management schools that are able (1) to determine most precisely which applicants demonstrate managerial skills, and (2) to improve significantly their performance of those skills. Unfortunately we continue to lack the means to choose effectively and systematically those people who will succeed in managerial jobs. Livingston provides some rather interesting evidence that the people most successful in M.B.A. programs are not necessarily the ones to succeed in management. He concludes: "There seems to be little room for doubt that business schools and business organizations which rely on scholastic standing, intelligence test scores, and grades as measure of managerial potential are using unreliable yardsticks" (1971: 81).

In fact, today the only way the management school can be safe

in its choices is to select experienced candidates who have already indicated success in managerial jobs. One wonders if we are any more effective in selecting people for jobs. How many managers who choose
and promote other managers place greater reliance on their own intuitive means of prediction than on the science of the personnel psychologist?[4] To conclude, we continue to grope for effective, systematic
methods to select people who will be successful managers.

Trait theory represents one major attempt to predict managerial
effectiveness. Early researchers in this field sought to isolate a unitary
trait or a constellation of traits that were basic to all effective managers.
But these efforts have largely been unsuccessful. There were difficulties
in measuring the traits and in relating them to effective managers.
Those that were isolated were often of such a general nature (such as
intelligence, empathy) as to be of little practical use. As a result, many
researchers have recently opted for situational or contingency theories
of leadership, in which they hypothesize that the particular situation
determines the set of traits that are desirable in the leader (Gibb,
1969, and Fiedler, 1966).

But what was at fault in trait theory? The concept that all successful managers exhibit a common set of personal characteristics? Or
the particular characteristics the researchers chose to measure? I
favor the second explanation, in the belief that the difficulty in
isolating and measuring general managerial traits should not stop our
search for personal characteristics that lead some people to succeed and
others to fail in a wide variety of managerial jobs. Two points in this
regard should be stressed. First, it has been argued throughout this
book that managerial jobs demonstrate variations superimposed on
basic similarities. This suggests that the effective manager exhibits specific personal characteristics related to his particular job superimposed on the general characteristics that he shares with all effective
managers. In other words, it is my personal belief that more powerful
theories of leadership effectiveness will have to consider both basic
and contingent personal characteristics of the leader.

Second, the focus on traits must be questioned. "Trait" is an in-
tangible concept, difficult to operationalize and to link to managerial
behavior. "Skill," on the other hand, is a more operational concept, directly related to behavior. A skill is simply a specific behavior that re-

---

[4] The lack of a systematic basis for selection has led to the persistence
of what may be called the "best salesman syndrome"—the choice of manager
based on the assumption that the man best at doing the work of the unit will
be best at supervising it. Clearly management skills are different from the
specialized skills of the worker. It is also interesting to note that during elections
for high political office (president, governor, prime minister, mayor), we hear
little analysis of the managerial skills of the candidates. Presumably these are
crucial determinants for success, but we do not yet understand them well enough
to analyze them.

sults in effective performance. If we seek to identify common (and contingent) managerial skills, instead of traits, then we shall be able to use behavior as a basis for measurement. For example, we can conclude from our list of skills presented earlier in this section that successful managers are likely to demonstrate a special ability to operate in peer relationships, to lead others in subordinate relationships, to resolve interpersonal and decisional conflicts, to deal in the verbal media, to make complex, interrelated decisions, to allocate resources (including their own time), and to innovate. The researcher might fruitfully spend his time trying to measure effectiveness in these general skills.

To summarize, if managerial training and development is to attain a reasonable level of efficiency, we must learn how to select those candidates who demonstrate the special skills that the job of managing requires.

IMPLICATIONS FOR THE MANAGEMENT SCIENTIST

Chapter 6 dealt at length with the role of the management scientist in reprogramming managerial work, ending with a summary statement. At this point the basic points are reiterated for the general reader.

The manager of today is overworked, and there is not much he can do to alleviate his load. It is the management scientist who will ultimately help him to redesign his working methods to improve his effectiveness significantly. But before the management scientist—be he systems analyst, planner, information systems designer, or operations researcher—can be of help to the manager, he must understand the job of managing. It is folly to believe that planners can help in the making of strategy if they do not understand the dynamics of managerial work, or that analysts can help the manager make decisions without an understanding of his information. The literature of management science has little to say about managerial work, and what it does say reflects the general meager state of understanding. The management scientist seems often to view managerial work in terms of the economist's simple model of "rational" decision-making—explicit goals, distinct alternatives, isolated choices made to maximize the net benefits—and he designs systems for the manager in accordance with this model. Then he wonders why the manager ignores his long-range plans or does not use his information system.

The management scientist must study and understand the work of the man for whom he designs systems and solves problems. He must gain access to the manager's hitherto undocumented information before he can be able to design useful systems for him. In this way, he will find that the manager generally has great need, not for the quantitative, routine, internal information that the information system has always provided, but for uncertain, ad hoc, external information. He will find that the manager can use, not static long-range plans, but flexible plans that can be modified en route. He will learn that "quick-and-dirty" analysis, providing results in real-time, can be more useful in the event of a crisis than statistically significant data.

Managers use programs that are not now well understood. The management scientist must help to reprogram the manager's work; he must specify the manager's programs in detail and redesign them with a view to better performance. Some of the manager's programs—those dealing with leadership, for example—do not lend themselves to reprogramming. A few may be extensively reprogrammed. The scheduling of the manager's time is one that merits careful attention by the management scientist. Scheduling, by its very nature, lends itself to analysis and reprogramming—the decisions are repetitive and the inputs are specific and to some extent quantifiable. For some managers the potential payoff of better scheduling is great.

Finally, much of the manager's work lends itself to partial reprogramming, whereby the manager can work with the management scientist (or with the computer) in a type of man–machine system. The manager defines the issues and provides some of the input information, the scientist provides the time and the analytical capability. Chapter 6 discussed a number of possibilities in this regard—monitoring and disseminating information, searching for problems and opportunities, conducting cost-benefit analyses, monitoring projects under the manager's supervision, producing adaptive strategic plans and contingency plans, providing models to aid in choice-making, and doing real-time analysis to aid in the handling of unanticipated events.

Management science has extended its influence up the organizational hierarchy since Frederick Taylor began experimenting late in the last century with methods to improve efficiency at the factory level. But a shift in orientation in the last decade has slowed its progress. The management scientist has sought elegance in his techniques. This may have been appropriate so long as he was dealing with highly structured problems. But those found at the policy level are not so neat, and it will take time for him to learn how to structure them. In his search for elegance the management scientist has hindered his ability to participate in solving policy problems. Without corrupting his science, the management scientist must be prepared to forego elegance, to adjust his technique to the problem rather than searching for problems that fit the technique. Management science must become once again the application of basic analysis—clear, systematic thinking with a reliance on explicit data—to the problems of management.

IMPLICATIONS FOR THE RESEARCHER

The success of the teacher of managers and of the management scientist in helping to improve the practice of managing will depend on the success of the researcher. He must provide them with better descriptions of the job. This study suggests a number of areas in which research might be done:

Open-ended Studies. We still know very little about managerial work and we are in greatest need of more studies in which the researcher seeks to develop basic understanding by the process of induction. Observational methods and the critical-incident method discussed in Appendix B appear to hold the best promise for this type of research.

Follow-up Studies. I have made a number of claims in this book that merit more careful investigation. Do the set of activities delineated here in fact have validity for describing the work of all managers? Can the roles described be specified in more precise, more operational terms so that we can more precisely compare the jobs of different managers? [5] Clearly, we need longer studies with larger and more diverse samples of managers to test the validity of these findings.

Studies of Job Differences. We must devote considerable attention to the study of job differences. How do the emphasis on roles and the characteristics of different managerial jobs vary, and why? We know almost nothing about work variations by culture or by style of incumbent and very little about other factors that cause variations in managers' jobs. We must study managers of staff groups, Japanese managers, managers elected to government, inexperienced managers, managers trained in different kinds of schools, managers in stable environments, managers who face endless crises, and on and on. Job sharing is a most interesting and important phenomenon; it merits careful study. The influence of situational factors on the manager's job and the effects of societal changes certainly require investigation.

Studies of Special Aspects of the Job. There is merit in focusing attention on specific aspects of managerial work, so long as the interrelatedness of the parts is not forgotten. We can profitably research various role configurations—the external roles, the informational roles, those roles that are primarily obligative in nature. We must learn more about the manager's acts of leadership, about his methods of handling crises, about decision-making as a sequence of episodes, about the pro-

[5] Appendix C discusses the issue of operationalizing the role set.

cess of developing contacts to bring in information, about the process of finding opportunities and problems. Every aspect of the manager's job requires intensive research.

Studies of Manager Effectiveness. We must find out what it is in their actions that distinguishes successful from unsuccessful managers. Our research studies must run the gamut from investigations of fatigue to analyses of disturbance handling. Somehow we must find out what the words "effectiveness" and "efficiency" mean in the manager's work.

Programming the Job. Finally, and perhaps most significant, we must describe managerial work as a system of programs. Our ability to prescribe improvement hinges on our ability to describe reality precisely. With our current understanding we can safely prescribe very little for the manager. Our most precise means of describing managerial work is to program it—to identify the programs managers use, to specify the content, to combine these into a simulation of managerial work. We shall develop a science of managing only when efforts of this type are successful.

Considering the upsurge in management research in the last decade, it is surprising that managerial work has received so little attention. It would appear that the contemporary researcher has reacted negatively to the early efforts in this area, trying to escape from the vague statements of principle and function made by the classical writers. He has often sought refuge in the functional areas, where the ambiguity is less, and where quantification is easier. We can no longer afford to ignore managerial work as an area of research. It is the researcher, feeding knowledge to the manager and management scientist, who will ultimately determine the ability of our large bureaucracies to cope with their immense problems.

I hope that this book will be received as a contribution to the beginning of a significant understanding of the manager's job. It can certainly be no more than that. I further hope that this investigation will stimulate others to engage in the interesting and important work of researching the job of the manager.

Appendix A: Major Studies of the Manager's Job

NEUSTADT'S STUDY OF PRESIDENTIAL POWER

In his book on the American Presidency Richard Neustadt (1960) analyzes the man and the office with particular reference to the immense set of forces acting on the officeholder. Neustadt studies three men who held the office—Roosevelt, Truman, and Eisenhower. Most of the book is devoted to an analysis of the personal power of these men, "what it is, how to get it, how to keep it, how to use it" (p. vii).

Along the way, however, much can be learned about the work of managing, particularly the collecting of information and the making of decisions. Neustadt argues, for example, that the President "must become his own director of his own central intelligence":

> A president is helped by what he gets into *his* mind. His first essential need is information. No doubt he needs the data that advisers can provide. He also needs to know the little things they fail to mention (p. 153).

In discussing time allocation, Neustadt emphasizes the demands of the office—the things the President has to do, the deadlines and the fires. If the President wants something done:

> He needs means of putting pressure on himself, of imposing new deadlines on himself, to come to grips with those things he would want to make his own if he were free to interfere and pick and choose at will. Deadlines self-imposed are no less helpful to a President than tangible details. The one informs his mind, the other arms his hand (p. 156).

Neustadt concludes: "Useful information, timely choices may not reach him; he must do the reaching. To do so is to help himself enhance his personal influence" (pp. 179–180). Roosevelt, who "had a love affair with power in that place," and Truman, who "loved to make decisions," helped themselves; Eisenhower, the "*anti*-politician," could not (pp. 161, 172, 180). A number of insights of this nature, sprinkled throughout this book, render it one of the most interesting studies of the work of the manager in politics.

HOMANS'S STUDY OF LEADERSHIP

In his book Homans (1950) devotes two important chapters to leadership. The first reviews the findings of William F. Whyte's famous study of *Street Corner Society* (1955). Whyte lived as a participant-observer in a slum society he named Cornerville, and he studied one gang in particular, the Nortons. He carefully described the gang's activities, and drew a number of conclusions about its internal structure and its relationship to the society in which it lived. Of interest is the existence of a clear, hierarchical leadership structure. As Homans notes:

> The Nortons, in short, developed on a small scale the same sort of pyramid of command—followers interacting with lieutenants, who interact in turn with leaders of a higher level—that we find on a larger scale in business and military organizations. . . . The pyramid evolved spontaneously, that is, through the dynamic relations between the norms of a group, its activities, sentiments, and interactions. The fact is that the organization of the large formal

enterprises, governmental or private, in modern society is modeled on, is a rationalization of, tendencies that exist in all human groups (1950: 186–187).

In his two chapters Homans draws a number of conclusions about the job of leadership in the Nortons and in general:

The higher a man's social rank, the larger the number of persons for whom he originates interaction, either directly or through intermediaries (p. 182).

The higher a man's social rank, the more frequently he interacts with persons outside his own group (pp. 185–186).

The leader is the man who comes closest to realizing the norms the group values highest. The norms may be queer ones, but so long as they are genuinely accepted by the group, the leader, in that group, must embody them (p. 188).

[The leader] is better informed than other men, and he has more channels for the issuing of orders (p. 188).

The leader brings his group from one social state to another through giving orders that govern, in greater or less degree, the behavior of the members. . . . In giving orders, the leader will use established channels . . . (p. 415).

[The leader] interacts most often with the persons nearest him in social rank, and his orders tend to be transmitted to the group through these men, his *lieutenants* (p. 429).

The leader is at the center of the web of interaction: much interaction flows toward him and away from him (p. 418).

The leader, whatever his rank, with whom the decision rests must in fact decide. Especially in an emergency that concerns the whole group, the members will expect the top leader to take charge and give the necessary orders with all the force at his command (p. 429).

And the job of a leader is twofold: (a) to attain the purposes of the group, and (b) in so doing to maintain a balance of incentives, both reward and punishment, sufficient to induce his followers to obey him (p. 423).

HODGSON, LEVINSON, AND ZALEZNIK'S "EXECUTIVE ROLE CONSTELLATION"

This is a penetrating and complicated study of the three senior executives of a large psychiatric hospital. The research was based on some intensive—although unstructured—observation of the executives and their environment. This resulted in an analysis that in his own complexity fully captures the complexity of managerial behavior.

The authors make very clear that their study is one of personal and interpersonal behavior, not of work per se. As a result, there is joint treatment throughout the book of the dimensions of work and of personality: "We make no attempt to divorce work style from work content" (1965: 98). Rather, the authors introduce the notion of *role-task work*—"the sustained and directed effort of mind in which a person seeks to synthesize the organizational requirements of his position with his own individual needs, interests, and aspirations" (p. 231).

The work of each of the three men is discussed, and the analysis then turns to their interrelationships, that is, to the formation and operation of the executive role constellation:

> The executives' roles in the organization tended to become specialized around the performance of certain tasks and the expression of certain emotions. Role specialization was seen to have important roots in the executive's personality and important consequences for his behavior in the organization. Several specialized roles were differentiated from one another in the top executive group, yet maintained a tightly integrated complementarity. They formed what we have called an *executive role constellation* (p. 477).

For the chief executive (superintendent) task specialization meant "relating the organization to its environment," while he expressed the emotions of "assertiveness and control." The clinical director specialized in "operating the clinical services inside the organization" and in expressing "love and supportiveness"; the comparable forms of specialization for the assistant superintendent were "innovative activities that resisted tight integration into the central flow of administrative routine" and "friendliness and equalitarianism" (all from p. 482).

In closing, the authors point out that a variety of administrative forms are likely to be found in different organizations—aggregates as opposed to constellations, and patriarch, dyad, and triad forms of leadership.

CARLSON'S LEADING DIARY STUDY

The first significant empirical study of managerial work, and the only one to generate wide interest so far is Sune Carlson's analysis of the work of nine Swedish directors (company presidents), published in 1951. Carlson expresses the aims of his study in the following terms:

> The purpose of this study has been neither to develop any normative rules as to how executives should behave, nor to describe their "typical" or "average" behaviour. But by studying a series of individual cases I have hoped to find certain common behaviour patterns and some general relationships which characterize these patterns (p. 10).

Carlson developed and used a method that was to gain wide popularity. He asked his managers to fill out time diaries to record their daily activities. For each activity they noted:

1. Place of work
2. Contact with persons or institutions (subordinates, customers, etc.)
3. Technique of communication (direct: personal observations, conversations, regular and ad hoc conferences, telephone calls; indirect: via persons, via papers)
4. Nature of question handled:
   a. Field of activity or functional area (finance, production, personnel, etc.)
   b. Development or current operations
   c. Policy or application
5. Kind (or content) of action (getting information, advising and explaining, taking decisions, giving orders).

Carlson's diary is reproduced in Figure 1, Chapter 2.

Carlson's conclusions are of three types—related to working time, to communication, and to work content.

Working Time. Carlson analyzed the place of work, the technique of communication, and the total working load. Best known is his finding about the rarity of uninterrupted time. Citing one example, Carlson indicates that although the executive averaged about one hour alone each day, the typical "alone" intervals were of only 10 to 15 minutes duration, and only 12 times during the 35 days was he alone for more than 22 minutes. "All they knew was that they scarcely had time to start on a new task or to sit down and light a cigarette before they were interrupted by a visitor or a telephone call" (pp. 73–74). Carlson also concludes in this section that the executives' working loads were heavy, averaging between 8.5 and 11.5 hours daily. These loads, Carlson points out, significantly precluded social and cultural activity. Carlson also concludes that the executives had little control over the design of their own workdays.

Communication Patterns. The greater part of Carlson's analysis deals with communication patterns of the chief executives. He found among other things that the executives initiated far fewer letters per day than they received, that median time with visitors was 3.5 hours per day, and that the layout of offices determined to some extent whom the executives saw and how frequently.

Work Content. In discussing the actual content of the executives' activities, Carlson is less sure of his conclusions and provides little of substance. He notes with reference to the "field of activity" data that different interpretations were made by different executives, and that many activities were recorded as multifield (personnel and production, for example). Similarly, with regard to the other categories of work content, Carlson points out:

> What one executive regards as a question of development, another may find to be a question of current operations, and there may even be inconsistencies in the markings of the individual chief executive during different periods. . . . It was much harder to determine whether a question was of a policy character or not (pp. 105–106).

Carlson's conclusions of the section are hardly illuminating: Production questions were more common than organization and planning questions; sales questions were usually defined as policy, whereas financial questions were usually defined as application. And finally, in discussing "kind of action," the data of central concern to us, Carlson states: "The study of the kind of action was, as I expected it to be, the most difficult part of our whole investigation, and neither the concepts nor the recording technique used are as yet sufficiently refined in this respect" (p. 49). Only one page is devoted to this topic, and only one major finding is presented:

> The main problem for the chief executive in dealing with questions brought up is to keep himself informed. Of the various headings on our questionnaire "getting information" was used at least twice as often as any of the others (p. 108).

FOLLOWUP DIARY STUDIES: BURNS, COPEMAN, DUBIN AND SPRAY, HORNE AND LUPTON, THOMASON

Carlson's study stimulated considerable followup activity, much of it in Great Britain.[1] In the mid-1950s Tom Burns published the results of two diary studies. In the first one (1954) he analyzed the relationships among four "closely associated" middle managers. He had them first estimate their time allocation and then use the diary method of recording for five weeks. His second study (1957) involved a larger sample, 76 senior and middle managers. Two of Burn's main findings were to be verified in virtually all of the subsequent studies—a high proportion of time spent in conversation, and much horizontal and lateral communication. Burns also notes the tendency of managers to spend considerable time with a select group of other managers:

[1] The head of a prominent French concern also adopted his method to study and redefine management work habits. This man argued that there was no reason for his managers to resist such a project when the factory worker's every motion was being studied by industrial engineers (Rolf Nordling "Work Simplification at the Level of the General Manager of a Company." Translated by the Management Consultation Services of General Electric from *Revue Mensuelle de l'Organisation,* June, 1954).

Perhaps the most striking of the results . . . is the uniform segrega-
tion of a senior management group of three, usually, or four persons. Of the total time spent in conversation with people within the
concern (i.e., the factory), the general manager might spend half
with the other two members of this group (1957: 60).

Following Carlson, Burns collected data both on area of activity
and on content (obtaining, giving, systematizing, and recording information, and explaining). But again the disclaimers appear: "Activities
may also be analysed according to another classification—that of content—though here we are on less sure ground" (1954: 75). Burns
presents no real conclusions in this area, although he does discuss at
length the finding that discrepancies occurred in one-third of the cases
between acounts of different people attending the same meeting. He
found also that the managers were poor judges of their own time allocation, particularly that spent on "human relationships."

Copeman (Copeman, Luijk, and Hanika, 1963) used the diary
to contrast the work of 29 chief executives with a like number of department heads. He found that the chief executives spent more time on
the job (53 versus 43 hours per week) and more time "writing" and
"planning," but less time drafting reports. The frequency of their contacts with subordinates was the same as for the department heads, but
they had fewer with superiors (1.5 percent versus 14.5 percent) and
more with their colleagues (16 percent versus 10.5 percent).

Dubin and Spray (1964) studied eight American managers for
two weeks and found that the higher-level managers were less likely
to concentrate their time on a single activity. But contrary to a finding
of Burns, these researchers did not find an increasing tendency at the
higher levels to spend time in horizontal relationships. Managers at all
levels studied spent substantial time in these relationships. Dubin and
Spray draw conclusions about other variations in managerial work
as well:

Top executives and those employed in client-centered industries
will be engaged more frequently in contacts with people outside
the organization than will their subordinates [while] . . . functional
specialization, like accounting, may permit the individual executive
to spend long periods of time doing his special tasks without need
for contact or coordination with others (p. 105).

Horne and Lupton (1965), who used diaries to study 66 British
middle managers for one week, conclude among other things that these
men were not overworked and that the time spent in particular functional areas indicated specialization by type of manager (for example,
personnel) but not by level. In addition, these researchers made an
explicit attempt to study content, using FOUR. A surrogate for
POSDCORB, FOUR stands for formulating, organizing, unifying and
regulating. The researchers reported that the managers spent the

"great bulk" of their time on nonformulating activities. The tables seemed to indicate wide discrepancies between companies, however, and all they appear to tell the reader is that managers list "regulating" somewhat more frequently and "organizing" somewhat less frequently.

Finally, we have the assortment of studies reported by Thomason (1966 and 1967). Carried out by students as field work assignments in a management course, these studies vary widely in sample size and in data sought by the students. In the first article, Thomason concludes that "the communication structure may look . . . like a patchwork quilt of centers and lacunae . . . with a cyclic pattern of communications extending down the hierarchy" (1966: 283). In his second article Thomason found interesting variations in jobs by functional area. For example, time spent on production decreased while time spent on policy increased as one moved up the hierarchy. His important conclusion is that the communication centers may be the focal points for specialized information:

> The overall hierarchy becomes a composite of different subject-oriented communications networks, with the centre of this network lying at the point in the hierarchy to which the subject is allowed or required to penetrate. The management structure may not operate as an arrangement of filters and amplifiers, but it may operate as a series of interconnected networks surrounding what have been called above the "hot centres" (the major centres of uncertainty absorption for the subject). Between these networks occur gaps or lacunae in the communications flow (1967: 29).

STEWART'S STUDY OF MANAGERIAL WORK DIFFERENCES

The major diary study among those so far carried out is reported by Rosemary Stewart (1967). Miss Stewart studied 160 senior and middle managers for four weeks each, with the aim of discovering similarities and differences in the way managers spend their time. She used the diary method, but she differed from her predecessors in one significant respect—she made almost no attempt to study work content.

> The main conclusions from [our] experiments with different types of diaries was that only simple, easily defined information can be collected if the information is to be comparable. In particular the kinds of action classification used in the studies described earlier was shown to be very unreliable. It is not difficult for a manager to be reasonably consistent in classifying his own work under such headings as "getting information" or "planning," but the discussions at the seminar and at the courses showed wide differences in what people understood by such terms. Even when the terms were de-

fined, differences in interpretation persisted. It was therefore decided to exclude a classification of kinds of action, such as planning or giving information, from the main diary (pp. 20–21).[2]

Each finding of this study is presented in the form of a histogram. Many of these suggest that most managers, but never all managers, exhibit a number of common work characteristics. Listed below are some of the main findings of this study with the figures representing arithmetic averages:

The managers averaged 42 hours of work per week.

75 percent of their time was spent in their own establishment, and 51 percent in their own offices.

60 percent of their time was spent in discussion—43 percent informal, 7 percent committee, 6 percent telephoning, and 4 percent social activity.

34 percent of their time was spent alone; 25 percent with their immediate subordinates, 8 percent with their superiors, and 30 percent with peers and others (of this, 12 percent with colleagues reporting to the same superior, 8 percent with fellows doing similar work elsewhere in the organization, 5 percent with other internal contacts, and 5 percent with external contacts).

Fragmentation in work was great, according to each of the three measures: in 4 weeks, the managers averaged only 9 periods of 30 minutes or more without interruption (and 4 out of 5 managers had less than 15 such periods); the managers averaged 12 fleeting contacts per day (i.e., less than 5 minutes duration); they averaged another 13 diary entries per day, for a total of 25.

"A manager's job is a varied one . . . in the place of work, in the contacts, in its activities and in its content" (p. 98).

Miss Stewart closes her report with an analysis of variations in work among the managers studied. Using cluster analysis on 25 of her variables, she delineates 5 basic job profiles:

Group 1: The Emissaries. These managers spend much of their time away from the company, dealing with and entertaining outsiders. They work longer hours, but their days are less fragmented than most. Typical of this group are the sales managers and senior manager who act as public figures.

Group 2: The Writers. These managers spend a greater share of their time in writing, reading, dictating, and figure work. They are soli-

---

[2] She did collect data on functional area, the "only part of the diary that attempted to analyse the content of the work," but these entries "proved unreliable" (p. 26).

tary "only by comparison" (p. 108). They tend to work shorter hours and are less subject to day-to-day pressures. By all appearances, these are the staff specialists or those who manage them—the assistant manager of a computing branch, the chief electrical engineer, and so on.

Group 3: The Discussers. These are the average managers. They spend much time with other people and particularly with their colleagues, and they carry out a diverse range of activities. Many types of managers fit in this group.

Group 4: The Trouble Shooters. These managers must spend more time coping with crises, hence their work is most fragmented. They spend much time with subordinates and less with peers. A relatively large share of their time is spent on inspection. Most of the production people fall into this group.

Group 5: The Committeemen. These managers spend a great share of their time in committee meetings. Their contacts are both vertical and horizontal but not outside the company. In the study these managers were found exclusively in larger companies.

STUDIES BY OBSERVATION: KELLY, PONDER, GUEST, JASINSKI

A number of researchers studied the job of the firstline factory supervisor using methods of observation. Four articles are reviewed below. Joe Kelly (1964 and 1969) used "activity sampling" to study the work of four section managers of the Glacier Metal Company. Activity sampling involves random, momentary observations of activity. Kelly made 2800 observations over a three-week period, collecting data similar to that of the diary researchers. His main findings, in his words, are as follows:

> A picture of the section manager can be built up from this study. He spends two-thirds of his time with other persons; a fifth of his time with his unit manager, a third with his colleagues; and half with his subordinates. . . . His work is mainly programming (a half), followed by technical (a quarter), and only a little personnel work (a tenth). Compared with other studies, he spends more time on the close details of work. In a phrase, he is a "task specialist" (1964: 284–285).

Kelly concludes, based on his findings, that the job, and not individual style, determines what managers do. "The important single conclusion to emerge from this study is the fact that the task is the principal determinant structuring the behavior of section managers. What follows as a corollary is that personal factors are of limited significance in determining his behavior" (1969: 355).

Ponder (1957) reports a study carried out at General Electric

company to distinguish work differences between effective and ineffective manufacturing foremen (as rated by superiors and subordinates). Each of 24 foremen was observed for a total of 16 hours,
spread over four-month periods. During observation, data similar to
that collected in the diary studies were recorded for all activities.
Ponder found that the "foreman's job is one of considerable discontinuity," with effective foremen averaging 200, and ineffective foremen
270 distinct activities per day. The two groups spent similar amounts
of time with subordinates, although the effective foremen concentrated
more on questions of personnel (23 percent versus 12 percent of
time), less on those of production (20 percent versus 40 percent). The
effective foremen spent more time with staff and service personnel
(32 percent versus 20 percent), initiated fewer contacts, and gave
more general work orders involving more delegation.

Guest (1956) and Jasinski (1956) report the results of an
observational study of 56 foremen for one day each. Minute-by-
minute records were kept of incident, time, topic, activity involved,
place, contact, and nature of the interaction. These subjects averaged
583 incidents per day, with a range of 237 to 1043. "Every 48 seconds
of the day the foreman was doing something different" (Guest: 48).
Guest notes the lack of idle time in their jobs, the constant interruption, the need to deal with pressing problems simultaneously. He also
highlights the variety of foreman contacts in a day, "rarely fewer than
25 and often more than 50" (p. 483) and the number of persons dealt
with in operating and service departments at different levels. Horizontal
and lateral relationships consumed about two hours per day.

THE OHIO STATE LEADERSHIP STUDIES

Certainly the most ambitious research on managerial work yet
undertaken is that of the Ohio State Leadership Group. The publication dates of their many books and articles span three decades,
beginning in the late 1940s and continuing into the middle 1960s. In
addition, these works prompted a number of other studies, many in
the 1950s and early 1960s. With the exception of one article in 1968,
however, interest in the Ohio State approach appears to have subsided
recently.

Carroll Shartle, the early director of the group, introduced the
studies in an article published in 1949 as follows:

At Ohio State University a research program is in progress on the
subject of "Leadership in a Democracy." One phase of the research
is concerned with the study of administrative positions in business,
industry, the armed services, and education. . . .
It is hoped that in the course of the 10-year study, facts and

techniques will be developed which will aid in the education, selection, training, and assignment of persons to leadership positions in business and industry, government, and education (p. 370).

The research method he described served as the prototpe for the studies that followed, although certain modifictions took place in the early 1950s. The method as evolved comprised three basic steps.

List of Statements. An extensive list of statements (sometimes 600 or more) was developed to cover all aspects of the job to be studied. Typical statements might be: "He [i.e., the manager] negotiates bank loans for the company." "He is capable of performing all the jobs of subordinates." "He coordinates the activities of others." Sources for these statements have included (a) personal experiences of the researchers, (b) the literature of management, (c) existing job descriptions, (d) the men to be studied, (e) their associates (superiors, subordinate, peers), and (f) evidence from observation of the men to be studied.

Questionnaires. The list of statements was administered to the managers under study (and/or to certain of their associates), with provision of a scale by which each statement could be rated (always, often, occasionally, seldom, never).

Reduction to Basic Factors. Some mathematical technique (generally factor analysis) was used to collect sets of related answers into basic dimensions of managerial behavior.[3]

This research method—or some variation of it—was used in a great number of studies carried out at the Ohio State University and elsewhere. Over the years studies have been reported on business managers of various types, foremen, military officers, labor union leaders, school administrators, government administrators, and senators.[4]

Factors have covered various aspects of managers and their jobs, including responsibility and authority, interpersonal activity, job satisfaction, managerial style, and managerial activity itself. These researchers first referred to the words that described homogenous groups of managerial activities as *functions;* more recently, the word *roles* has come into popular usage. "The concept frequently invoked to link the system and the individual is that of role, that is, a set of

---

[3] In some of the earlier studies, this distillation of statements was carried out subjectively in advance. Managers were then asked to make direct estimates (e.g., time spent) on each factor.

[4] See Shartle (1949), Fleishman (1953), Brooks (1955), Stogdill, Shartle and Associates (1956), Stogdill, Scott, and Jaynes (1956), Jerdee and Mahoney (1957), Stogdill and Coons (1957), Creager and Harding (1958), Hemphill (1959, 1960), Peres (1962), Mahoney, Jerdee, and Carroll (1963), Prien (1963), Stogdill, Goode, and Day (1963a, 1963b, 1964) Stogdill (1965), Katzell et al. (1968).

activities and responsibilities associated with a particular position or job" (Katzell et al., 1968: 22).

Various categorizations of managerial activity have been presented in these studies, the number ranging from 2 to 14. The 14 were presented first, in Shartle's study of 1949:

1. Inspection of the organization
2. Investigation and Research
3. Planning
4. Preparations of Procedures and Methods
5. Coordination
6. Evaluation
7. Interpretation of plans and procedures
8. Supervision of Technical Operations
9. Personnel Activities
10. Public Relations
11. Professional Consultation
12. Negotiations
13. Scheduling, Routines, Dispatching
14. Technical and Professional Operations

For a number of years following, researchers used this same typology or a modification of it. Some reduced Shartle's categories, first to four and then to two groups. Fleishman (1953a), for example, worked initially with 150 items (which had actually been reduced from an original list of 1800). Using "expert judges," he distilled from these items nine dimensions of leadership behavior—integration, communication, production emphasis, representation, fraternization, organization, evaluation, initiation, and domination. Finding from a first administration of his questionnaire that these dimensions lacked independence, Fleishman readministered it to 300 air force crew members (who described their commanders), to 220 foremen (who described their supervisors), and to 394 workers (who described their foremen). The result after factor analysis was that "practically all the variation could be accounted for by . . . two major dimensions" (p. 4).

> Items in the "Consideration" dimension were concerned with the extent to which the leader was considerate of his workers' feelings. It reflected the "human relations" aspects of group leadership.
>
> Items in the "Initiating Structure" dimension reflected the extent to which the leader defined or facilitated group interactions toward *goal attainment*. He does this by planning, communicating, scheduling, criticizing, trying out new ideas, etc (Fleishman, 1953a:2).

Thus, in a paper entitled "The Description of Supervisory Behavior" the prime conclusion is that all the work can be described as "consideration" and "initiating structure!" This result was repeated again and again. Prien (1963) reported on his study of foremen and their supervisors ten years after Fleishman: "It seems, from this analysis, that the role of the first-line foremen in this manufacturing operation involves two basic functions; namely, dealing with people and production" (p. 13).[5]

One Ohio State Leadership study—that of Hemphill (1959 and 1960)—merits detailed review because of the nature of its sample and its explicit focus on managerial work. Hemphill began his study by surveying the literature, interviewing executives, and examining job descriptions. This resulted in 1500 statements from which he eventually selected 575. This list of statements was administered to 96 executives in five large companies, across three position levels (upper management, middle management, and beginning management not including first-line foremen), and across five functional areas (research and development, sales, manufacturing, general administration, and industrial relations).

Responses (from 93 of the managers) were carefully evaluated against each other. No statistically significant differences or similarities among the five companies or across the three levels of management could be found. Moreover, job title told little about job features. Only when the data were analyzed in terms of the five functional areas did similarities appear. For example, industrial relations positions appeared to show distinct similarities with each other.

Hemphill then performed a factor analysis, which isolated ten clusters of statements, or factors:

Factor A: Providing a Staff Service in Non-Operational Areas. Renders various staff services to supervisors: gathering information, interviewing, selecting employees, briefing superiors, checking statements, verifying facts, and making recommendations. Sample positions: director of personnel services, assistant treasurer.

Factor B: Supervision of Work. Plans, organizes, and controls the work of others; concerned with the efficient use of equipment, the motivation of subordinates, efficiency of operation, and the maintenance of a work force. Sample positions: works manager, district traffic manager.

Factor C: Business Control. Concerned with cost reduction, maintenance of proper inventories, preparation of budgets, justification of capital expenditures, determination of goals, definition of supervisor

---

[5] With the repetition of results such as these, one can understand what prompted Campbell et al., in their review of this literature, to comment:

The many studies using questionnaires and check lists for rating and describing managerial job behavior led, through factor analysis, to just two basic dimensions of managerial behavior. Certainly, this must be an oversimplification of the characteristics and full range of behaviors demanded by managerial jobs! (1970: 85).

responsibilities, payment of salaries, enforcement of regulations. Sample positions: budget administrator, operations manager.

Factor D: Technical Concerns with Products and Markets. Concerned with development of new business, activities of competitors, contacts with customers, assisting salesmen. Sample positions: division director of research, vice president sales.

Factor E: Human, Community, and Social Affairs. Concerned with company goodwill in the community, participation in community affairs, speaking before the public, etc. Sample positions: regional manager, general manager retail division.

Factor F: Long-range Planning. Broad concerns oriented toward the future; does not get involved in routine and tends to be free of direct supervision. Sample positions: assistant vice president engineering, section supervisor research division.

Factor G: Exercise of Broad Power and Authority. Makes recommendations on very important matters; keeps informed about the company's performances; interprets policy; has high status. Sample positions: divisions manager, general sales manager.

Factor H: Business Reputation. Concerned with product quality and/or public relations. Sample positions: employment manager, chief of process engineering division.

Factor I: Personal Demands. Incumbent senses obligation ot conduct himself according to the stereotype of the conservative businessman. Sample positions: director of purchases, controller.

Factor J: Preservation of Assets. Concerned about capital expenditures, taxes, preservation of assets, loss of company money. Sample positions: assistant treasurer.

Hemphill tabulated his ten factors against the three management levels and the five functional areas. His data indicate, for example, that upper management tended to rank highest on human affairs, planning, and broad power, while the lowest levels appeared highest on staff services, work supervision, and technical products and markets. Among the functional areas, research and development (R&D) appeared particularly strong on staff services, planning, and technical products and services, while manufacturing and sales were both strong on business control.

There has been little followup of Hemphill's work. The only study uncovered is that of Katzell et al. (1968) who studied 194 army civilian executives, with the aim of relating roles to job situational factors. They found that executives in organizations primarily concerned with administration emphasized controlling and staffing activities, but not planning. Those in production-type organizations emerged higher on the planning, staffing, and the time-spent-with-others dimensions, whereas those in research organizations were high on planning but low on these other two. Executives at higher levels were less prominent on staffing and controlling dimensions; those in small organizations were prominent on planning.

In noting the little followup of the Hemphill study, Campbell et al. speculate that this may be due to "the complexities implied by his dimensional analyses" (p. 98) or due to his having

> left so much of his executives' jobs undefined from a behavioral standpoint. Job dimensions with labels such as "providing staff services," "supervising work," or "long-range planning" are so behaviorally sterile that they offer few, if any, suggestions about the human qualities necessary for effectively carrying them out (p. 98).

In drawing to a close our review of the Ohio State Leadership studies, two possible reasons are suggested as to why these studies have not generated interest commensurate with the effort expended.

Inappropriate Data. The method used consistently in these studies was such that the researchers were studying *perceptions* of the managers' jobs rather than the *jobs themselves*. Shartle claimed:

> There are two aspects of executive performance. First are events as shown in the duties, functions and responsibilities which are required in the organization and are expressed in writing or orally. Second, we have what the executive actually does. These events may vary from what is officially expected of him (1956: 100).

What Shartle did not appear to recognize is that standing between (a) what the manager is supposed to do and (c) what he actually does is (b) what he thinks he does. Thus Shartle is simply incorrect when he claims in this book that "We shall now discuss what executives actually do" (1956:81).

The difference between managers' perceptions of their work and the work itself has been clearly demonstrated in the studies of Burns (1954), Horne and Lupton (1965), and Harper (1968). Each first asked managers to record what they thought they did and then measured, by the diary method, what they actually did. Each concluded that managers are poor predictors of their own activities.

Inappropriate Dimensions. In each study, a small set of dimensions describing managerial work was distilled from many hundreds of statements of all different kinds. Inevitably, the dimensions emerge as a mix of the vague POSDCORB-type terminology, some very specific work activities, and a series of style and personality characteristics (for example, coordination, public relations, concern for production). In the final analysis, this mélange of terminology is vague and confusing.

In assessing the reasons for this one can conclude that the important inductive research was done, not in the filling out of questionnaires or in the factor analysis, but in the development of the list of statements in the first place. For it was here that the researchers constrained their findings. Any important elements of managerial work inadvertently excluded at this point could not reappear later. From this point on, the studies simply *weighted* given job elements. It is surprising, therefore, that these researchers gave so little attention in their reports to the choice of statements, and so much to the routine mathematical manipulations of data.

In his paper, Hemphill comments that, on showing the questionnaire to the men to be studied, "The fact that no new elements were suggested confirmed the view that the list was comprehensive" (1959: 61). But can one take this statement seriously? Faced with a list of 575 statements, what manager has the stamina to add more? And even if he wanted to, could he? There is ample evidence in the biographical literature and even in a book by one of Hemphill's own associates (Shartle, 1956: 82–83; the opening quotation of Chapter 1) that managers have difficulty describing their own jobs. As Jackson and Messick (1965) note in their analysis of creativity:

> There is some evidence that at least in some fields the most sensitive people cannot articulate their awareness with any degree of precision. Their sensitivity is *intuitive;* the person who behaves intuitively is sensitive to cues that cannot be identified verbally (1965: 325).

As anyone who has programmed a computer well knows, the output of a system can be no better than the input, no matter how elegant the program. If the input here was unduly influenced by the traditional literature, and POSDCORB in particular, rather than by systematic, inductive research, then it should surprise no one that the output of the Ohio State Leadership studies has generated little interest.

STIEGLITZ'S STUDY OF THE CHIEF EXECUTIVE'S JOB

A study recently completed for the National Industrial Conference Board, although not a derivative of the Ohio State Leadership studies, shares a common methodology. Stieglitz (1969) administered questionnaires to 280 chief executive officers, more than half of them non-American. A number of conclusions emerge:

> Although most were accountable to boards of directors, a number discussed this as merely formal.
> One-quarter reported that no set standards existed by which they were evaluated. Most of the rest could provide only vague standards such as "performance in general." Few could even

claim standards by which they planned to measure their own success in the job after retirement.

Only 30 of the executives claimed to allocate their time to correspond with the importance they attached to certain activities. Planning was one example of this—only 106 out of 183 who ranked it as most important claimed to spend most of their time on it.

The reported workdays and workweeks were long, and the executives found it difficult to separate their private and working lives.

The questionnaire also dealt with the chief executives' views of their own jobs. Three questions were posed:

1. What do you consider to be your primary responsibilities?
2. What are the factors or bases that determine what you delegate?
3. What aspects of your job—if any—do you believe cannot be delegated and must be reserved to you as chief executive? (1969: 10).

The answers uncovered, in the author's words, "a body of duties that almost all chief executives recognize as reserved to their office" (p. 10).

1. Determining overall objectives and plans
2. Establishing priorities and allocating resources
3. Formulating policy
4. Organization and key executive selection and development
5. Development and designation of a successor
6. Relationships with board of directors
7. Key external relationships
8. Control

Leadership, described as related more to the man than to the job, is emphasized as an additional critical factor in understanding the work of these men.

These eight categories come close to replicating POSDCORB. This is not surprising, for here again the researcher abdicated his responsibility to the manager. It was the managers who described what they did; the researcher simply tabulated the results. And since managers read rather than do research, it stands to reason that they give back in the questionnaire what they find most prevalent in the literature—POSDCORB.

TWO STUDIES OF FOREMEN: WIKSTROM AND WALKER, GUEST AND TURNER

Two empirical studies of foremen, using very different methodologies, merit review in this section. In *Managing at the Foreman Level,* another Industrial Conference Board study, Walter Wikstrom (1967) describes the results of four company studies. Of primary interest to him is the question "Is the foreman a manager?" In a section entitled "Everybody Gets into the Act" Wikstrom describes the erosion of the foreman's responsibility by teams of specialists—production engineers, quality control experts, maintenance men, personnel experts, and labor relations experts. Company policy may be an additional constraining factor. The result is the appearance "that there is really little left for the foreman to do. . . . [he] has little authority to decide anything. Rather, he serves as an interpreter of the rules and instructions of his superiors and of the staff" (1967: 7). Wikstrom contrasts this general view with specific cases in his study where foremen maintained authority and established new forms of relationships with subordinates, superiors, and staff personnel.

> Obviously, then, the specialization necessitated by the complexity of today's manufacturing operations does not in itself rob the foreman's job of stature and significance. Rather it is a matter of how the roles of specialists and line managers are fitted into a total management structure (p. 7).

According to Wikstrom the key element is coordination. "Whether or not [the existence of specialists] reduces the managerial aspects of the foreman's job depends upon whether or not the foreman coordinates the work of the specialists with whom he shares these responsibilities" (p. 7). Some foremen manage, others are "master workers supervising others" or "are merely straw bosses, because the firm believes that coordination must be provided at a higher level" (p. 9).

The second study of the work content of foremen is reported in the book, *The Foreman on the Assembly Line,* by Walker, Guest, and Turner (1956). Fifty-five foremen were interviewed in the study. "Every aspect of the foreman's situation was covered as far as practicable, with emphasis given to actual duties and what he thought of them, and to his relationships with other people and with his environment" (p. 2).

Among work duties discussed, one set involves relations with the workers—the development of personal relationships, teaching and promotion, absorbing pressure without transmitting it ("be a shock absorber"), standing up for the men, consulting them, and delegating work to them. A second set involves the foreman's relationship with others, particularly with staff and service departments, other foremen, the foreman's own boss, and senior management. Foremen tend to judge these people according to their "helpfulness."

The foremen studied were concerned primarily with staffing, and particularly absenteeism; with quality—"the essence of a foreman's job is to promote 'quality-mindedness' and to minimize human error wherever possible" (p. 74–75); and the meeting of emergencies, his "primary role" (p. 81). Emergencies arise largely because of fluctuations in schedules, and are accentuated by "the complexities of the products and the technical imperatives of the assembly line" (p. 81).

Most of this book deals, not with the nature of the work itself, but with the foreman's feelings about it and with the influence of sophisticated technology on these feelings. Detailed observational analysis of one foreman's day is presented for purposes of illustration.[6]

SAYLES'S STUDY OF MANAGERS AT LOWER AND MIDDLE LEVELS

One study stands apart from all the others. In his book, *Managerial Behavior* (1964), Leonard Sayles sheds much light on the subject of managerial work. He discusses his research as follows:

> The field work was conducted by techniques of anthropological studies: The researcher endeavors by living within a culture for extended periods of time to comprehend significant relationships and attitudes—even those which may depart from his predispositions and expectations . . . (p. vii).
>
> We make no pretence of having conducted a scientific experiment, so we are not proposing scientific hypotheses backed by systematically collected validating data. Rather we have looked and pondered for a long time and then developed a scheme of analysis, by which we mean simply that minimum number of concepts which would "explain" what was happening (p. viii).

This study can be criticized on grounds quite opposite to those used to critique the work of Hemphill. Sayles's study is loose—there is no evidence of systematic research tools, no hard data are presented, and the findings are not backed up with much evidence from the field. The reader is told little more than that 75 lower- and middle-level managers in a large American corporation were observed and interviewed. But it is clear from his book that Sayles is one of the few researchers whose writings demonstrate that he appreciates the complexities inherent in managerial work.

Defining the administrator's primary purpose as "to maintain the regularity or the sequential pattern of one or more of the work processes underlying the division of labour" (p. 49), Sayles describes three aspects of managerial work in his analysis:

---

[6] This developed into the work reported by Guest and Jasinski, discussed above.

1. The manager as a participant in external work flows
2. The manager as leader
3. The manager as monitor

As a *participant* in external work flows, the manager engages in seven basic relationships with people outside of his immediate managerial responsibility:

Trading relationships. Purchasing and selling arrangements with other members of the organization to get the work done.

Work flow relationships. Contacts concerning the work preceding or following that supervised by the manager.

Service relationships. Contacts concerning the giving or receiving of services or support by specialist groups (for example, typing pool or maintenance department).

Advisory relationship. Provision of counsel and advice to line managers by experts (for example, industrial relations department).

Auditing relationships. Contacts with those who evaluate or appraise organizational work (for example, quality control).

Stabilization relationships. Contacts with those who are empowered to limit or control the manager's decisions in accordance with organizational policy (for example, production scheduling).

Innovative relationships. Contacts with groups especially isolated to perform a research function.

Sayles stresses that these external contacts are time-consuming and that they require negotiation rather than the use of authority. The manager's concern for these relationships reflects his quest for stability and the avoidance of internal disruptions in the pace of work.

The *leadership* role focuses on the manager's relationships with his subordinates—his hierarchical, as opposed to horizontal and lateral, duties. Sayles points to three basic types of leadership behavior:

1. *Leadership as direction,* getting subordinates to respond simultaneously to the actions of the manager.
2. *Leadership as response* to initiations from subordinates who are seeking aid or support.
3. *Leadership as representation* or as *intervention* for subordinates in contacts with other parts of the organization (p. 53).

As *monitor,* the third aspect of his work, the manager appraises his internal and external relationships, looking for situations requiring his intervention. Sayles argues that monitoring is carried on, not by measuring results, but by following the progress of work through the system. The manager initiates verbal or observational checks, receives subordinate reports, and reviews numerical records. He detects variations. If he decides that they are not random, but that significant shifts are occurring, he initiates action.

The crucial factor in imposing change is to maintain what Sayles calls "moving equilibrium," a balance between stability and change.

> The manager's objective, then, is not a static system of human relations. Rather, he is seeking a dynamic type of stability, making adjustments and readjustments to both internally generated and externally imposed pressures. By these responses to variations in the environment, he hopes to maintain a *moving equilibrium* (p. 163).

Short-term change—in which the manager takes corrective or stabilizing action—is simpler, but long-term change is necessary when problems persist or compound themselves, when they are of great magnitude, or when they spiral to other parts of the organization.

In his summary Sayles critiques the classical view of managerial work, with its neat, compartmentalized responsibilities, its precise lines of authority, its notions of maximization. To Sayles the usual job descriptions "lie dormant in unused files" because "the dynamic elements of his job are left unspecified" (p. 34). In contrast, Sayles's view of the job stresses the openness of the system, the need for continual marginal adjustments to it, and the dynamic nature of the network of interrelationships with its mutual dependencies and reciprocities:

> [The manager] must adopt a variety of administrative patterns to fit the varying requirements of the interface: where his job meets others. . . .
> Superimposed on these day-to-day administrative patterns is the requirement that the manager evolve an adequate control mechanism to assess the functioning of his subpart of the total organization. As a manager, he must assess his direct subordinates' responsiveness to his initiations, just as he must check the behavioral pattern of his lateral relationships. For the most part, the manager operates on a contingency basis, trying to detect where the system of human relations may break down. Insofar as his control measures enable him to identify the problems, he seeks through remedial changes to return the system to equilibrium. This requires changes in his behavior and efforts to change the behavior of others. Failing here and in situations where such deviations occur with significant frequency, the manager seeks to introduce structural change (pp. 256–257).

Appendix B:
Seven Research
Methods
Used to
Study
Managerial Work

Described below are seven of the research methodologies that have been used to study managerial work. The advantages and disadvantages of each are pointed out and conclusions are summarized in Table 6 at the end of Appendix B.

SECONDARY SOURCES

Neustadt's study of the U.S. Presidency (1960) demonstrates the value of using secondary sources, such as correspondence and interviews with informants, to gain insight into the work of specific managers. It must, however, be recognized that this method suffers from some rather severe limitations. It does not allow the researcher to be comprehensive—he cannot know what is missing from the secondary sources that are studied. Second, only a very special kind of manager (a political leader, for example) is of sufficient importance to have generated the quantity of data required for analysis. Nevertheless, secondary sources provide the only means of studying the very important manager who is unavailable for more direct forms of research.

INTERVIEW AND QUESTIONNAIRE

It would appear that the simplest way to find out what managers do is to ask them, by way of interviews or questionnaires. This approach was used in most of the Ohio State Leadership studies and by Stieglitz in his NICB study. The results have been disappointing. As noted in Appendix A, to ask the manager what he does is to make him the researcher; he is expected to translate complex reality into meaningful abstraction. There is no evidence to suggest that managers can do this effectively; in fact there is ample evidence from empirical studies cited in Appendix A that managers are poor estimators of their own activities. Despite their convenience, the interview and questionnaire methods should be recognized as useful only in the study of managers' perceptions of their own jobs.

CRITICAL INCIDENT AND SEQUENCE OF EPISODES

One approach to the study of managerial work, discussed by Flanagan (1951, 1954) and by Kay (1959), is to collect and analyze descriptions of "critical incidents." Flanagan describes this method in his 1954 article in the *Psychological Bulletin,* citing studies dealing with teachers, air traffic controllers, dentists—even mothers. Only a few of the studies concern managerial work. To Flanagan the critical incident method "consists of a set of procedures for collecting direct observations of human behavior in such a way as to facilitate their potential usefulness in solving practical problems and developing broad psychological principles" (1954: 327).

The researcher collects information on a series of specific incidents by studying records, using interviews and questionnaires, and so on. He then analyzes these incidents and produces a set of basic work factors. Flanagan claims the technique has been used for measuring proficiency, for training, for job design, for equipment design, and for psychotherapy, among other things.

In his 1951 article Flanagan discusses two studies. In one, military officers reported on 2907 incidents "they had observed in which what was done was especially effective or ineffective" (p. 29). Results were distilled into 54 critical job requirements, which fell into 6 groupings—handling administrative details, supervising personnel, planning and directing action, organizational responsibility, personal responsibility, and military occupational specialty. A second study involved research executives who described effective and ineffective incidents for research workers. Among the general findings of the two studies, Flanagan reports that supervising subordinates emerged as a key factor in both jobs. Kay (1959) reports a study of effective and ineffective foremen.

The critical incident technique is interesting and useful because it focuses on concrete examples, allowing the manager to describe what he knows best (actual events), and leaving interpretation of data and development of theory to the researcher. Its main disadvantage is that one can never be sure that important parts of the job are not missing from the description. There may be a tendency to ignore activities that are routine, complex, or sensitive, or to focus on special activities to the detriment of comprehensive research. Flanagan indicates this problem in the report of one study made to determine the critical requirements for instructors of general psychology courses. The researchers found "substantial differences between the patterns of critical incidents reported by students and faculty" (1954: 333).

In an article entitled "Studies of Managers—A Fresh Start?" D. L. Marples (1967) proposes a method that lies halfway between the critical-incident and diary approaches. Criticizing the diary studies for their focus on "input" rather than "output," Marples suggests that the manager be viewed as a problem-solver/decision-maker, and that sequences of episodes (rather than isolated episodes) become the researcher's focus of attention. Marples's paper is exploratory and presents results from only a pilot study. A thorough assessment of his method will have to await the presentation of fuller results. At this time one can only suggest that the sequence-of-episodes method exhibits the same basic strengths and weaknesses of the critical-incident method. Both are potentially useful because they enable the researcher to probe deeply into important aspects of managerial work. But both may be misleading in that the researcher may unknowingly but consistently exclude from study certain important aspects of the manager's work.

DIARY

The diary method of Carlson (1951), Stewart (1967), and others has proven to be a useful tool for the study of managerial work characteristics, but a useless one for the study of work content. The reason for this, as indicated in Chapter 2, is that the diary is designed to determine only the time distribution among *known* job factors. As the method has been applied, managers are given precoded pads on which to record details of each activity. (Carlson's form is shown in Figure 1 of Chapter 2.) Because of the manager's time pressures, these forms must be simple and must enable him to record events quickly. Hence the diary method cannot be used to categorize work, only to allocate time among known categories. Where the categories are known (work characteristics such as place of work, participants, and so forth), the diary method is useful. Where they are not (work content), it is of no help. Rosemary Stewart, who tried to collect data on work content in her trial studies, comments:

> The most important conclusion that I reached was that it is impossible to design a diary of kinds of action. . . . This conclusion imposes a very important limitation on the possible scope of analysing managers' jobs by means of diaries, since it means that if one wants comparable results—and that surely must be the aim—one is severely restricted in analyzing what the manager does, as distinct from where, how, or with whom he does it (1965: 230).

Hence we must conclude that the diary method is most useful where we wish to study the time distributed among known job factors. The method uses the manager to record data, and hence is most efficient for collecting data on large numbers of managers.

A number of other shortcomings of the diary method should be noted here. Unreliability is one that has been discussed by Burns (1954 and 1957), Stewart (1965, 1967, 1968), and Marples (1967). One cannot be sure, first of all, whether or not the manager clearly understands the words on the diary form. Some categories such as "place of work," involve no difficulty. Others, such as "functional area," have led to problems of interpretation. Stewart (1967) collected this kind of data but rejected it as unreliable; Burns (1954 and 1957) discusses the finding that in almost 40 percent of the episodes involving the manager and a subordinate, different interpretations of "functional area" were given. (A possible explanation for this is given in Appendix C.)

One must also ensure that the managers are recording their activities consistently and continuously. Stewart (1967) carried out tests of reliability over the four-week periods, but Carlson (1951) indicated concern with reliability after a week or two of recording. And Burns, claiming that his method "yields information which is at bottom no more objective than that obtained in interview" (1957: 48), comments:

> Concerning the results, there are three provisos to be made. First, and most important, the records are in no way objective; they are statements made by individuals about what they thought—or thought I ought to know—they were doing. Secondly, the records vary greatly in precision and accuracy. While it was suggested that

brief, trivial episodes (for example, an unsuccessful telephone call) might safely be ignored, but that episodes lasting two or three minutes or upwards, or briefer episodes if important, should be recorded, the diligence with which individual recorders adhered to this general ruling varied a great deal. Moreover, thirdly, some recorders tended to run episodes together more than others, using one sheet to record two or more consecutive affairs involving two or more subjects and two or more respondents (1957: 47).

Finally, there is the problem of the pace and density of work. The pace of their work may be such that managers simply lack the time to record certain events (a brief contact, a stack of mail processed quickly). Marples (1967) presents data to indicate this loss of data by the diary method. And Rosemary Stewart built a "fleeting contacts" section into her diary form. No doubt this alleviated the problem. But, as discussed in Appendix C, it is doubtful that it solved the problem. The pace of work is at times simply too hectic.

ACTIVITY SAMPLING

Another approach is that used by Kelly (1964) and Wirdenius (1958). Here managerial activity is observed at random time intervals by the researcher. When a statistically significant sample is built up, analysis is undertaken. Hans Wirdenius's book provides a most thorough discussion of this method. In his own application of activity sampling—which he discusses in great detail, paying particular attention to questions of validation—the researcher observed 10 to 12 production supervisors by following predetermined, randomly selected touring circuits. Each subject was observed and then interviewed briefly an average of once every two hours. Wirdenius describes a simple example as follows:

> With his visiting sequence list to guide him, the observer heads for the supervisor next in line, approaching the latter's section along a route that he randomly picks out of several available. On arriving at one of the section entrances, also randomly selected, the observer makes note of the time. Upon entering the room or the area (the observation point), the observer promptly assures himself *at a glance* whether his man is there or not ("one-step" observation). If so, the subject's behavior is observed at the exact instant of the observer's glance. This done, he immediately moves toward the subject and continues observing the unfolding of the event at closer quarters. Then, when he deems the time appropriate, he interviews the supervisor, records the behavior, and repeats the procedure for the next supervisor on his list (1958: 132).

To test reliability, Wirdenius used two researchers to study the same supervisor at the same time, although they followed different paths.

Referring to studies carried out in three firms, Wirdenius devotes considerable space to various analyses of reliability, including a comparison of single and paired observers, an assessment of the reliability of observation by superiors, and the influence of the observer's presence on the subject's behavior. Many of these results are inconclusive or mixed, but the author does state that observer influence was probably insignificant, except perhaps in a few cases and then only at the beginning of the study period.

Using the activity-sampling method, one in effect photographs the action periodically. The researcher is not exposed to the activity continuously, hence interpretation of complex aspects of it becomes difficult. Like the diary method, activity sampling is effective when the topic under study is well understood and can be coded simply and quickly. The method appears to be best when known aspects of a variety of jobs must be studied in one location.

UNSTRUCTURED OBSERVATION

This method, used by Sayles (1964), Dalton (1959), and Hodgson, Levinson, and Zaleznik (1965), has proven an effective one to deal with the complexity of managerial work. The researcher lives in the system, either as a participant or as an independent observer, and records all observations that interest him. This generally includes a mixture of events, anecdotes, views and attitudes of those observed, documentary evidence, and so on. The rich array of data that results is then taken from the scene, arranged, rearranged, and studied intensively. Hodgson and his coworkers point out the value of such an approach:

> By deliberate decision, we gave free reign to an unstructured, clinical wonder over what we observed taking place as the executives went about their work in the hospital. In some ways it would have been easier to establish an orderly pattern for gathering coded data right from the start. Looking back, we believe it was fortunate that we held our anxieties in abeyance, and remained open to unfolding events. Many of the data that proved to be analytically most useful were gathered unexpectedly, almost despite our attempts at systematizing the data collection (1965: 20).

This method has two great strengths. First, the researcher can be purely inductive. He imposes on himself no artificial constraints or premeditated structure. Nothing need stand between the work he observes and the theory he develops save his own ability to interpret. Second, the researcher is in a position to probe deeply into the work that he observes. If an incident is unclear, he is there and he has the time to find out more.

But unstructured observation suffers from one major disadvantage—too much is asked of the researcher. He cannot replicate his research, and he must support his findings by anecdote rather than by systematic evidence. The theory he produces cannot be validated scientifically, and the reader is asked to show great faith in his honesty and reliability.

Of further concern to us is comprehensiveness. Can we be sure that the researcher captures all parts of the job, or just what interests him or catches his attention? Carlson makes clear the problems of the unstructured study:

> Before we go out in the field in order to make our observations we must know what to look for and how to describe and measure the things we observe. . . . Without such a conceptual framework, there would be no way of selecting among the infinite number of factual observations which can be made about any concrete phenomena. . . . In the reporting of our fact finding we must state the operations by which our data are arrived at (1951: 19).

STRUCTURED OBSERVATION

A few researchers have used a variety of more systematic forms of observation. These include Guest (1956), Jasinski (1956), Ponder (1957), O'Neill and Kubany (1959), Landsberger (1962), Radomsky (1967), as well as myself (as reported in Appendix C). However, in most of these studies an approach similar to that of the diary researchers was used—the recording categories were predetermined. The only real difference was that recording was done by the researcher instead of the manager. This avoided some of the problems of the diary studies, but not the basic one of being able to find out only about the time distribution of those dimensions of the job already understood. Hence this approach offers, at a higher cost, little more than the diary method.

But structured observation can draw also on the chief strength of unstructured observation, namely, the development of categorization schemes during and after observation. Joseph McGrath, in a paper entitled, "Toward a 'Theory of Method' for Research on Organizations," cites this as the essence of field study research. "The investigator needs to know (or assume) less about the phenomena before he starts[;] . . . the field study investigator imposes a 'strong' structure *after,* rather than before, he collects his data" (1964: 554).

For certain purposes such an approach can offer the best of both worlds—the inductive power of observation coupled with the structure of systematic recording. Sayles's method deals with the complexity of managerial work, Carlson's with the need for hard data. Structured observation can deal with both. My own study, reported in Appendix C, was designed with these two purposes in mind.

We might look briefly at the problems of the structured observation method, as outlined by Rosemary Stewart (1965). First and most significant is inefficiency—the researcher must be present at all times; as a result, the sample size is severely limited. Second, the researcher may be excluded from some confidential work and may have difficulty understanding some of what he sees. Rosemary Stewart notes that with the diary method:

> Classification is made by the man who knows what he is doing. It is hard for an observer to follow all that is being done, without interrupting the manager, even if he is familiar with the job he is observing. The difficulties of classification become much greater when observing an unfamiliar, and especially a highly technical job. (I speak from experience.) (1965: 235).

One unique application of the observational methodology merits attention at this point because it circumvents the second problem mentioned above and because it enhances the power of the research significantly. Interested in studying the decision processes managers use to schedule their time, John Radomsky (1967) focused a videotape camera on them at their desks as they went about making scheduling decisions. He recorded both their images and the verbalizations of their thoughts at the moment of recording. (This technique of capturing the decision-maker's "protocols" has been used by Clarkson (1962) and others to study decision processes ranging from determination of an investment portfolio to choice of a chess move.) On the following day, as Radomsky reviewed the tapes with the managers, he was able to ask a number of specific questions about their reasons for certain decisions.

Radomsky found that this method of replaying the image and sound of the activity within twenty-four hours aided his subjects' recall considerably:

> In our opinion video equipment is a valuable aid to observation of decision processes. It picks up nuances missed by the observer and unnoticed by the respondent. The recall stimulus is pronounced. One respondent remarked that he had the same feelings during the reviews that he had at the time the events occurred (1967: 25).

What is especially powerful about Radomsky's methodology is that, first, it captures with great reliability the manager's actions (at least while he is behind his desk), and, second, it provides a most effective means for extracting background information by way of leisurely interviews.

To conclude, structured observation is an expensive research method but perhaps the only one that enables us to study systematically and comprehensively those parts of managerial work that are not well understood.

Table 6. Seven Methods to Study Managerial Work

Method	Applications	Major Advantage(s)	Major Disadvantage(s)	Appropriate Use
Secondary Sources	Neustadt	Convenient; draws on analyses of others	Data frequently unavailable, inappropriate, or incomplete	To study job of inaccessible manager
Questionnaire and Interview	Ohio State Leadership Group	Convenient	Data of questionable reliability	To study manager's perception of his job
Critical Incident and Sequence of Episodes	Flanagan, Marples	Allows for intense probing	Parts of job not covered by the data	To study certain aspects of job in depth (e.g., decision-making)
Diary	Carlson, Stewart	Efficient (i.e., large sample possible relative to researcher's time investment)	No help in developing understanding of new dimensions; some problems with interpretation, consistency, and reliability	To study characteristics of large sample of differing managerial jobs
Activity Sampling	Kelly, Wirdenius	Efficient; recording by researcher	Little help in developing understanding of new dimensions; noncontinuous, hence interpretation difficult	To study observational aspects of different jobs in one location
Unstructured Observation	Sayles, Dalton, Hodgson et al.	Enables researcher to understand new dimensions and to probe	Nonsystematic (may lose important data; cannot replicate); inefficient	To study the most complex, least understood aspects of manager's job (content)
Structured Observation	Guest, Ponder, Mintzberg, Radomsky	Enables researcher to understand new dimensions, to probe, to be systematic	Inefficient (consumes much researcher time); difficult to interpret some activities	To study at same time content and characteristics of small sample of managers' jobs

Appendix C: A Study of the Work of Five Chief Executives

This appendix reports my own research on the work of managers, carried out in 1967–1968. A review of the literature undertaken before designing my study revealed a lack of descriptive material on the *content* of managerial work. In simple terms, there was little to tell us what managers actually do. Hence, this study was designed to focus (1) on the job rather than the man, (2) on basic similarities in managers' work rather than on differences, and (3) on the essential content of the work rather than its peripheral characteristics.

These objectives led to the choice of a research methodology that is inductive, comprehensive, and intensive. It had to be *inductive* because the purpose was to describe what we did not know, to develop from a study of specific managers a general statement of managerial roles. The research had to be *comprehensive* to capture, not what might interest me or draw my attention for the moment, but the whole job of managing. And it had to be *intensive* in that it had to probe deeply, not superficially, into the complex set of managerial activities.

In this appendix we look first at the research methodology and then at the research sample. Following this the data are presented, in some detail. We next examine the differences in the work of the five men studied. This is followed by some comments on the nature of the analysis that led to the theory discussed in Chapters 3 and 4 (the theory of roles in particular). The appendix concludes with some comments on the use of the research methodology.

STRUCTURED OBSERVATION APPLIED [1]

Structured observation was chosen as the method for this study because it made it possible to develop theory inductively, to observe and question intensively where necessary, and to be systematic. The method restricted the sample size, and, as a result, less quantitative data on job characteristics was generated than would have been done by a comparable diary study. But I was happy to trade off this kind of data in return for more powerful data on activity content. The trade-off was for depth at the expense of breadth, a necessary one given the objective of describing work content.

This method necessitated walking a tightrope between using structure and excluding it. Too little structure would have resulted in an inability to record much of the important data, tabulate the findings, and reproduce the research. Too much structure could have led to the problem inherent in diaries—an inability to develop an understanding of the things we knew nothing about.

The label *structured observation* is used here to refer to a method that couples the flexibility of open-ended observation with the discipline of seeking certain types of structured data. The researcher observes the manager as he performs his work. Each observed event (a verbal contact or a piece of incoming or outgoing mail) is categorized by the researcher in a number of ways (for example, duration, participants, purpose) as in the diary method, but with one important difference. *The categories are developed during the observation and after it takes place.* In effect, the researcher is

[1] Weick's paper in *The Handbook of Social Psychology* (1968), entitled "Systematic Observational Methods," provides an excellent and detailed account of the applications, advantages, and disadvantages of *structured observation*.

influenced in his coding process, not by the standing literature or his own prior experience, but by the single event taking place before him. In addition to categorizing events, the researcher is able to record detailed information on important incidents and to collect anecdotal materials.

The field study proceeded through three basic stages—preliminary data collection, recording of observations, and coding of observations.

Collection of Preliminary Data

For each manager studied, a body of preliminary data was collected before the actual observation began.

One Month of Scheduled Appointments. From the calendar pad, usually with the help of the manager's secretary, information was collected on all scheduled meetings (place, duration, participants) that took place during one month. This information was compared with that collected during the study.

Information About the Organization. Information collected included the organizational chart, reprints of appropriate articles, speeches by the manager, annual reports, books about the organization. This information was used to develop an understanding of the environment of the manager, to give insight into some of the strategy questions that might arise during observation, and to become familiar with the names of members of management who might interact with the manager during observation.

Information About the Manager. Information was collected on the manager's background, personality, approximate working hours, work-related activity at home, managerial style, and so on. Copies of his personal résumé were obtained, as well as published information about him. Interviews were held with him, his secretary and/or his personal assistant. This information enabled me to familiarize myself with the man and to prepare for the actual week of observation.

Recording and Coding of Observations

During observation two types of data were collected. The "anecdotal data" comprised materials on specific activities. Critical or otherwise interesting incidents were described in considerable detail; exhibits of actual correspondence were obtained; background notes were recorded during informal discussions with the managers. These anecdotal materials were used to facilitate coding and to develop and support some of the theory.

"Structured data" were collected on the pattern of activity throughout every minute of the workday and on all mail and verbal contacts. Three records were used to record these data. *The chronology record* described activity patterns and cross-referenced the other two records. The *mail record* described each piece of incoming and outgoing mail. The *contact record* described each verbal contact. During observation, raw data were collected in each of these three records with no special concern for consistency. Whatever words were needed to describe an observation were used. Each evening the data of each of the three records were tabulated. Here, all descriptions were reduced to a few words or a short phrase, although it was still not yet considered vital to establish consistent terminology. Finally, when the research was completed, the data of these three records were then recorded (more times than this researcher cares to remember), with the aim of producing accurate, tidy, and concise categories. (The results of this process appear in the tables presented later in this appendix.) It should be noted that the essence of the inductive process is in the successive iterations of the processing of raw field data—recording, tabulating, coding and recoding, analyzing these results—until meaningful conceptualizations appear.

To clarify this process for the reader, we reproduce below a detailed example of a manager's morning, using incidents experienced by the different managers of the study. We show the tabulation of this data in the three records in an intermediate stage—as it would have been done on the evening following the observation of the work.

> As Mr. M. enters his office at 8:20 A.M. and greets Janice, his secretary, the telephone rings. It is the manager of the local manufacturing operation and the call is put through. "We had a fire in the plant last night," Mr. M. is told, "and the damage amounted to $30,000; we should be back in operation by next Wednesday."
>
> As he hangs up, Janice enters and reminds him of an 11 A.M. appointment and of his intention to call the company lawyer. "Joe dropped by and would like to see you, and, oh yes, that flight to Paris is booked, so I put you on the 4 P.M. leaving on the fifth. Nothing much in the mail except for that letter from Antwerp." The seven pieces of mail are processed immediately:
>
>> The invitation to speak to a trade organization is declined with a note to Janice to reply that Mr. M. will be abroad.
>>
>> The advertisement for a magazine on mergers and acquisitions is thrown away.
>>
>> A notice informs Mr. M. of the date of the board meeting and the date is noted on the calendar.
>>
>> *Fortune* magazine is skimmed, and an advertisement for certain production equipment is clipped.
>>
>> The head of the organization's Antwerp office has written to complain that the treasurer will not release funds for his tenth anniversary celebration. Mr. M. calls to Janice to ask the treasurer to drop by today.
>>
>> The internal financial statement for the month is glanced at and put in the "out" basket for filing.

Without reading it, Mr. M. signs a document received from his vice president of research and development. It is a request for funds under a federally supported program, and Mr. M. must sign it before it goes to Washington.

The time is 8:40 and Mr. M.'s assistant looks in: "It looks like there will be trouble at the meeting—they think Mike was forced out, and they are prepared to make a stink about it." They proceed to discuss the situation.

At 8:55 Mr. M. calls the chairman of the board. "There'll be trouble at the meeting, George," and Mr. M. goes on to repeat the information he has just received.

The conversation ends precisely at 9:00, and a Mr. Jamison is ushered in with a member of the personnel department. Mr. Jamison is introduced to Mr. M. who asks, "Well, what will you do when you leave us?" After some discussion about Mr. Jamison's camp in New Hampshire, he is presented with a plaque commemorating 30 years of service to the organization.

At 9:30 the treasurer, who has been waiting at the door, enters. "John, look at this," says Mr. M. as he hands him the Antwerp letter. "What's the story?" The treasurer explains his side to Mr. M.'s satisfaction; when the treasurer leaves at 10 A.M., Mr. M. immediately writes a letter to Antwerp explaining that he cannot interfere with the decision of the treasurer.

Ten minutes later, Janice is called in: "Now who are these people coming at 11?" Once told, he asks Janice to arrange for his assistant to be present at the meeting.

At 10:10 A.M., Mr. M. walks through the executive offices toward the plant. On the way he passes the medical center and appears to note something. Once in the plant, he stops by various machines to watch the operations and chat with the workers. He stops at the office of the production superintendent, who is not there. He hands the assistant superintendent the advertisement clipped from *Fortune* magazine, commenting, "Jerry may find this worthwhile to use for production scheduling."

Back in his office at 10:45 A.M., Mr. M. finds a message to call the executive vice president, who is in Los Angeles. "They are asking 13 million? Tell them we won't go a penny over 10, but, Joe, let's be prepared to settle for 12."

This telephone call is followed by one to the controller. "Have you been through the medical department lately? They don't need that new wing—they are not using the space they have now."

The 11 o'clock meeting, which carries on over lunch, is held in the board room, with Mr. M., his assistant, and two members of a consulting firm in attendance. These meetings are held monthly for the duration of a consulting contract. After brief pleasantries, it becomes clear that there is friction here. The consultants are trying to justify their fees, while the assistant questions them. Mr. M., who has been silent, suddenly asks, "What about the charge for reprogramming? I don't think it should be borne by us." After some negotiation, a settlement is reached at lunch.

The *chronology record* notes times and basic activities, and is cross-referenced with the other two records. It would represent the activities of this morning as shown in Table 7.

The chronology record was designed to provide basic data on the design of the working day, and to provide a cross reference to the other two records. It shows at a glance the distribution of telephone calls, scheduled and unscheduled meetings, tours, and desk work. In the Reference column meetings, telephone calls, and tours are annotated with sequential letters, and pieces of mail, with numbers.

Meetings are defined as *unscheduled* if they are arranged hastily, as when someone just "drops in." *Tour* refers to a chance meeting in the hall, or to the promenades taken by the manager to observe activity and to deliver information. *Desk work* refers to the time the manager spends at his desk, processing mail, scheduling activities, writing letters, and communicating with his secretary. *Duration* is recorded to the nearest tenth of an hour; activities lasting less than three minutes are recorded as lasting 0.02 hours.

The *mail record,* detailing the nature of the mail received and generated by the manager, would be developed as shown in Table 8. *Form, sender,* and *attention* are straightforward categorizations. (If the manager receives a copy of correspondence not addressed to him, the original addressor and addressee are noted.) Recorded in columns headed *purpose* and *action taken* are short descriptions of the purpose, from the manager's point of view, of each piece of mail and

Table 7. The Chronology Record

Time	Medium	Reference[a]	Duration (in hours)
8:20	Call	A	0.02
8:22	Desk work	1-7	0.3
8:40	Unscheduled meeting	B	0.2
8:55	Call	C	0.1
9:00	Scheduled meeting	D	0.5
9:30	Unscheduled meeting	E	0.5
10:00	Desk work	(5)	0.2
10:10	Tour	F	0.1
10:40	Tour	G	0.2
10:45	Call	H	0.2
10:55	Call	I	0.1
11:00	Scheduled meeting	J	2.0
1:00	End of meeting	–	–

[a]Cross references to items in Tables 8 and 9.

Table 8. The Mail Record

Reference	Form	Sender	Purpose	Attention	Action Taken
1	Letter	Trade organization	Request to speak	Read	Reply: decline
2	Clipping	Salesman	Solicitation	Skim	–
3	Letter	External board	Notice of meeting	Read	–
4	Periodical	–	Business news	Skim	Forward advertisement to production supervisor
5	Memo	Foreign vice president	Request resolve staff conflict	Read	Reply: explain
6	Report	Controller	Financial data	Skim	–
7	Letter	R&D vice president	Request signature	–	Sign

the manager's reaction to it (if it occurs during the same day). Note that mail originated by the manager is recorded in the same way.

The *contact record,* providing detail on meetings, telephone calls, and tours, would be developed as shown in Table 9. *Medium* is recorded as in the *chronology record* except that the number of participants is also noted. *Participants, duration,* and *place,* are straightforward categorizations. *Initiation* describes the ostensible stimulus for the contact—"self" for the manager, "opposite" for the other person in a two-person contact, "clock" if the contact is a regularly scheduled one. *Purpose* is recorded as in the mail record. The *ed* suffix refers to a passive action by the manager (inform*ed* means that he receives information), while the *ing* suffix refers to an active one (inform*ing* means that the manager gives information.) I.C. means "instant communication," the rapid transmission of important, current information.

CHOOSING MANAGERS TO BE STUDIED

As noted above, structured observation imposed strong restrictions on the research sample size. It was, therefore, decided to study five managers in all, for one week each. This was clearly a small sample, but one in keeping with the resource constraints and with the imposition on the research subjects.[2]

With a sample of five managers, it clearly made no sense to seek a comprehensive mix of managerial types to study. Hence it seemed best to limit the research to experienced chief executives of medium to large organizations:

> *Position: Chief Executive.* Chief executives were chosen as the subjects for study because (a) it would be less difficult to understand the work of a man who relates his organization to the outside society than of one who relates his unit to others within an organization, (b) acceptance of the researcher's presence and "right to know" would follow with the approval of only one man, and (c) any published materials on the organizations would provide direct insight to the chief executive's job. Perhaps most important was a personal reason—an interest in the policy-making process and in drawing conclusions on the possible role of management science at the policy level.
>
> *Experience: Substantial.* Managers recently appointed to their positions were excluded because of the possibility that their activities would not yet have stabilized.

[2] As this research was undertaken in the form of a doctoral dissertation, the time of only one researcher was available, and that for only 12 months or so. The reliability of the results is discussed later in this appendix.

Table 9. The Contact Record

Reference	Medium	Purpose	Participants	Initiation	Duration	Place
A	Call	Informed (event)	Manufacturing manager	Opposite	0.02	Office
B	Unscheduled meeting 2	Informed (I.C.)	Assistant	Opposite	0.2	Office
C	Call	Informing (I.C.)	Chairman	Self	0.1	Office
D	Scheduled meeting 3	Ceremony	Retiring employee; Personnel staffer	Opposite (personnel staffer)	0.5	Office
E	Unscheduled meeting 2	Informed (action taken)	Treasurer	Self	0.5	Office
F	Tour	Observation	Plant employees	Self	0.5	Medical plant
G	Tour	Informing (idea)	Assistant superintendent	Self	0.1	Plant
H	Call	Strategy	Executive vice president	Opposite	0.2	Office
I	Call	Informing (decision)	Controller	Self	0.1	Office
J	Scheduled meeting 4	Negotiating	Assistant, consultants	Clock	2.0	Board room

Organization: Middle- to Large-sized in Various Industries. The study focused on the chief executives of middle- to large-sized organizations. (A subsequent study, reported in Chapter 5, dealt with chief executives of small ones.) Organizations of very different types were chosen (public, consumer goods, and so on).

Three men—the president of a small printing firm, the dean of a major management school, and the vice chairman of a large food-retailing chain—participated in a preliminary study. The first man was observed (unstructured) for three days, and the other two described one month of their scheduled activity. This led to the choice of factors to be used during structured observation. Finally, the five men to be studied were chosen.

Manager A was chairman and chief executive officer of a major consulting firm. He had held this position for three years before the study, and had joined the firm at a senior level six years before that. This man was a well-known figure in American public affairs. His firm was one of the largest in its field, with important foreign operations and a major reputation for innovative research activities.

Manager B, an engineer by training, was president of a firm that carried out research and development activities and produced sophisticated technological products for industry and defense. He was one of the original members that formed the firm shortly after World War II; he became president two years before the study. At the time of the study the firm was growing rapidly, partly through acquisition activity, and its sales were in the range of $60–$70 million, up from less than $10 million in 1959.

Manager C was head of a large, important urban hospital that he had joined as an intern in 1951. He became general director five years before the study at a remarkably young age. He was widely known as a hospital administrator, and had published a number of books and articles on technical medical subjects as well as on hospital administration. His institution was an old one, with a world-wide reputation in medical teaching and research. At the time of the study, its expenses totalled $31 million annually.

Manager D was president of a firm producing consumer goods in a sophisticated and highly competitive industry. At the time of the study he had held that position for eight years, coming from the marketing department. His company had been the dominant firm in its industry until the 1950s, and was in difficulty when Manager D took over the presidency. He had since revitalized it. Sales at the time of the study were in excess of $100 million.

Manager E was superintendent of a large suburban school system. Like Manager C, he had joined it at the operating level (as a teacher) and had assumed the office of chief executive at a young age. (He had taken off time to earn a Ph.D. in education.) His school system was widely known for its innovative activities and the quality of its work. At the time of the study the system had 18,000 students in 33 schools and a junior college, and an annual budget of $15 million.

Common to all these men at the time of study were four basic factors. (1) Their position: Each was in name and in fact the chief executive of his organization. (2) The basic organization: In each case a large line and staff organization reported to the chief executive, and there was an active board of directors. (3) The success of their organizations: The commercial organizations were profitable, growing rapidly, and among the largest in their fields. The hospital and school system were judged to be among the best in America. All five organizations were working at the forefront of modern scientific development, and four of them (all but organization D) had deeply rooted ties to leading academic institutions. (4) Certain basic aspects of their backgrounds: All these men were experienced chief executives; all worked in their own organizations before assuming their present positions; all were college educated (but only one had had formal management training—Manager D who held an M.B.A).

THE RESULTS OF THE STUDY

Each of these men was observed at work for one week. In total, 659 pieces of mail reached their desks, 231 pieces were sent out, and 368 distinct verbal contacts were made. In all, the mail and contact records contained 1258 entries, categorized in a number of ways. In this section these results are described and tabulated for each of the five managers and for the composite.

The Chronology Record

Table 10 presents the results of the analysis of the *chronology records*. The first group of figures are totals—202 hours of work during the five weeks in which 547 distinct activities were performed.

Data on the five major types of activities follow. Note that *desk work* refers to periods when the managers worked alone, or with their secretaries, in the confines of their offices. This work consumed only 22 percent of their time. Much of it involved scheduling activities and dealing with documents (sorting and processing mail, reading and editing reports, replying to correspondence, signing letters, writing speeches, and so on). The data on *tours* give the only indication of the time the managers spent on relatively open-ended activity—strolling about the organization, greeting people in the hall, and so on. This amounted to 3 percent of the total working time.

On the average, each day these managers engaged in 7 desk-work sessions in which they processed 36 pieces of mail, and they had 5 brief telephone calls, 4 scheduled meetings (which took 59 percent of their total time), 4 unscheduled meetings, and 1 tour. A final section in the chronology record indicates activity duration. Half of all activities observed averaged less than 9 minutes duration and only one in ten lasted longer than 60 minutes.

The Mail Record

Tables 11 and 12 contain the results of the analysis of the mail records. In Table 11 the incoming mail is categorized according to format, attention received, sender, and purpose. Note that 61 percent of the mail was sent by outsiders, and 39 percent by people within the organization. As discussed later in this appendix, it was not possible to categorize insiders except to call them "subordinates." [3] Table 12 presents similar figures for mail that the managers sent out. Note here that only 25 pieces of output mail during the five weeks were self-generated by the manager (that is, not responses to input). The managers received 659 pieces and reacted to about one-third of these with acknowledgements or replies, or by forwarding them to subordinates. Note also that subordinates, who sent 39 percent of the managers' mail, received 55 percent (most of it forwarded mail), and that directors of the organizations sent only 7 pieces and received only 5 during the five weeks of observation. In evidence here is a strong net flow of documented information to these managers from all sources. Moreover, it appears that these managers acted as filtering devices in transferring information from the environment into their organizations.

The key to our study was the categorization of the *purpose*. This describes the essential content of managerial activity—in raw form, what five managers did—and it is what led to the development of the theory on roles. Twelve categories were chosen to describe the purposes of input mail; each is discussed in detail below:

1. *Acknowledgements.* Letters formally acknowledging a visit, a favor, some information received, a completed job, and so on, made up 5 percent of the mail received. It was with outsiders, most often with peers, that this formal correspondence was traded. Some of this mail was forwarded to subordinates.
2. *Status Requests.* One-eighth of the managers' mail brought inconsequential requests made of them because of their positions. These were of three types: (a) Peers made half of these requests —for the manager to speak, to send information, to donate funds, and so on. (b) Letters and reports, prepared for the managers' signature by subordinates, constituted another one-third of this mail. Some of it was formality (for example, Manager E signed all letters offering teaching appointments), some was because of the manager's prestige (Manager A was asked

[3] This is an undesirable term. But none could be found that would be better understood.

Table 10. Analysis of the Chronology Record
Based on five weeks of observation

Category	Composite	Manager A	Manager B	Manager C	Manager D	Manager E
Total Hours Worked	202 hrs	28[a]	36	45	53	40
Hours in Travel to Outside Meetings (not included)	18 hrs	5.4	7.1	4.5	0.3	0.3
Hours of Evening Meetings (included)	24 hrs	–	3	3	7	11
Total Amount of Mail	890 pieces	161	165	230	222	112[b]
Average Amount of Mail Processed Per Day	36 pieces	32	33	46	44	22[b]
Total Number of Activities	547	101	86	96	160	104
Desk Work						
Number of sessions	179	36	31	25	54	33
Time on desk work	44 hrs	10.6	8.3	8.3	10.7	6.4
Average duration	15 min	18	16	20[c]	12	12
Proportion of time	22%	38%	23%	18%	20%	16%
Telephone Calls[d]						
Number of calls	133	27	27	30	22	27
Time on telephone	13 hrs	2.4	3.2	3.0	1.9	2.4
Average duration	6 min	5	7	6	5	5
Proportion of time	6%	9%	9%	7%	4%	6%
Scheduled Meetings						
Number of meetings	105	16	14	27	18	30
Time in meetings	120 hrs	10.6	20.6	29.1	29.5	29.8
Average duration	68 min	40	88	65	98	60
Proportion of time	59%	38%	57%	65%	55%	75%

Unscheduled Meetings					
Number of meetings	101	10	14	10	55	12
Time in meetings	20 hrs	1.7	3.5	4.0	9.6	1.2
Average duration	12 min	10	15	24	10	6
Proportion of time	10%	6%	10%	9%	18%	3%

Tours						
Number of tours	29	12	–	4	11	2
Time on tours	5 hrs	2.9	–	0.5	1.5	0.2
Average duration	11 min	14	–	8	8	6
Proportion of time	3%	10%	0%	1%	3%	1%

Proportion of Activities Lasting Less Than 9 Min	49%	44%	40%	45%	56%	51%
Proportion Lasting Longer Than 60 Min	10%	5%	12%	13%	9%	12%

[a] It was decided to exclude a seven-hour trip that Manager A took to Washington in connection with congressional hearings.

[b] Manager E commented that his mail was significantly lighter at the time of observation—the last week of classes.

[c] Manager C spent Saturday processing much of his mail. He was largely uninterrupted, spending one 3.1-hour session and one 0.7-hour session. Excluding these, the average duration of his desk work sessions would have been 12 minutes.

[d] Telephone calls screened or made by the secretary were excluded.

Table 11. Analysis of the Mail Record: Input
Based on five weeks of observation

Category	Composite	Manager A	Manager B	Manager C	Manager D	Manager E
Number Pieces Received	659	112	142	164	172	69
Form of Input (%)						
Letter	29%	28	15	40	26	43
Memo	10%	14	1	9	14	13
Report	25%	12	28	32	23	28
Periodical[a]	16%	13	41	6	14	3
Copy of letter	9%	16	6	7	8	9
Copy of memo	6%	11	4	2	10	2
Clipping	4%	5	4	3	5	2
Book	1%	1	1	1	1	–
Attention (%)						
Skim	31%	32	63	34	13	6
Read	63%	65	33	57	80	94
Study	6%	4	4	9	7	–
Sender (%)						
Subordinate	39%	49	21	30	47	62
Director	1%	1	1	2	1	1
Peer[b]	16%	17	9	31	12	6
Trade organization	9%	2	10	20	2	6
Client[c]	5%	11	9	1	3	3
Supplier or associate	8%	2	14	4	13	4
Independent[d]	6%	6	1	6	10	3
Publisher	11%	10	27	2	13	3
Government	5%	3	9	4	2	12
Purpose of Input Mail (%)						
Acknowledgments	5%	7	2	7	6	4
Status requests	12%	10	5	15	8	30
Solicitations	5%	4	9	3	5	3
Authority requests	5%	3	3	4	3	12
Total Requests	21%	17	18	23	16	45
Reference data	14%	8	11	20	17	9
General reports	8%	6	5	18	5	1
Periodical news	15%	12	42	5	12	3
Events	8%	4	6	12	8	7
Reports on operations	18%	30	12	8	25	12
Advice on situations	6%	7	2	3	6	14
Problems and pressures	2%	4	1	3	2	3
Ideas	2%	4	1	2	2	1
Total Information	74%	76	80	70	78	51

[a]Periodicals received and read at the managers' homes were not included.

[b]Refers to executives of organizations having no direct relationships with those of the managers (e.g., personal contacts, competitors, codirectors on external boards).

[c]Includes buyer of consumer goods or service, patient in hospital, parent associated with school system.

[d]Refers to individual with no relevant organizational affiliation (e.g., job seekers, students doing research, members of the general public).

Table 12. Analysis of the Mail Record: Output
Based on five weeks of observation

Category	Composite	Manager A	Manager B	Manager C	Manager D	Manager E
Number reactions to inputs	206	34	20	65	49	38
Number self-initiated	25	15	3	1	1	5
Total output	231	49	23	66	50	43
Output as percent of of input	35%	44	16	40	29	62
Self-initiated as percent of output	11%	31%	13%	2%	2%	12%
Form of output mail %						
Letter	47%	53	39	56	30	51
Memo	19%	14	22	9	30	26
Report	2%	4	9	–	–	2
Forwarded letter	18%	22	30	8	28	9
Forwarded memo	5%	2	–	9	4	5
Forwarded clipping, report, periodical, book	9%	4	–	18	8	7
Target of output mail %						
Subordinate	55%	41	57	45	68	67
Director	2%	6	4	–	–	2
Peer	17%	22	22	24	12	2
Trade organization	5%	–	–	12	6	–
Client	7%	22	4	3	–	5
Supplier or associate	3%	4	4	–	8	–
Independent	5%	2	4	9	6	–
Government	7%	2	4	6	–	23
Purpose of output mail %						
Acknowledge input	12%	12	9	17	10	7
Reply to written request	33%	20	39	33	26	51
Reply to information received	10%	4	4	14	18	7
Forward information to subordinate	23%	24	13	27	34	9
Forward request to subordinate[a]	7%	2	13	8	6	12
Write to 3rd party re input	3%	6	9	–	4	2
Acknowledge or reply to verbal contact	6%	18	4	–	–	9
Write report	2%	4	9	–	–	2
Originate letter or memo	3%	8	–	1	2	1

[a] That is, delegate task of handling the request to a subordinate.

to sign a letter to a client), and some, because of legal restrictions (Manager E validated a statement of expenditures). (c) Finally, independents made a number of requests of the managers: Manager C was asked by a girl who saw him on television to explain why she was having difficulty in becoming a nurse, and Manager D received a number of requests for free merchandise. Surprisingly, the managers reacted to almost all of this mail, and these reactions accounted for nearly one-third of the output.

3. *Solicitations.* Similar to status requests were solicitations. One-third of solicitations came from trade organizations, universities, and consultants who requested that the organizations participate in seminars; another third from manufacturers, lawyers, publishers, and so on, who attempted to sell products or services; and one-fifth came from people seeking employment. Of the 33 solicitations received, only 2 were judged to be consequential—an offer to sell a nearby piece of property to the hospital, and an offer of financing, which came on the heels of a discussion calling for just such an arrangement. Again, the managers reacted frequently. The reactions to solicitations and to status requests, taken together, accounted for a full 40 percent of the managers' output.

4. *Authority Requests.* An average of once per day the managers received a written authority request from a subordinate (a) seeking authorization for an *exception* to normal operating procedures (to show a client an internal report, to allow a teacher to take a leave of absence), (b) seeking approval for a *new program or procedure* (to approve a new pay scale), or (c) seeking acceptance for a *decision or report,* usually associated with a resource or policy commitment (to give the go-ahead on construction or to bring in a consultant). In essence, the manager was presented with one alternative, and was asked to give a yes-or-no answer. As would be expected, most of these received replies, half containing immediate affirmations.

5. *Reference Data.* A large proportion of mail—1 piece in 7—contained information which was to be used for reference only. (a) Some came from the organization—meeting agendas, résumés of new employees, for example. (b) Another large portion came from outside organizations, not so much for the manager as for his organization: annual reports of clients, address changes, statements of industrial policy by trade organizations, and so on. (c) Finally, trade organizations and external boards of directors sent correspondence concerning scheduling arrangements. Reference mail received cursory attention. Much of it was skimmed; only one-fifth stimulated responses.

6. *General Reports.* Each day an average of 2 reports, clippings, or books of general interest crossed the managers' desks. (a) More than one-third of these come from subordinates and were related to topics in which the manager had expressed an interest. (b) The remaining two-thirds of the general reports were received without direct or indirect solicitation. They came either as internal reports which a subordinate felt the manager should see, or as external reports which an outsider felt the manager or his organization should have (a report on nursing wages from a trade organization, a report on optimum advertising expenditures from a trade organization). About half of

this information was skimmed, and 19 percent was studied in depth. One piece in 5 elicited a reaction; most often, information was forwarded to a subordinate.

7. *Periodical News.* A large amount of mail consisted of magazines and commercial newsletters from trade organizations and private services. These were classified as: (a) general news (*New York Times*), (b) management journals and newsletters (*AMA Management Review*), (c) trade journals and newsletters (*Massachusetts Hospital Association Newsletter*), (d) business and financial news (*Wall Street Journal*), (e) political news (*Washington Reports*), (f) technological journals (*Journal of Public Health, Science*), and (g) house organs. These were handled in an almost ritualistic manner—very few were studied, two-thirds were skimmed, and action was taken on only 4 of the 102 received during the five weeks.

8. *Events.* Subordinates, trade organizations, and a variety of personal contacts dispatched about 2 pieces of mail daily designed to keep the managers informed of events in their environments. (a) Some of this mail related the *organization to its environment* (a clipping of an article mentioning the organization). (b) Some noted *upcoming events at trade organizations.* (c) Another large group referred to *personal contacts* (notice of a friend receiving a new appointment), *competitors* (a clipping discussing research finding of a competitor, letter from trade organization announcing unionization of a hospital), or *clients* (letter on progress of newly formed client). (d) A final group informed the manager of *political events* (report on state delegation to Washington). As the examples indicate, this information came in a variety of forms as direct letters and memos, as letters forwarded by subordinates, and as reports and clippings. Some of the information was forwarded to subordinates.

9. *Reports on Operations.* Mail relating to the operations of the managers' organizations accounted for 18 percent of the total input. (a) *Regular internal reports* averaged 2 per day (annual report of company's medical center, transcript of accounts). (b) *Ad hoc reports* on specific programs averaged almost 3 per day (progress on client contact, action taken on legal suit, report on development of new social studies unit). (c) Furthermore, it was common for the manager to receive *unsolicited letters from clients and independents* commenting on service (praise for a consulting report, complaint about a salesman, reaction to a television advertisement). Although much of this last type of correspondence was addressed simply to "The President," it was read faithfully.

Reports on operations received varying degrees of attention —a few were studied, most were read or skimmed. Surprisingly, of the 40 routine operating reports received, in only 2 cases did the manager react overtly to something he read. Ad hoc reports on progress elicited somewhat more frequent response (7 out of

65), as did client comments (4 out of 11). The response usually was a forwarding of the information to a subordinate, or an acknowledgement.

10. *Advice on Situations.* Subordinates and, to some extent, retained experts were used by the managers to give advice on current, usually strategic, situations. The advice often included background data resulting from an investigation, a listing of alternatives, an analysis, and *specific* recommendations. Examples were: a memo on the desire of a firm to affiliate, with the comment, "I conclude that there appears to be no ready avenue for [our] participation"; a report on a joint venture in a foreign country; a report on the costs of keeping playgrounds open in the summertime. This mail was treated carefully—all reports were read, and most of the information was used in strategy-making meetings.

11. *Problems and Pressures.* An infrequent but important type of mail was the correspondence that carried information related to *clearly-defined* problems, demands, and pressures. These came from subordinates, and from outside associates, like clients and suppliers. The managers reacted frequently, replying or forwarding the correspondence to a subordinate. The examples were varied: a charity organization asking why the firm did not make a donation, a change demanded by a client in work done, a petition from department heads requesting creation of a new committee, a clipping of a competitor's advertisement with a letter noting infringement of copyright, a request by a parent to redistrict so that his children could attend school closer to home.

12. *Ideas.* Occasionally—on the average of twice per week—a letter containing an unsolicited idea reached the managers' desks. Some of these came from subordinates, others from personal contacts, still others from independents hoping their ideas would receive consideration. These ideas were not ignored. Most were acknowledged or replied to, or were forwarded to the appropriate person. In one case a letter came from a friend of Manager A advising him of the opportunity for a consulting contract in a large school system; in another case a consultant gave Manager B information on a possible acquisition; Manager D was informed of a new invention.

13. *Self-initiated Mail.* Only once per day, on the average, the manager initiated a piece of mail. More often than not it was an inconsequential one—acknowledging a visit, a presentation, or a verbal request, or scheduling an appointment. The few more important pieces of self-initiated mail were designed to (a) pressure a subordinate to complete overdue work, (b) inform directors of the docket for a meeting (one included the chief executive's annual statement), and (c) inform subordinates of the events of a recent trip.

The Contact Record

Table 13 contains the results of the analysis of the 368 *contact records*. In most parts of the table, data are recorded in two ways—by frequency and by proportion of time. Thus, for example, telephone calls accounted for 36 percent of all contacts and 8 percent of all time in verbal contact. The figures are broken down in terms of media, number of participants, form of initiation, location, and purpose.

The managers' days were characterized by a large number of brief, informal two-person contacts (telephone calls and unscheduled meetings), and relatively few scheduled meetings, which nevertheless took most of their time. Subordinates consumed about half the managers' contact time and were involved in two-thirds of the contacts. Other contacts were distributed among a wide variety of outsiders, many of them peers, associates, and codirectors on outside boards. The managers initiated less than one-third of their contacts, and only 5 percent were scheduled regularly. Their offices were used for many of the short contacts, while longer-lasting contacts often occurred in the conference rooms or away from the organizations.

Again, the key results derive from the categorization of purpose. Thirteen categories are described in detail below, a few of which parallel directly those of the mail analysis. Seven deal with secondary activities and requests, four with information flow, and two with decision-making. This material forms the basic description of what five chief executives did during observation.

1. *Nonmanagerial Work.* In only one case did a manager undertake work that was considered to be nonmanagerial—in this instance he was involved in the specialized work of his organization. Even in this case it was his managerial skill that caused the manager to become involved. Manager A was asked to "role play" director of a company to which a consulting report of his firm was submitted for preliminary review. The work was part of a consulting contract; his time was billed to the client; and although he was acting as manager, Manager A was actually performing as consultant.

2. *Scheduling.* Brief, informal contacts for purposes of scheduling time (telephone calls and unscheduled meetings) were frequent. Most were conducted with subordinates; less than half were initiated by the managers; and most took place while the managers were at their desks.

3. *Ceremony.* One-eighth of the managers' time was consumed by ceremonial events that were usually scheduled, populous, and time-consuming. The examples of these were varied: dropping in to greet a new employee or saying farewell to a departing teacher, presenting a plaque to a retiring employee, speaking to a group visiting the hospital, attending the funeral of an

Table 13. Analysis of the Contact Record
Based on five weeks of observation

Category	Composite	Manager A	Manager B	Manager C	Manager D	Manager E
Total time in verbal contact	158 hrs	17	28	37	42	34
Total number of verbal contacts	368	65	55	71	106	71
Media: Percent of Contacts/Percent of Time						
Telephone calls	36%/8%[a]	42/14	49/12	42/8	21/5	38/7
Scheduled meetings	29%/76%	25/60	25/75	38/79	17/69	42/88
Unscheduled meetings	27%/13%	15/10	25/13	14/11	52/23	17/4
Tours	8%/3%	18/16	-/-	6/1	11/4	3/1
Size of: Scheduled Meetings/Unscheduled Meetings/Tours						
Percent with 2 people	44%/92%/17%	37/100/67	29/93/-	61/100/67	28/88/89	48/100/100
Percent with 3 people	14%/4%/12%	25/-/25	14/-/-	4/-/-	22/4/-	11/-/-
Percent with 4 people	9%/3%/4%	13/-/-	14/7/-	4/-/-	11/3/11	7/-/-
Percent with more than 4 people[b]	34%/1%/8%	25/-/8	43/-/-	32/-/33	39/2/-	33/-/-
Participants: Percent of Contacts/Percent of Time						
Subordinate	64%/48%	66/60	59/34	54/50	77/39	65/61
Director	6%/7%	6/2	4/5	14/10	-/-	11/17
Codirector	5%/5%	9/19	14/12	3/3	1/0.3	1/0.3
Peer and trade organization	3%/11%	-/-	-/-	10/28[c]	2/16	3/1
Client	2%/3%	8/9	-/-	-/-	-/-	6/10
Supplier and associate	9%/17%	8/6	20/48	1/0.3	9/24	10/9
Independent and other	9%/8%	3/3	4/1	18/8	12/21	4/2
Form of Initiation: Percent of Total Contacts						
Manager	32%	52	25	27	27	30
Opposite party	57%	43	66	58	64	52
Mutual	5%	2	5	-	6	10
Clock	7%	3	4	15	3	8

Location: Percent of Contacts/Percent of Time

	Percent of Contacts/Percent of Time					
Manager's office	75%/39%	87/39	86/38	66/41	75/38	85/47
Office of subordinate	10%/8%	22/18	11/11	8/6	10/9	1/0.3
Hall or plant	3%/1%	3/3	2/1	7/1	4/1	–/–
Conference or board room	3%/14%	3/19	5/28	8/16	4/10	1/4
Away from organization	8%/38%	5/21	7/23	10/36	8/43	13/48

Purpose of Contact: Percent of Contacts/Percent of Time

Organizational work	.3%/2%	2/17	–/–	–/–	–/–	–/–
Scheduling	15%/3%	14/5	18/3	12/1	22/4	11/1
Ceremony	6%/12%	9/12	–/–	4/5	5/15	10/25[d]
External board work	2%/5%	6/19	7/13	1/3	–/–	–/–
Total Secondary	23%/21%	31/53	25/16	17/9	27/19	21/26
Status requests and solicitations	5%/1%	5/3	4/1	11/2	3/0.5	4/1
Action requests	17%/12%	8/3	20/9	25/22	13/5	20/16
Manager requests	12%/5%	12/7	11/3	10/6	14/9	10/2
Total Requests and Solicitations	34%/18%	25/13	35/13	45/30	30/15	34/19
Observational tours	2%/1%	6/4	–/–	1/0	3/1	–/–
Receiving information	14%/16%	9/4	7/5	10/22	24/29	11/7
Giving information	10%/8%	14/8	9/3	14/13	4/5	13/9
Review	10%/16%	11/10	5/3	13/25	10/22	8/11
Total Informational	36%/40%	40/26	21/11	37/60	41/57	32/27
Strategy	6%/13%	5/8	13/24	1/2	3/8	10/22
Negotiation	1%/8%	–/–	5/36	–/–	3/8	3/5
Total Decision-making	7%/21%	5/8	18/60	1/2	3/8	13/27

[a] This means 36% of all verbal contacts and 8% of all time in verbal contacts were spent on the telephone.
[b] Most involved more than eight people.
[c] Includes one seven-hour conference.
[d] Includes a number of year-end dinners.

employee's brother. A majority of these meetings were held with subordinates, the rest with various outsiders. Most were arranged by subordinates, but others, such as retirements and funerals, were scheduled by the clock! These meetings usually took the managers away from their offices to specially designated locations.

4. *External Board Work.* The managers were involved to a limited extent in the work of the boards of directors of other organizations. In addition to actual board meetings, there were occasional contacts with codirectors on issues facing the boards. This work was infrequent but of long duration, and it generally took the managers from their offices and gave them the opportunity to interact with their peers. Once they had made the initial decision to join a board, the managers had little control over the scheduling of time devoted to external board work.

5. *Status Requests and Solicitations.* On the average of almost once per day the managers were approached (usually by the telephone) by peers, suppliers, or other outsiders, who wished to make inconsequential requests of them. Related largely to their status, these requests included invitations to attend or speak at some function, to join boards, to send documents, and to make contacts. They also included simple solicitations. Manager C received a few telephone calls from personal and professional associates asking that friends in the hospital be given special care. In one case a man set up an appointment with the chief executive by telling his secretary he was "an old friend"— and then attempted to sell him soap to wash the floors of his hospital.

6. *Action Requests.* Far more important, frequent, and time-consuming were the "action" requests of various types made of the managers: (a) One-third were requests by subordinates for *authorization*—that the manager approve a new program or policy, or an exception to an existing policy. Manager D was told about a sales plan for one product line and was asked to give a go-ahead. Manager E was approached by a teacher who was applying for Fulbright funds and needed the official sponsorship of his school system: "They said the next step is to see you, to see if we can garner your support."

(b) Another 42 percent of these requests were for *information:* current information to which the managers had access; special organizational information, such as plans, policies, or costs; opinions and values; and advice on personal problems. In one case an executive telephoned Manager B to find out what occurred at a meeting that he had left a half hour early.

(c) In another 10 percent of the cases the managers were asked to *initiate* something. Could Manager C make a certain point at the meeting of the Ladies Auxiliary?

(d) Finally, 18 percent of the requests consisted of *influencing pressures*—attempts to influence the manager with regard to pending or unresolved decisions. Related to a vacancy, Manager B received a number of telephone calls from various employees who made suggestions and requests (for example, "appoint a local man"). Manager E received a parent who wished to complain about a teacher, and two principals who wished to complain about an overlooked promotion. These requests often came in the form of telephone calls and unscheduled meetings; they took an average of 18 minutes and consumed one-eighth of the managers' contact time.

7. *Manager Requests.* In 12 percent of their contacts the managers made requests of the opposite parties. Thus the managers made about half as many requests as others made of them, and they made these requests quickly—these contacts averaged 11 minutes in duration. The managers used the telephone for half of their requests, but they also made frequent use of tours and scheduled and unscheduled meetings. Manager requests were of three types:

(a) Half the time subordinates were asked for *information or advice.* "Can you use an engineer, a friend of mine, who is out of work?" "Do you know anything about the advertising display in Geneva?"

(b) In another 40 percent of the cases the manager asked an aide to take action on an issue or idea of current interest (that is, the manager *delegated* a task). In one lengthy meeting a foreign associate was asked to begin negotiations on the acquisition of a supplier. Manager D asked an assistant to investigate a promotional idea that he had been considering.

(c) The remaining manager requests were *follow-ups* on previous requests—"I was thinking about the lead; I wonder if we shouldn't follow it up more aggressively."

8. *Observational Tours.* Occasionally the managers left their offices for brief periods of time, to greet someone in the hall, to see something of interest, or just to tour the organization.

9. *Receiving Information.* Many of the managers' activities, taking 16 percent of their total contact time, were devoted strictly to the receiving of information of various kinds. (a) More than one-third of this was *instant communication* [4]—very current information rushed to the manager by telephone or unscheduled meeting while it was still "hot." In one case a deputy [5] rushed into the manager's office and declared: "Harry Jamison will call—Elmwood man—feels that Mr. Flagdale was forced out—wished to object—wants a hearing."

Few of these "instant communication" interactions brought widely known, well-defined, or factual information. Rather, the information often took the form of gossip, hearsay, and opinion —for example, "I don't like to bear rumours but—Larry

---

[4] This term is borrowed from Manager C.
[5] See No. 11 below for a description of the term "deputy."

Holmes just got back last night and he spent the night with Tremblay!" This type of information flow appeared to be rather important to the managers.

(b) Another 28 percent of these informational sessions took the form of *briefings,* usually at scheduled meetings and usually by subordinates or hired experts such as consultants. The executive staff of organization D attended a presentation by a market research consultant on consumer reactions to its products; Manager E was briefed on an analysis related to keeping gymnasium facilities open.

(c) In the remaining cases, the managers obtained information by interviewing prospective employees, by attending conferences, and by listening to advice and to various comments of subordinates.

10. *Giving Information.* The managers spent 8 percent of their time in contacts where they simply gave information to the opposite party. Half as much time was spent here as was spent in contacts where the managers simply received information. The former averaged 20 minutes' duration as contrasted with 30 minutes for "receiving information" sessions. "Giving information" sessions may be categorized as follows:

(a) The largest group, taking 43 percent of contact time, involved the passing of *instant communication* from the manager to the opposite party. For example, Manager A went to a staffer's office to tell him about some information he had received at a board meeting about a possible contract.

The balance of the information given verbally by the manager divided approximately equally between (b) *plans and policies* (Manager B telling a meeting of salesmen about a sales policy to be enforced), (c) *advice* (Manager B advising a subordinate how to handle an acquisition negotiation), and (d) various other kinds (telling about a trip abroad). Much of this verbal output was directed at subordinates, although associates, directors, and various others received a share. This informing was frequently undertaken on the managers' own initiative, in their own offices, and on the telephone (half the cases).

11. *Review.* In all, 16 percent of the managers' time was taken by review sessions—contacts characterized by the discussion of a wide range of issues and by a clear, *two-way* process of information flow. Review sessions tended to be long, averaging 40 minutes' duration, and were frequently initiated by the clock. About half occurred in the managers' offices. Six distinct types seemed to recur:

(a) One-third are labeled *deputy reviews.* Certain close subordinates met with the chief executive periodically to discuss many issues that both felt were current and important. In the words of the participants, they met "to clean the slate" or to check to see if there was "anything on the griddle." These sessions generally occurred regularly or after a prolonged absence of one party.

It appeared common for the manager to designate implicitly one subordinate as deputy—the man with whom all important events and problems could be discussed, against whom all possible strategies could be tested, and from whom much important instant communication, especially related to the workings of the organization, could be received. Most meetings with him tended to be open-ended and general (that is, review sessions), while a meeting with one of the others tended to have one specific purpose (making a request, giving information, receiving information).

Deputy review sessions, while regularly held, were seldom explicitly scheduled, and could take place in the office of either participant.

An example will serve to illustrate this kind of activity. In one of these sessions the deputy (the president) began by informing Manager A (the chairman) of a meeting he had had. The deputy then gave his views on the type of planning function he thought the organization should have, ending with a recommendation that the subject be put on the agenda of an upcoming meeting. Manager A concurred. Mention was made of negotiations on a foreign joint venture, and then the men discussed certain scheduling arrangements. Manager A showed the president a copy of a letter of praise from a client, and then the discussion returned to the foreign venture. Manager A asked if the deputy thought the return-on-investment might be higher than predicted, and the deputy commented that he thought not but that the venture would be an effective means of developing contacts in that part of the world. The discussion then turned to the congressional hearings, the chairman expressing his concern to the president, and the latter giving advice.

In one deputy review session, Manager E and an executive discussed fully 15 distinct issues in the 18 minutes that the meeting lasted.

(b) Over one-third of the review sessions fall under a second heading, *functional review*. These sessions usually involved a large number of people at scheduled meetings, and were used to review one functional area of the organization's operations. For example, the hospital had a number of special weekly staff meetings; at Organization D, the visit of the new IBM representative was taken as an opportunity to review various aspects of the data-processing operation. In general, these sessions involved a wide variety of purposes—information flowed to and from the manager, requests were made of him to give authorization or to express value judgments. Work was delegated by the manager, and strategic decisions were made. In fact, these sessions often combined many of the purposes of contacts discussed in the previous and following points, although *receiving* and *giving information* tended to predominate.

(c) Three other kinds of review sessions were held, although less frequently. During *contact review,* the manager met, usually in a social milieu, with a personal contact—an old employee, a peer, a competitor—to discuss the events and the problems of the trade. One chief executive commented before one of these meetings, "We'll trade rumors."

(d) When a man joins a new organization, he accumulates a large number of questions on organizational procedures, special arrangements that he requires, and so on. In the *new-man reviews,* the chief executives met with new, high-ranking subordinates to clear up these questions and decide on the requests for special attention. In addition, they discussed the problems and the future of the departments that the new man would run.

(e) *Post-meeting review* sessions brought the manager and another participant, usually a deputy, together, often for only moments, to review the events of the meeting. Such sessions often turned into deputy reviews when other topics were discussed.

(f) Finally, two of the review sessions observed were in the form of *organizational board meetings.* These were large meetings, held in the board room. Such meetings were usually scheduled on a clocked basis. These two meetings followed fairly well-defined patterns. First, the chief executive presented his report, which included current information (for example, correspondence), a report on the outlook for the organization, and briefings on results of operations and particular programs. The chief executive then requested a number of formal authorizations from the board—to pass on the appointment of certain new executives, to amend a retirement plan, and so on. Special issues ("old business") were then discussed, board members expressed their opinions, and decisions were made. Finally, the directors took the opportunity during "new business" to question the chief executive on various issues of concern to them and to raise new problems for discussion.

Two features of the board meetings that were observed are worth noting. The board meetings focused on the chief executive. He had the information, he understood the issues, and it is to him that the responsibility for action was delegated by the board. The directors played rather passive roles, spending most of their time simply receiving information from the chief executive. There was an atmosphere of formality at these sessions. In particular, the requests by the manager for authorization were primarily formal ones that were rubber-stamped without much consequential discussion.

12. *Strategy.* During the five weeks of observation, there were a total of 21 meetings that were classified as dealing with strategy (important organizational decisions). Because these were particularly long meetings, they consumed 13 percent of the managers' contact time. Various kinds of strategy sessions were observed.

(a) Some were concerned with the making of a *key decision* about an organizational program to be undertaken, to solve a particular problem or to exploit a particular opportunity. For example, Manager A met with a number of his senior executives to decide whether or not to proceed on a foreign joint venture. (b) In some sessions, the managers handled particular *crises,* for example, a severe conflict between two subordinates. (c) In a few cases, explicit *operational planning* (budgeting, allocation of resources, or target-setting) was undertaken. For example, Manager D met with his marketing executives to set the annual sales targets. (d) Finally, in only one case was open-ended *strategic planning* conducted. Manager E met with a group of teachers (he did regularly) in a "think group" atmosphere, to look for general problems and discuss new opportunities.

Strategy was usually developed with subordinates, and occasionally with directors or with outside experts (for example, underwriters). Usually more than four people were involved and the meetings were scheduled. Few sessions were initiated by the manager, and their locations varied widely.

Two points should be noted. First, strategy-making was very much intertwined with the activities categorized elsewhere (giving and receiving information, requests for authorization, even scheduling). Second, in observing the strategy sessions, it was possible to note a number of their characteristics: Major decisions were broken into a number of component decisions; the manager took full charge in the event of a crisis; the manager juggled a large number of strategy issues; the manager, not the group, tended to make the major decisions; timing and delay were key factors in these decisions.

13. *Negotiation.* The managers were involved occasionally in negotiation sessions. In these cases they met with outsiders in attempts to reach agreements between their two organizations. Manager B spent some time negotiating with firms that his organization wished to acquire; Manager E with two members of a consulting organization to work out a costing conflict. All negotiation sessions were of long duration, averaging over two hours. They involved a number of participants from both organizations, and usually took place in the office of a subordinate or in the board or conference room.

Reliability of the Results

At this point, before closing our discussion of the results of the field work, we address ourselves to the question of the reliability of the research sample. Evidence from this study and from other work suggests (a) that the one-week periods were representative of each man's work, (b) that these men were, in their work, typical of chief executives of large organizations, and (c) that important basic similarities exist between the types of jobs studied here and those of other managers.

First, there is reason to believe that the observational periods were representative of the usual mix of work for these men. Data on the scheduled meetings of a previous month were compared with what was observed during the one week. The frequency of meetings, the types of participants, and the duration of meetings were similar for the two samples. The five research subjects, as well as their secretaries, commented on the representativeness of the observational periods. Thus, the small sample chosen was probably as "typical" of these men's dynamic jobs as any could be.[6]

Second, some support for the choice of only five chief executives is provided by the surprising amount of consistency in the data collected during the five observational periods. Although each of the five men was observed for a period of only one week, and although their five organizations were quite different, the results indicate that there were remarkable similarities in their work activities. For the most part, each was active in each of the areas that were categorized. Each man interacted with the same types of people—each formally reported to a board of directors (even if it was not specifically called that); each dealt with a number of trade organizations; each interacted with suppliers and some equivalent of clients; each found it necessary to deal directly with the federal government; each interacted with peers and independents. Not only did the five men seem to do the same kinds of things, but for many of the activities the same general proportions held for all five men. Strong similarities appeared, for example, in the following: the frequency of documented and verbal contact with subordinates, the quantity of mail on internal operations, the frequency of desk work sessions, the number and duration of telephone calls, the proportion of time spent in scheduled meetings, the proportion of activities lasting less than 9 and more than 60 minutes, the quantity of self-initiated mail, the proportion of mail in reply to written requests, the average size of meetings, the proportion of activities initiated by contacts, the location of activities.

A variety of differences were also present. Some of these do not detract from the common conclusions. For example, although one man had relatively short scheduled meetings (average duration of 40 minutes), and another, relatively long ones (98 minutes), it was still

---

[6] There was once clear bias in the choice of observational period. Although some of the chief executives' time was spent in long-distance travel, it was obviously necessary to choose a week in which intercity travel was limited. Nevertheless, there was some travel, the appropriate data were recorded, and I was satisfied that no activity which differed in kind from that recorded was undertaken during periods of travel. Obviously, the mix of activities would vary during travel periods as would the quantity of correspondence processed.

possible to conclude that, compared with the other media, scheduled meetings were by far of the longest average duration. Some other differences were of greater significance, and here of course one could not draw general conclusions. These differences are discussed in detail in the next section.

Third, other empirical studies suggest that the basic work of these five men, as observed, is similar to that of managers in other jobs. As we saw in Chapter 3, the findings on job characteristics are supported by the diary studies. Furthermore, most of the conclusions on job roles, as they derive from the analysis of work content, are supported by a number of studies reported in the literature (particularly in that of Sayles, 1964) and by two followup studies—one on chief executives of small businesses and one on middle managers in industry and government. The reader's attention is drawn particularly to the first of these—the structured-observation study of the chief executives of three small firms by Irving Choran (1969), which showed results surprisingly similar to my own in many ways.

WORK DIFFERENCES AMONG THE FIVE CHIEF EXECUTIVES

The work of the five men of my study was analyzed as to differences. The sample was too small to draw any firm conclusions. Nevertheless, a number of interesting, if speculative, findings emerged which led to some of the hypotheses presented in Chapter 5. The unique features of each of the five managers are described below.

Manager A. Compared with the other four chief executives of my study, Manager A (of the consulting firm) exerted far more control over his activities, taking more tours (12 versus 4)[7] and initiating more of his letters and contacts (31 percent and 52 percent versus 6 percent and 28 percent). Furthermore, he spent more of his time with external contacts, particularly clients (9 percent versus 2 percent) and codirectors (19 percent versus 3 percent), and he wrote more frequently to clients (22 percent versus 3 percent of output mail).

Three factors could enter into the analysis of these differences— the liaison needs of a consulting firm, Manager A's reputation, and the existence of a president who reported to him, the chairman and chief executive officer. In this case the president probably involved himself more deeply in internal issues, leaving the chief executive with free time to initiate more of his own activities, to spend more time touring, and to develop, maintain, and use his system of contacts. Manager A

[7] All figures compare the results for one man with the average for the other four. See Tables 10–13 above for the presentation of the actual data.

participated actively on external boards of directors; he reacted to many status requests; he developed his reputation. His role as critic of governmental strategy was clearly relevant in this last regard. His reputation helped him in his search for contract leads; it was also of use to his organization in that prospective clients were brought to meet him, and certain important letters were sent out over his signature.

Turning to other differences in his work, there is clear evidence that Manager A preferred short contacts. His scheduled meetings were brief (40 versus 74 minutes on average), and very few of his activities lasted longer than 60 minutes (5 percent versus 11 percent). This apparent preference for brevity was in all likelihood nothing more than personal style, as his secretary noted at the start of the research. Manager A also received more mail dealing with internal operations (34 versus 21 pieces). This reflects the fact that he maintained close watch on a number of contracts in which he was personally involved. But, then, one would expect a consulting firm to emphasize internal communication of a formal and analytical nature—operating reports, periodic briefings on projects, and such.

Manager B. The work of Manager B, president of the firm producing industrial technological products, was characterized by emphasis on strategy and negotiation (60 percent versus 13 percent of contact time). Much time was spent for these purposes in large meetings, often with suppliers and associates. In fact, the company was, at the time of the study, deeply involved in an expansion program, and the president spent a very great proportion of his time (1) working out acquisition and negotiation strategies with his staff, (2) negotiating with people on acquisitions, and (3) making associated arrangements concerning expansion financing.

Manager B engaged in no internal touring or ceremony; he forwarded little of his mail into the organization; and he spent little time solely for purposes of verbal information transfer. These characteristics may be attributed in part to a lack of time due to his efforts in the expansion program. However, considering that he received little mail from his subordinates, the suggestion can be made that his organization placed relatively little emphasis on internal formal communication. (In fact, this point was verified by a company study that I read after drawing this conclusion.)

The same cannot be said for external communication. There was much mail from suppliers and associates, (20 versus 8 pieces), a good part of this dealing with acquisition activity, and much from the government (13 versus 5 pieces). Because of the technological nature of the industry, the government was a key client and participant in the company's affairs. Manager B received a great number of periodicals (58 versus 12); this fact may be explained by the nature of the industry—the president was forced to keep abreast of a rapidly changing technology. Finally, his high incidence of contact with co-directors (14 percent versus 3 percent of contacts) is explained by Manager B's executive position in the local chamber of commerce.

Manager C. A divergent array of work differences appear for Manager C of the hospital. However, a close examination indicates that they may fall into three groups.

1. Due to the particularly high status in the field of medicine of both the hospital and its director, Manager C was required to interact frequently with peers and trade organizations (10 percent versus 1 percent of contacts). Many status requests and solicitations were made of him (11 percent versus 3 percent of verbal contacts) and a large number of trade publications were submitted to him for review (20 percent versus 5 percent of mail from trade organizations). No doubt all hospital administrators receive a large number of status requests from members of the communities they serve. Furthermore, there appears to be a well-developed communication system in the hospital community, particularly with regard to the distribution of medical reports. The prestige of Manager C and his hospital served to magnify these characteristics.

2. The internal workings of this organization (and no doubt, of hospitals in general) were characterized by a very high level of internal democracy. The professional staffers were highly trained, high-income individuals who conducted many of their affairs as they alone saw fit. In simple terms, there tended to be much internal "political" activity, and this influenced the chief executive's work. His unscheduled meetings were longer (24 versus 11 minutes on average)—people who dropped in had to be allowed to state their cases. As might further be expected in this milieu, the flow of documented information was lighter, while verbal information flowed more freely. Information related to organizational politics is seldom documented. Thus, one found in this organization a high frequency of meetings in the hall (7 percent versus 2 percent of contacts), a high frequency of two person (tête-à-tête) scheduled meetings (61 percent versus 45 percent), a large proportion of Manager C's verbal contact time devoted to information processing (60 percent versus 34 percent), and little mail concerned with internal operations (8 percent versus 21 percent).

3. The similarities between the hospital and the school system with regard to a number of factors, such as the frequency of clocked meetings and contacts with directors, suggest the existence of a number of dissimilarities between business and public-service organizations. These are discussed in the section on Manager E.

Manager D. Manager D of the firm that produced consumer goods engaged in much more informal activity (55 versus 12 unscheduled meetings) for purposes of receiving or giving information. Of the five organizations in which my study took place, this was perhaps the one that found itself in the most competitive environment. Competitor actions had to be monitored continually to detect events—a new advertising program, the marketing of a new product, a price cut—that could signal the need for an immediate readjustment of strategy.

As a result, the prominent characteristics of the organization were flexibility and informality, and the organization equipped itself with a chief executive who spent much of his time receiving information (29 percent versus 11 percent of contact time), particularly instant communication. Much of this information was transmitted by subordinates who had ready and informal access to the chief executive through the medium of the unscheduled meeting. Furthermore, Manager D took more tours (11 versus 5) during which information was transmitted, and he spent much time interacting with external contacts for the purpose of trading current industry information.

It would appear that informality had become a way of life at his organization. The unscheduled meeting was used frequently, even when the information to be transmitted could easily wait. For example, in a number of cases a subordinate who developed an idea came unexpectedly to the office of the president to tell him about it. He did not schedule a meeting or transmit his idea in memo form.

It is interesting to note that at this organization, which was characterized by informality, a good many of the chief executive's contacts were devoted to scheduling of his activity (22 percent versus 8 percent). This may be contrasted with the findings for the chief executives of the two public-service organizations. They attended a much larger number of clocked meetings (15 and 8 percent versus 3 percent for Manager D) and spent little time scheduling their activity (1 percent each versus 4 percent for him). Thus, as might be expected, Manager D paid the price of informality—the need to spend more time just to coordinate his efforts with those of his executives.

Two other points might be noted. At the time of the study the firm lacked a vice president of marketing, and the president assumed that role. Perhaps this explains why Manager D spent such long hours at work (53 versus 37 hours), many of which were devoted to scanning marketing reports. Finally, the length of his scheduled meetings (98 versus 62 minutes) reflects Manager D's enjoyment of discussion and his desire to seek information whenever and wherever possible.

Manager E. The activities of Manager E of the public school system were in direct contrast to those of Manager D. His work was characterized by greater formality—for example, a higher incidence of scheduled and clocked meetings (30 and 6 versus 18 and 3 for Manager D). Many of these took place in the evening. Many of Manager E's meetings were with directors and clients (11 percent and 6 percent versus 5 percent and 1 percent of contacts for the others), and many were devoted to ceremony and strategy-making (10 percent and 10 percent versus 5 percent and 5 percent of all contacts). Furthermore, Manager E received a large number of status and authority requests in the mail (30 percent and 12 percent versus 10 percent and 4 percent).

Perhaps it might be argued that public organizations adopt formalized patterns of behavior because of the complex system of forces in which they find themselves. While Manager D may have to answer occasionally to powerful shareholders, Manager E is continually dealing with the mayor and other municipal authorities, the state educational department, the school committee, the parent-teachers association, individual parent, and individual residents. Certain kinds of informal behavior might lead to communication problems where formal behavior might not. Thus, in Manager E's work there were more scheduled meetings, more clocked meetings, more formal authority requests, and a tendency to present analyses in the form of printed reports. Manager E received more status requests and he spent more time with clients (that is, parents) simply because he had to make himself easily available to outsiders. At the hospital, which may be considered a quasi-public organization, Manager C's work exhibited the same tendencies, particularly with regard to the frequency of written status requests and the frequency of scheduled and clocked meetings.

The work of Managers C and E was also characterized by relatively frequent contact with the organizations' directors (17 percent and 10 percent versus 2 percent, 5 percent, and 0 percent for the other three). It would appear that the role of the director in overseeing activity and relating it to the wishes of member groups is somewhat more significant in the public organization. Aside from well-defined groups of owners and employees, few people would be directly concerned if the business firms made a serious mistake in strategy. In contrast, the public of the city, the medical profession that looks to the prestige hospital, and the local medical school, all were deeply concerned in special ways about the decisions taken at the hospital. At the school system the concerns were even more pronounced. The municipal politicians, the parents, state government officials, and a variety of others, all looked very carefully over Manager E's shoulder. The decisions that he took in his organization affected the quality of education of a community of students who, for the most part, had no alternative source of formal education. The school committee (or board of trustees at the hospital) attempted to reflect the diverse and pronounced concerns of these groups; therefore, the school committee interacted more frequently with the chief executive.

Some other points about Manager E's work may be noted. He attributed his light mail (69 versus 148 pieces) to the fact that he was observed during the last week of the school year. And he participated in a number of ceremonial activities related to the yearend (25 percent versus 8 percent of contact time). Finally, one might note the quantity of mail Manager E sent to and received from governments (16 percent versus 4 percent of all mail). In a school system that received research and operating funds from various federal and state agencies, this quantity of mail was to be expected.

Clearly, this analysis is far from conclusive. The research was not designed to compare or categorize different types of managers' work. Nevertheless, the analysis does suggest that a number of variables influence the work of managers, including the following:

Nature of the industry: importance of liaison role in consulting; requirement for informality where competition is strong; reading of trade journals where technology is sophisticated.

Nature of the organization: many status requests at high-status hospital; more formality and more frequent contacts with directors and clients in public or quasi-public organizations; climate favoring little formal communication at one organization and much political activity at another.

Nature of the man's style: Manager A's preference to serve as liaison man, leaving operations to the president; Manager D's enjoyment of long discussions.

The needs of the moment: acquisition strategy at organization B; yearend dinners at Organization E.

The contingency theory introduced in Chapter 5 derives in part from these conclusions.

DEVELOPMENT OF THE THEORY

Figure 19 shows the development of the theory of this book. First, the data of observation were coded in terms of the three records. Then categories of components of the work were developed (as shown in Tables 10–13), and these were described in detail (as above). These findings formed one basis for the four bodies of theory presented in Chapters 3 through 6. The development of the theory on work characteristics was simple enough. The quantitative data suggested their own conclusions, and these were combined with those reached by the diary researchers to develop the six sets of characteristics presented in Chapter 3.

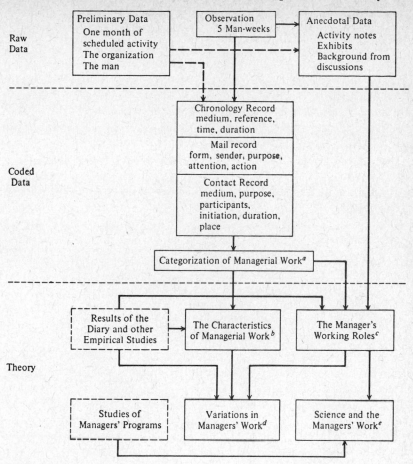

Figure 19. Outline of the Analysis

[a] See Tables 11–14.

[b] See Chapter 3.

[c] See Chapter 4.

[d] See Chapter 5.

[e] See Chapter 6.

The theory presented in Chapter 4, on the manager's working roles, involved a more complex analysis. We deal with this in some detail below. The theory of Chapter 5, on variations in managers' jobs, drew on the characteristics and roles of Chapters 3 and 4 as a basis for analyzing differences. Here I relied primarily on the findings of other empirical studies, but made some use of an analysis of the differences in work among the five managers of my study. Finally, the theory of Chapter 6 on the manager's programs was derived from studies of the managers' programs and indirectly from my theory of roles.

The basic framework of 10 managerial roles was derived from my own findings, particularly the 13 categories of the purposes of verbal contacts and mail. Results of other empirical studies were then used to enrich the theory and to support the contention that the basic content of all managers' work can be described in terms of these ten roles. I discuss below in some detail the derivation of the role set from the results of my study.

In developing my statement of managerial roles, I straddled two objectives—the provision of clear description to the general reader interested in understanding managerial work, and the establishment of a scientifically valid framework for further research. One objective required simplicity, the other precision. I achieved some of each, at the expense of each.

At best, role is a fuzzy concept. *Program* is a better concept, but it demands a greater knowledge of the subject than we now have. A statement of roles represent one attempt, among many that are possible, to slice up a job. There can be no correct or incorrect categorization of roles, just tighter and looser, more or less useful ones. The pragmatist will judge the usefulness of a theory by attempting to use it, the scientist, by the validity of the approach used to arrive at it. Both demands—that the theory be applicable and that it derive from rigorous methods—are reasonable.

But science can inhibit itself by being too demanding. The inductive process can never be rigorously explained. Bronowski argues this point eloquently on behalf of all inductive theorists in a classic article in *Scientific American* entitled "The Creative Process" (September, 1958). Pointing out that "A fact is discovered, a theory is invented. . . ." (p. 58), Bronowski states:

> The creative activity of science lies here in the process of induction. For induction imagines more than there is ground for and creates relations which at bottom can never be verified. Every induction is a speculation and it guesses at a unity which the facts present but do not strictly imply.
>
> To put the matter more formally: A scientific theory cannot be constructed from the facts by any procedure which can be laid down in advance, as if for a machine. To the man who makes the theory, it may seem as inevitable as the ending of *Othello* must have seemed to Shakespeare. But the theory is inevitable only to him; it is his choice, as a mind and as a person, among the alternatives which are open to everyone (p. 62).

The theory on manager's roles derives from the statements of *purpose* of the managers' mail and contacts, discussed at length above. For each distinct type of activity one question was asked repeatedly—

why did the manager do this? Why did he partake in ceremonial events; why did he collect and give out certain kinds of information; why did he make certain kinds of decision? A collection and categorization of the answers—some obvious, others not—led to a statement of roles.

For purposes of illustration, consider the following sequence of two episodes: A chief executive attends a meeting of an external board on which he sits. Upon his return to his organization, he immediately goes to the office of a subordinate, tells of a conversation he had with a fellow board member, and concludes with the statement, "It looks like we shall get the contract."

The purposes of these two contacts are clear—to attend an external board meeting, and to give current information to a subordinate. But why did the manager attend the meeting? Indeed, why does he belong to the board? And why did he give this particular information to his subordinate?

Basing analysis on this incident, one can argue as follows: The manager belongs to the board in part so that he can be exposed to special information that is of use to his organization. The subordinate needs the information but has not the status that would give him access to it. The chief executive, on the other hand, has the status necessary to interact with other chief executives who can provide this information. Board memberships bring chief executives into contact with one another for this purpose.

Two roles can be seen to emerge from this brief analysis—the *liaison* role (associated with the manager's status) in which he interacts with peers for the purpose, in part, of gaining information; and the *disseminator* role in which the manager transfers privileged information into his organization.

A repeat of this type of analysis for 368 verbal contacts and for 890 pieces of mail, categorized in various ways as to purpose, led to development of the theory of the manager's roles. In essence, it was found that most activities could be characterized as essentially interpersonal, informational, or decisional in nature. Hence our roles are divided into these three groupings.

In looking at the theory of roles for purposes of future work, researchers may ask how operational it is. Our simple answer is that it is not fully operational in the form presented, but that to make it so should not be a difficult task. The chief problem in doing so, as is made clear in the summary table at the end of Chapter 4, is that there is not a simple one-to-one mapping of activities onto roles. Some activities, such as "ceremony," link to one role (*figurehead*). Others, such as a meeting with an outsider, can link several roles (*liaison, spokesman, negotiator*). The *leader* role links to every activity involving subordinates, and the *monitor* role, to every activity involving information inputs to the manager, no matter what the main purposes of any of these activities.

Hence, the researcher interested in studying precisely how much time a given manager spends in each of these ten roles—an obvious next step for comparative research—must first develop some clearer mapping of activities onto roles. This should not be a difficult task. It may involve the making of a few arbitrary decisions, but the overall result should be generally valid and useful. One should have little difficulty observing a manager and then estimating the time he spends in the *figurehead, disseminator, liaison, spokesman,* and *negotiator* roles (although there may be some overlap in these last three). The *entrepreneur* and *disturbance handler* roles overlap at the margin (as discussed in Chapter 4), and it may be difficult to distinguish some activities in terms of these roles and the *resource allocator* role. However, most of these problems can probably be handled in a simple and reasonable way. It will be somewhat more difficult to determine how much time the manager spends in the *leader* role (and, to a lesser extent, the *monitor* role). The proportion of his work with subordinates that is expressly for interpersonal purposes will probably give a good *relative* indication of his involvement with the *leader* role (just as the amount of time spent expressly receiving information will probably provide a reasonably accurate estimate of his attention to the *monitor* role).

In closing, I should note that the theory of Chapter 4 was presented in the spirit of the opening quotation of that chapter—in the hope that it may serve to get us to better theories of the content of managerial work.

COMMENTS ON THE USE OF STRUCTURED OBSERVATION

Structured observation produced all the results expected of it. Induction was possible and facilitated by the structuring, and there were some problems in data collection and coding. Four issues merit attention—the difficulties of collecting certain kinds of data, unanticipated consequences due to the presence of an observer, difficulties due to the pace of the work, and the problems of coding.

Problems in Data Collection

Five kinds of activities presented difficulties in collecting data and therefore required improvisation.

Telephone calls: It was not possible to hear the other end of the conversation.

Evening work: Work at the manager's home could not be observed.

Activities away from the organization: It was frequently not possible to accompany the manager to meetings at other organizations (to board meetings, for example).

Missed meetings: From time to time the researcher was not allowed to attend a meeting. Interestingly, it was seldom because the meeting was confidential. Rather, these were meetings involving sensitive personal issues (for example, an employee explaining his departure). The chief executives appeared to have no qualms about my being exposed to strategically sensitive issues. It is also worth noting that in only one known case was correspondence withheld, and that, because it was officially designated as "secret" by the U.S. government.

Complex meetings: At times, a meeting was one of a series that took place over many months, involving intricate negotiations or problem-solving. Part of what took place was not understandable to an outsider. Only the highly structured data (duration, participants) could be recorded. It was difficult to infer the purpose of the meeting and impossible to record meaningful anecdotal notes. The same problem occurred, although less frequently, with telephone calls and mail.

One procedure was used to circumvent these five problems. The executive was asked to summarize, in a sentence or two, the information that was needed. After a short period of time each man came to understand what kinds of data were sought, and he had little trouble providing it. For example, after a telephone call in which the chief executive did little talking, I was told (1) who called and (2) the purpose of the call. For missed meetings, distant meetings, and complex meetings, a short, general résumé sufficed, while evening work was discussed during the next day.

In general, only a few specific questions could be asked during the day, but between 5 and 6 P.M. the manager and I would frequently converse for periods of one-half hour or more. At these times details on missed or confusing contacts and mail could be asked for, and the previous evening's activities could be reviewed. This was a time to learn also about the chief executive's thoughts—his impressions of his job and its related problems, his strategies and aspirations.

Effects of Presence of Researcher

Does the presence of a researcher influence the work that the manager does? There is reason to believe that it does not, although it may influence his style of performing the work.

The basic events of any manager's week are not subject to major change simply because a researcher is present. Scheduled meetings are set up well in advance, and incoming telephone calls and mail are not influenced by the presence of an observer. Perhaps it could be argued that fewer unscheduled meetings and originated calls would take place, but given the kinds of information to which I was exposed, there was no reason to believe that activities were delayed to avoid my being exposed to them.

There were some interesting consequences during scheduled meetings. Clearly the manager could get used to my presence as the week progressed, but to most participants at meetings, with the exception of a small bank of deputies who had frequent unscheduled contacts, the presence of a researcher was unexpected. In almost every case (the exceptions being very large meetings where my presence would not be noticed), introductions were necessary. When the manager was unsure whether the opposite party would agree to my presence, he usually asked about this during the introduction. This, of course, put the caller on the spot; and one chief executive would meet the man in the hall and put the question to him before the introduction. In no case, to my knowledge, did anyone express misgivings about my presence. Most of the time the only questions asked reflected an interest in the research being undertaken.

Once introductions were completed, various patterns set in. A few people were self-conscious, and would steal quick glances in my direction as if they did not believe the expressed explanation for my presence. Others sympathized with my mission and would direct some comments to me, particularly for purposes of clarification. In the vast majority of meetings, however, my presence seemed to be quickly forgotten.

In spite of the adjustments that took place during meetings, the main topic of research interest—purpose of activity—appeared to be unaffected. The presence of an observer will not change the basic purpose of a meeting, although it may change the style that the manager uses during the meeting. Since this was a study of work activity rather than of style, I conclude that the effects of the presence of the researcher were inconsequential.

Hectic Pace of the Work

Of particular relevance to those who plan research on managerial work—and here I especially include followers of both the diary and observational methods—is the workload associated simply with recording managerial activity.

Recording turned out to be a hectic, full-time job. There was an immense amount of data to be collected, and it frequently came in short, dense bursts. In effect, the researcher is tied to the schedule of the manager, which is often a hectic one. Related to *one* particular week of observation 334 pages of notes were collected, consisting of

124 pages of preliminary data (magazine articles, speeches, public relations releases, and so on), 5 sheets of chronology records, 72 sheets of mail records (60 raw rata, 12 coded), 119 sheets of contact records (111 raw data, 8 coded), and 14 pages of general notes.

Two factors that can have an important bearing on future research became very clear during observation. (1) The neat categories required for diary recording are not characteristic of managerial work. (2) The manager is far too busy to record properly. During the research one meeting of two people lasting 18 minutes covered 15 distinct topics; often a manager had a number of chance and very brief contacts in the hall; in a number of cases managers processed large quantities of mail at rates of 30 per hour. The following sequence of events occurred in one case—a one-minute unscheduled meeting, a one-minute telephone call, five minutes of desk work, a two-minute call. Imagine one of these managers faced with a diary pad! Managing is a complex, full-time job, and, as I was to learn, so is recording.

Problems of Coding

In the social sciences, where measuring tools are crude, it is often difficult to categorize observations. Eggs can easily be measured and graded, using well-defined criteria, but managerial activities frequently cannot. There follows a description of the various difficulties of categorizing and the means used to resolve them.

Activity. How is one to define the term *activity*? To an industrial engineer, the term is used for the physical act of grabbing a machine tool, while to people at NASA, the Apollo program was an activity. To Homans, potato planting, speaking, and confirmation are all activities (1950: 34). I needed a tighter definition, and therefore took as the start of a new activity any point at which there was a change in the basic participants and/or the medium (a meeting, a telephone call, desk work, a tour). But two difficulties were encountered. The first arose with very brief contacts. I decided that every contact, no matter how brief, should be recorded. This was a difficult rule to maintain. Consider the case when a passer-by looks into the manager's office to say a quick "hello." Does this merit inclusion? I found that by including all contacts, some difficult problems were alleviated. An exception was made only in contacts that the manager had with his secretary, since they were very numerous and different from others. (All were excluded.)

A second difficulty arose with social activity. Clearly it was inappropriate to include telephone calls from the manager's wife. The difficulty arose with certain other extra-organizational contacts. Where was the line to be drawn in such cases as lunch with a competitor to discuss trade gossip, a board meeting of an organization in an unrelated industry, a board meeting of the golf club? The manager may or may not have received important information related to the running of his organization at each of these meetings. A specific case was Manager A's testimony as a private individual at congressional hearings. He emphasized that all his activities were related to his work, and he explicitly included those associated with the hearings. The difficulty with this view was that it meant I would have to study every verbal and written contact, social and otherwise. But clearly this could not be done, both because of the great imposition that would have to be made on the managers and because of the irrelevance for my study of so many of the social activities.

The rule I used was simply to include business-like work (for example, Chamber of Commerce board meeting) and exclude work that was ostensibly social in nature (golf club board meeting). I also decided, perhaps arbitrarily, to exclude the work associated with the hearings.

The issue of what to exclude merits discussion, in part because of the difficulties presented, but also because of the need to deal with it more carefully if this type of research is undertaken again. More importantly, the issue is raised because it highlights the point that high-level executives tend to relate much of their social activity to their work.

Medium. Distinguishing between tours and unscheduled meetings proved to be difficult at times. In the case of a subordinate entering the manager's office to deliver information, and in the case of a manager who spent ten minutes walking about his plant looking for no one in particular, it was clear that the former could be called an unscheduled meeting and the latter, a tour. Problems arose when the manager ambled down the hall toward the plant and met a subordinate to whom he gave some specific information. In general, if the manager's goal when he embarked on the trip was basically to observe something, to greet someone informally, or simply to tour, I called the activity a tour. (Note, however, that if the manager did end up passing information, the purpose of the tour was recorded as "giving information," not "observational tour.")

Attention to Mail. "Skim," "read," and "study" are vague words, but were used respectively to imply (1) that a piece of mail reached the manager's desk, but, with the possible exception of one brief section, it was given cursory attention, (2) that a good part of the item was read at standard reading speeds, and (3) that more time was spent on the item than was necessary simply to "read" it. This categorization had some meaning in the cases of long reports and periodicals. But it was difficult to decide what sort of attention the manager gave to short letters and memos. Therefore most of these were recorded simply as having been "read."

Duration of Contact. Since I did not feel that it was worthwhile or appropriate to use a stopwatch, duration was recorded to the nearest tenth of an hour (maximum possible error due to rounding was three minutes). I do not believe that this rule introduced important inaccuracies. A small problem arose, however, with contacts that lasted less than three minutes. If I recorded them as having lasted 0.0 hours, then they would not appear in the time analyses. I felt that it was appropriate to record them as having lasted 0.02 hours (just over one minute), since of those activities lasting less than three minutes a great majority lasted less than one minute.

Participants in Contact. The categorizing of participants proved to be a difficult and time-consuming task. Eventually I found a means of categorizing, to my satisfaction, the outsiders with whom the manager interacted. I could not, however, appropriately categorize the employees of the managers' organizations and was forced to call them all "subordinates," an unfortunate term, but one without a good synonym.

Contrary to much of the traditional literature, the lines of authority in the organizations were not clear, at least not to the researcher who planned a brief stay. A priori, one would expect most of the chief executive's contacts to be with his vice presidents, and only certain contacts (ceremonial ones, for example) with lower-level employees. Such was not the case. Relatively low-ranking employees fed information directly to the chief executives and were fed information directly by them. They also made fairly routine requests of him. If I had defined the position of people by the nature and frequency of their contacts with the chief executives, I would not have produced the organizational charts. Rather, I would have drawn wheel-like structures. At the hub, with an enormous span of control, would have stood the chief executives.

Thus it was found to be necessary to beg the whole question of categorizing subordinates. The only distinction made was to designate one man as the manager's "deputy"—that person who had distinctly frequent and open-ended contact with him.

Initiation of Contact. For the majority of contacts there was no difficulty in defining the form of initiation. But who could be recorded as the initiator of a meeting that a subordinate called to present the findings of a study requested by the manager? Or who was to be recorded as initiator when the manager chose to attend a conference to which he was invited by a trade organization? I was therefore forced to use a somewhat arbitrary, although convenient, rule—to record the apparent initiator and ignore previous contacts. (Thus, in the first case, I recorded the subordinate, in the second case, the manager.)

Functional Area. Like Rosemary Stewart I began the research with the intention of recording the *functional area* associated with each contact and piece of mail. However, it soon became clear that the difficulties of categorizing this would not be overcome. For example, was I to record a monthly report containing sales and production figures as "marketing," "manufacturing," or "control"? In the case of a meeting to sort out a conflict between two manufacturing executives, was I to record "manufacturing" or "personnel"?

The neat functional categories that we tend to use appear to be of little help in the study of managerial work, simply because the manager's work involves such a complex intermingling of these functions. Thus, I present no information on functional area, and we would question its validity in the studies that do.

Purpose of Mail and Contact. By far the most important categorization process was the determination of "purpose," since this provided the basis for the theory on work content. Choosing these categories was a most difficult and time-consuming process. I felt that this set of categories should (1) represent a logical partitioning of the manager's work, (2) be easily understood by the reader who has never studied the manager's work, and (3) include all observed activity in as few categories as possible. These proved to be very difficult conditions to satisfy, and the categorization of "purpose" required many, many hours of thought and a number of reclassifications of the data.

Given a set of purposes, how is one to determine which was most appropriate for each activity observed? Most mail, telephone calls, and tours had fairly overt raisons d'être. People tended to write or telephone the manager for clear and simple reasons. However, meetings, because they were of longer duration and because of certain characteristics of face-to-face discussion, frequently presented categorizing difficulties. Therefore, I found it necessary to develop a number of special rules.

The scheduled meeting tends to proceed through three stages— an opening period of pleasantries and gossip, the discussion of the core issue, and a closing discussion of side issues. (See discussion of this in Chapter 3.) Naturally, in categorizing the purpose of a meeting, I had to concentrate, not on the opening and closing comments, but on the core issue—the request made, the negotiations conducted, the ceremony taking place. Here, five types of situations presented categorization problems:

1. *Sequential Purpose.* To accomplish one purpose, one may first need to accomplish another purpose. For example, to make a request, one may first need to give information. (Before asking the manager to approve a new sales plan, there is a need to brief him.) To come to a strategic decision, long briefings may first have to take place.

2. *Overt-Covert Purpose.* There is the problem of double-talk:

    A man requesting advice (Should I take the job?) may simply be trying to inform (I've been asked to take the job), or he may be requesting authorization (Will you allow me to take the job?).

    A man giving information (Look at the layout of this promotion center) may be requesting authorization (You had better speak now because if there is a problem later, I'll claim you had your chance to stop it).

    A manager seeking advice (What do you think of Martin for the job?) may be trying to feed the grapevine (Let Martin know I'm considering him for the job).

    A manager giving information (I don't like the report) may be requesting or demanding something (Change the report).

    A manager giving one kind of information (I'm holding the meeting even though you cannot be there) may be giving a different kind of information (I don't want you at the meeting).

    A man giving one kind of information (I would like to recommend a policy change in our promotion procedures) may be seeking another kind of information (Why didn't you promote my subordinate?).

3. *Ostensible Purpose.* At times a man will use an excuse to gain access to the office so that he can raise a different issue. (A subordinate comes to leave a reprint, and, before leaving, comments, "By the way, I hear that the controllership position is open in Los Angeles and I would like to have it.")

4. *Multiple Purpose.* In certain cases a contact may have more than one overt purpose: Social events can be used to transfer certain kinds of information. (At a cocktail party a number of subordinates find the manager to tell him of their accomplishments.) A speech may be both ceremonial and informational. (The manager must make a speech to a visiting group, but views this obligation as an opportunity to inform a segment of the public of the reasons behind a recent price increase.)

5. *Changed Purpose.* Finally, an important bit of instant communication may change the whole nature of a meeting. (At a board meeting, news of a competitor's move, or news of anticipated moves by the public, may turn a relatively informal meeting into a high-pressure strategy session.)

To deal with these and associated problems, the following rules were used in coding *purpose:*

1. The incidental flow of information in stages one and three of meetings were ignored, except in the cases where the discussions assumed great importance in terms of time consumed and issues discussed. In those cases, the meetings were categorized as "review" sessions.

2. The ostensible and overt purpose of a meeting was used for coding unless covert purposes were obvious. In other words, the doubletalk was ignored unless it was not very subtle. When there was real doubt, the manager was asked for his interpretation of purpose.

3. When meetings had more than one purpose, the one thought to be most important was used. Thus, a speech on the hospital's history would be called ceremonial; one on the reasons for its rising costs, informational.[8]

4. In the case of a request for information being made and satisfied, if both took place at the same time, the *contact record* would show "request" (for example, newspaper man interviewing chief executive). If they took place separately, then the first meeting was recorded as a "request," and the second, "giving information" or "receiving information" (for example, manager asks subordinate to conduct study; subordinate reports back one week later).

5. When the discussion focused on one area (the computer facility) but a number of purposes appear to be equally important (making requests, transmitting information, making strategic decisions), the meeting was categorized as a "review" session.

6. A change in the classification of a meeting was made when some "instant communication" changed the course of the meeting. In two actual cases, the meetings were categorized as strategy sessions. Similarly, when the manager started on an observational tour and ended up transmitting information, the purpose was changed to "giving information."

In summary, I did all I could to find the most logical classification for the purpose of each meeting, without trying to close my eyes to important data and thereby paying a high price for categorizing, and without trying to search for trivial subtleties.

[8] Note that the categories of "strategy," "receiving information," and "giving information" were used for certain contacts. This is in no way meant to imply that all strategy-making and information transmission took place during these contacts. Rather, the implication is that these purposes were explicitly highlighted during these contacts. Clearly all contacts involved the transmission of information, and many, categorized elsewhere, involved strategy-making of various kinds. Even "scheduling," for example, involved strategy-making of one kind.

In conclusion, let me emphasize my strong belief that with our present understanding we cannot rely on the indirect methods of research, such as diaries, questionnaires, and interviews. Managerial work is complex; we know too little about it. Once we have an appropriate theoretical understanding of managerial work, the diary method may prove useful to collect data efficiently and to compare many types of managers. But first we must have the basic understanding. Early use of the highly structured forms of research that presuppose much knowledge of the subject and that do not enable the researcher to create new structure as he goes along is likely to perpetuate the naive views that we now have of managerial work.

Bibliography

Aguilar F. J. (1967) *Scanning the Business Environment,* New York: Macmillan.

Ansoff H. I. (1965) *Corporate Strategy,* New York: Mc-Graw-Hill.

Anthony R. N. (1965) *Planning and Control Systems: A Framework for Analysis,* Boston: Harvard Business School, Division of Research.

Argyris C. (1953) *Executive Leadership: An Appraisal of a Manager in Action,* New York: Harper & Row.

Bailey J.C. (1967) "Clues for Success in the President's Job," *Harvard Business Review,* 45, May–June: 97–104.

Barnard C. I. (1966) *The Functions of the Executive,* Cambridge, Mass.: Harvard University Press. First Published 1938.

Bavelas A. (1960) "Leadership: Man and Function," *Administrative Science Quarterly, 5:*491–498.

Berle A. A. and Means G. C. (1968) *The Modern Corporation and Private Property,* New York: Harcourt Brace Jovanovich. First published 1932.

Blake R. R. and Mouton J. S. (1964) *The Managerial Grid,* Houston, Tex.: Gulf.

Blau P. M. and Scott W. R. (1962) *Formal Organizations,* San Francisco: Chandler.

Braybrooke D. (1964) "The Mystery of Executive Success Re-examined," *Administrative Science Quarterly, 8:*533–560.

Braybrooke D. and Lindblom C. E. (1963) *A Strategy of Decision,* New York: Free Press.

Brewer E. and Tomlinson J. W. C. (1964) "The Manager's Working Day," *The Journal of Industrial Economics, 12:*191–197.

Bronowski J. (1958) "The Creative Process," *Scientific American, 199,* September: 59–65.

Brooks E. (1955) "What Successful Executives Do," *Personnel, 32:*210–225.

Burns T. (1954) "The Directions of Activity and Communication in a Departmental Executive Group," *Human Relations, 7:*73–97.

Burns T. (1957) "Management in Action," *Operational Research Quarterly, 8:*45–60.

Burns T. and Stalker G. M. (1961) *The Management of Innovation,* London: Tavistock Publications.

Business Week (1967) "How Johnson Brings the World to His Desk," March 4:178–182.

Campbell J. P., Dunnette M. D., Lawler E. E. III, and Weick K. E., Jr. (1970) *Managerial Behavior, Performance, and Effectiveness,* New York: McGraw-Hill.

Carlson S. (1951) *Executive Behaviour: A Study of the Work Load and the Working Methods of Managing Directors,* Stockholm: Strömbergs.

Cartwright D. (1965) "Influence, Leadership, and Control" in J. G. March, ed., *Handbook of Organizations,* Chicago: Rand McNally.

Centre Emile Bernheim pour l'Etudes des Affaires (1959) *Les cadres supérieures des entreprises: leur origine, leur carrières, leur caractéristiques,* Bruxelles: Université Libre de Bruxelles.

Chapple E.D. and Sayles L. R. (1961) *The Measure of Management,* New York: Macmillan.

Charnes A. and Cooper W. W. (1962) "Management Science and Managing," *Quarterly Review of Economics and Business, 2,* May: 7–19.

Choran I. (1969) *The Manager of a Small Company,* Montreal: McGill University. Unpublished M.B.A. thesis.

Churchman C. W. (1961) *Prediction and Optimal Decision,* Englewood Cliffs, N.J.: Prentice-Hall.

Clarkson G. P. E. (1962) *Portfolio Selection: A Simulation of Trust Investment,* Englewood Cliffs, N.J.: Prentice-Hall.

Collins O. F. and Moore D. G. (1970) *The Organization Makers*, New York: Appleton.

Collins O. F., Moore D. G., and Unwalla D. B. (1964) *The Enterprising Man*, East Lansing, Mich.: Michigan State University Press.

Copeland M. T. (1951) *The Executive at Work*, Cambridge, Mass.: Harvard University Press.

Copeman, G. H. (1959) *The Role of the Managing Director*, London: Business Publications Ltd.

Copeman G. H., Luijk H., and Hanika F. deP. (1963) *How the Executive Spends His Time*, London: Business Publications Ltd.

Cordiner R. J. (1965) "The Work of the Chief Executive" in Moranian T. et al., *Business Policy and Its Environment*, New York: Holt, Rinehart & Winston.

Costin A. A. (1970) *Management Profiles in Business and Government*, Montreal: McGill University. Unpublished M.B.A. thesis.

Courtois Abbé G. (1961) *L'art d'être chef*, Paris: Editions Fleurus.

Creager J. A. and Harding F. D., Jr. (1958) "A Hierarchical Factor Analysis of Foreman Behavior," *Journal of Applied Psychology*, 42:197–203.

Cyert R. M. and March J. G. (1963) *A Behavioral Theory of the Firm*, Englewood Cliffs, N.J.: Prentice-Hall.

Dale E. (1960) *The Great Organizers*, New York: McGraw-Hill.

Dale E. and Urwick L. F. (1960) *Staff in Organization*, New York: McGraw-Hill.

Dalton M. (1959) *Men Who Manage*, New York: Wiley.

Davis R. T. (1957) *Performance and Development of Field Sales Managers*, Boston: Harvard Business School, Division of Research.

Dill W. R. (1959) "Environment as an Influence in Managerial Autonomy" in J. D. Thomson et al. *Comparative Studies in Administration*, Pittsburgh: University of Pittsburgh Press.

Dill W. R. (1964) "Decision-making" in *Sixty-third Yearbook of the National Society for the Study of Education, Part II*, Chicago: Behavioral Science and Educational Administration, 199–222.

Dill W. R. (1964) "The Varieties of Administrative Decisions" in H. J. Leavitt and L. R. Pondy, eds. *Readings in Managerial Psychology*, Chicago: University of Chicago Press.

Dimock M. E. (1945) *The Executive in Action*, New York: Harper & Row.

Drucker P. F. (1954) *The Practice of Management*, New York: Harper & Row.

Drucker P. F. (1967) *The Effective Executive*, New York: Harper & Row.

Drucker P. F. (1967) "How the Effective Executive Does It," *Fortune*, February: 140–143.

Dubin R. (1962) "Business Behavior Behaviorally Viewed" in G. B. Strother, ed. *Social Science Approaches to Business Behavior*, Homewood, Ill.: Irwin-Dorsey.

Dubin R. and Spray S. L. (1964) "Executive Behavior and Interaction," *Industrial Relations*, 3:99–108.

Elliott O. (1959) *Men at the Top,* New York: Harper & Row.

Ewing D. W. (1964) "The Knowledge of an Executive," *Harvard Business Review, 42,* March–April: 91–100.

Ewing D. W. (1964) *The Managerial Mind,* New York: Free Press.

Fayol H. (1950) *Administration industrielle et générale,* Paris: Dunod. First published 1916.

Feigenbaum E. A. and Feldman J. (1963) *Computers and Thought,* New York: McGraw-Hill.

Fiedler F. E. (1966) "The Contingency Model: A Theory of Leadership Effectiveness" in H. Proshansky and B. Seidenberg, eds. *Basic Studies in Social Psychology,* New York: Holt, Rinehart & Winston, 538–551.

Filley A. C. and House R. J. (1969) *Managerial Process and Organizational Behavior,* Glenview, Ill.: Scott, Foresman.

Flanagan J. C. (1951) "Defining the Requirements of the Executive's Job," *Personnel, 28:*28–35.

Flanagan J. C. (1954) "The Critical Incident Technique," *Psychological Bulletin, 51:*327–358.

Fleishman E. A. (1953) "The Description of Supervisory Behavior," *Journal of Applied Psychology, 37:*1–6.

Fleishman E. A. (1953) "Leadership Climate, Human Relations Training, and Supervisory Behavior," *Personnel Psychology, 6:*205–222.

Forbes Magazine (1971) "The Buck Stops Here: The Role of the Chief Executive Office," *15:* May: whole issue.

Forrester J. W. (1961) *Industrial Dynamics,* Cambridge, Mass.: M.I.T. Press.

Fortune editors (1956) *The Executive Life,* Garden City, N.Y.: Doubleday.

Galbraith J. K. (1967) *The New Industrial State,* Boston: Houghton Mifflin.

Gaudet F. J. and Carli A. R. (1957) "Why Executives Fail," *Personnel Psychology, 10:*7–22.

Gibb, C. A. (1969) "Leadership" in G. Lindzey and E. A. Aronson, eds. *The Handbook of Social Psychology,* 2nd ed., Reading, Mass.: Addison-Wesley, vol. 4.

Goodman R. A. (1968) "A System Diagram of the Functions of a Manager," *California Management Review, 10:*27–38.

Gore W. J. and Dyson J. W. eds. (1964) *The Making of Decisions,* New York: Free Press.

Gross B. M. (1964) *The Managing of Organizations,* New York: Free Press.

Guest R. H. (1955–1956) "Of Time and the Foreman," *Personnel, 32:* 478–486.

Gulick L. H. (1937) "Notes on the Theory of Organization" in L. H. Gulick and L. F. Urwick eds. *Papers on the Science of Administration,* New York: Columbia University Press.

Hacker A. (1967) "The Making of a (Corporation) President," *The New York Times Magazine,* April 2: 26–27, 126–132.

Haire M. ed. (1959) *Modern Organization Theory,* New York: Wiley.

Haire M., Ghiselli E. E., and Porter L. W. (1966) *Managerial Thinking: An International Study,* New York: Wiley.

Hamblin R. L. (1958) "Leadership and Crises," *Sociometry, 21:*322–335.

Harbison F. and Myers C. A. (1959) *Management in the Industrial World: An International Analysis,* New York: McGraw-Hill.

Harper W. K. (1968) *Executive Time: A Corporation's Most Valuable, Scarce and Irrecoverable Resource,* Boston: Harvard University, Graduate School of Business Administration. Unpublished D.B.A. thesis.

Harrell T. W. (1961) *Managers' Performance and Personality,* Cincinnati, Ohio: South-Western.

Harrington A. (1959) *Life in the Crystal Palace,* New York: Knopf.

Hekimian J. S. and Mintzberg H. (1968) "The Planning Dilemma," *The Management Review, 57:* May: 4–17.

Hemphill J. K. (1959) "Job Descriptions for Executives," *Harvard Business Review, 37,* September–October: 55–67.

Hemphill J. K. (1960) *Dimensions of Executive Positions,* Columbus: Ohio State University, Bureau of Business Research. Research Monograph Number 98.

Hitch C. J. (1965) *Decision-Making for Defense,* Berkeley: University of California Press.

Hitch C. J. and McKean R. N. (1960) *The Economics of Defense in the Nuclear Age,* Cambridge, Mass.: Harvard University Press.

Hodgson R. C., Levinson D. J., and Zaleznik, A. (1965) *The Executive Role Constellation: An Analysis of Personality and Role Relations in Management,* Boston: Harvard Business School, Division of Research.

Homans G. C. (1950) *The Human Group,* New York: Harcourt Brace Jovanovich.

Homans G. C. (1958) "Social Behavior as Exchange," *American Journal of Sociology, 63:*597–606.

Horne J. H. and Lupton T. (1965) "The Work Activities of 'Middle' Managers—An Exploratory Study," *The Journal of Management Studies, 2:*14–33.

Inkson J. H. K., Schwitter J. P., Pheysey D. C., and Hickson D. J. (1970) "A Comparison of Organization Structure and Managerial Roles: Ohio, U.S.A., and the Midlands, England," *The Journal of Management Studies, 7:*347–363.

Jackson P. W. and Messick S. (1965) "The Person, the Product, and the Response: Conceptual Problems in the Assessment of Creativity," *The Journal of Personality, 33:*309–329.

Jasinski F. J. (1956) "Foremen Relationships Outside the Work Group," *Personnel, 33:*130–136.

Jennings E. E. (1960) *An Anatomy of Leadership,* New York: Harper & Row.

Jennings E. E. (1965) *The Executive in Crisis,* East Lansing, Michigan: Michigan State University, Graduate School of Business Administration.

Jerdee T. H. and Mahoney T. A. (1957) "New Way to Look at Manager's Jobs," *Factory Management and Maintenance*, December: 110–112.

Katz D. and Kahn R. L. (1966) *The Social Psychology of Organizations*, New York: Wiley.

Katzell R. A., Barrett R. S., Vann D. H., and Hogan J. M. (1968) "Organizational Correlates of Executive Roles," *Journal of Applied Psychology, 52:*22–28.

Kaufmann W. W. (1964) *The McNamara Strategy*, New York: Harper & Row.

Kay B. R. (1959) "Key Factors in Effective Foreman Behavior," *Personnel, 36*, January–February: 25–31.

Kay E. and Meyer H. H. (1962) "The Development of a Job Activity Questionnaire for Production Foremen," *Personnel Psychology, 15:* 411–418.

Kelly J. (1964) "The Study of Executive Behaviour by Activity Sampling," *Human Relations, 17:*277–287.

Kelly J. (1969) *Organizational Behavior*, Homewood, Ill.: Irwin–Dorsey.

Klahr D. and Leavitt H. J. (1967) "Tasks, Organization Structures, and Computer Programs" in C. A. Myers, ed. *The Impact of Computers on Management*, Cambridge, Mass.: MIT Press.

Knight F. H. (1921) *Risk, Uncertainty, and Profit*, Boston: Houghton Mifflin.

Koontz H. and O'Donnell C. (1968) *Principles of Management: An Analysis of Managerial Functions*, New York: McGraw-Hill.

Krech D., Crutchfield R. S., and Ballachey E. L. (1962) "Leadership and Group Change" in *Individual in Society*, New York: McGraw-Hill, 422–454.

Landsberger H. A. (1962) "The Horizontal Dimension in Bureaucracy," *Administrative Science Quarterly, 6:*299–332.

Lawler E. E. III, Porter L. W., and Tennenbaum A. (1968) "Managers' Attitudes Toward Interaction Episodes," *Journal of Applied Psychology, 52:*432–439.

Learned E. P. et al. (1951) *Executive Action*, Boston: Harvard Business School, Division of Research.

Leavitt H. J. and Whistler T. L. (1958) "Management in the 1980's," *Harvard Business Review 36*, November–December: 41–48.

Lewis R. and Stewart R. (1958) *The Boss*, London: Phoenix House.

Light H. R. (1961) *The Business Executive*, London: Pitman.

Likert R. (1961) *New Patterns of Management*, New York: McGraw-Hill.

Lindblom C. E. (1959) "The Science of 'Muddling Through,'" *Public Administration Review, 19:*79–88.

Lindblom C. E. (1965) *The Intelligence of Democracy*, New York: Free Press.

Lindblom C. E. (1968) *The Policy-Making Process*, Englewood Cliffs, N.J.: Prentice-Hall.

Livingston J. S. (1971) "Myth of the Well-Educated Manager," *Harvard Business Review, 49*, January–February: 79–89.

Livingston R. T. and Waite W. W., eds. (1960) *The Manager's Job*, New York: Columbia University Press.

McGrath J. E. (1964) "Toward a 'Theory of Method' for Research on Organizations" in W. W. Cooper, H. J. Leavitt, and M. W. Shelly, eds. *New Perspectives in Organization Research*, New York: Wiley.

McGregor D. (1960) *The Human Side of Enterprise*, New York: McGraw-Hill.

McGregor D. (1967) *The Professional Manager*, New York: McGraw-Hill.

Mackenzie R. A. (1969) "The Management Process in 3-D," *Harvard Business Review, 47*, November–December: 80–87.

McMurry R. N. (1965) "Clear Communications for Chief Executives," *Harvard Business Review, 43*, March–April: 131–147.

Mahoney T. A., Jerdee J. H., and Carroll S. J. (1963) *Development of Managerial Performance—A Research Approach*, Cincinnati, Ohio: South-Western. Monograph C9.

Manley R. and Manley S. (1962) *The Age of the Manager*, New York: Macmillan.

March J. G. and Simon H. A. (1958) *Organizations*, New York: Wiley.

Marples D. L. (1967) "Studies of Managers—A Fresh Start?" *The Journal of Management Studies, 4:*282–299.

Martin N. H. (1956) "Differential Decisions in the Management of an Industrial Plant," *Journal of Business, 29:*249–260.

Melcher R. D. (1967) "Roles and Relationships: Clarifying the Manager's Job," *Personnel, 44*, May–June: 33–41.

Mills C. W. (1956) *The Power Elite*, New York: Oxford University Press.

Mintzberg H. (1967) "The Science of Strategy-making," *Industrial Management Review, 8:*71–81.

Mintzberg H. (1968) *The Manager at Work—Determining his Activities, Roles, and Programs by Structured Observation*, Cambridge, Mass.: M.I.T. Sloan School of Management. Ph.D. thesis.

Mintzberg H. (1970) "Structured Observation as a Method to Study Managerial Work," *The Journal of Management Studies, 7:*87–104.

Mintzberg H. (1971) "Managerial Work: Analysis from Observation," *Management Science, 18:*B97–B110.

Mintzberg H. (1972) "The Myths of MIS," *California Management Review, 14*, Fall: 92–97.

Mitchell W. N. (1965) *The Business Executive in a Changing World*, New York: American Management Association, Inc.

Moonman E. (1961) *The Manager and the Organization*, London: Tavistock Publications.

Morris D. (1967) *The Naked Ape*, New York: McGraw-Hill and London: Cape.

Myers, C. A. (1965) "The Impact of EDP on Management Organization and Managerial Work," *MIT Working Paper 139-65*, Cambridge, Mass.: Sloan School of Management, M.I.T.

Myers C. A., ed. (1967) *The Impact of Computers on Management*, Cambridge, Mass.: M.I.T. Press.

Nealey S. M. and Fiedler F. E. (1968) "Leadership Functions of Middle Managers," *Psychological Bulletin, 70:*313–329.

Neustadt R. E. (1960) *Presidential Power: The Politics of Leadership,* New York: Wiley.

Newcomer M. (1955) *The Big Business Executive,* New York: Columbia University Press.

Newell A. and Simon H. A. (1972) *Human Problem Solving,* Englewood Cliffs, N.J.: Prentice-Hall.

Nordling R. (1954) "Work Simplification at the Level of the General Manager of a Company" (translated by the Management Consultation Services of General Electric from *Revue Mensuelle de l'Organization,* June).

Ohmann O. A. (1957) "Search for a Managerial Philosophy," *Harvard Business Review, 35,* September–October: 41–51.

O'Neill H. E. and Kubany A. J. (1959) "Observation Methodology and Supervisory Behavior," *Personnel Psychology, 12:*85–95.

Papandreou A. G. (1952) "Some Basic Problems in the Theory of the Firm" in B. F. Haley, ed. *A Survey of Contemporary Economics,* Homewood, Ill.: Irwin, vol. 2: 183–219.

Peres S. H. (1962) "Performance Dimensions of Supervisory Positions," *Personnel Psychology, 15:*405–410.

Ponder Q. D. (1957) "The Effective Manufacturing Foreman" in E. Young, ed. *Industrial Relations Research Association Proceedings of the Tenth Annual Meeting,* Madison, Wisconsin, 41–54.

Prien E. P. (1963) "Development of a Supervisor Position Description Questionnaire," *Journal of Applied Psychology, 47:*10–14.

Radomsky J. (1967) *The Problem of Choosing a Problem,* Cambridge, Mass.: M.I.T., Sloan School of Management. Unpublished M.S. thesis.

Radosevich R. and Ullrich R. A. (1971) "Program Design Strategies for Graduate Professional Learning," *AACSB Bulletin,* April: 18–29.

Redlich F. (1951) "Innovation in Business," *The American Journal of Economics and Sociology, 10:*285–291.

Rockwell W. F., Jr. (1971) *The Twelve Hats of a Company President,* Englewood Cliffs, N.J.: Prentice-Hall.

Rubin I. M., Stedry A. C., and Willits R. D. (1965) "Influences Related to Time Allocation of R & D Supervisors," *IEEE Transactions on Engineering Management, 12:*70–78.

Sarbin T. R. and Allen V. L. (1968) "Role Theory" in G. Lindzey and E. Aronson, eds. *The Handbook of Social Psychology* 2nd ed., Reading, Mass.: Addison-Wesley, vol. 1: 488–567.

Sayles L. R. (1964) *Managerial Behavior: Administration in Complex Organizations,* New York: McGraw-Hill.

Scholefield J. (1968) "The Effectiveness of Senior Executives," *The Journal of Management Studies,* May: 219–234.

Schumpeter J. A. (1947) "The Creative Response in Economic History," *The Journal of Economic History, 7:*149–159.

Schumpeter J. A. (1961) *The Theory of Economic Development,* Cambridge, Mass.: Harvard University Press. First published 1934.

Scott W. R. (1965) "Field Methods in the Study of Organizations" in J. G. March, *Handbook of Organizations,* Chicago: Rand McNally.

Selznick P. (1957) *Leadership in Administration*, New York: Harper & Row.

Senger J. (1971) "The Co-Manager Concept," *California Management Review, 13*, Spring: 71–83.

Shartle C. L. (1949) "Leadership and Executive Performance," *Personnel, 25*:370–380.

Shartle C. L. (1956) *Executive Performance and Leadership*, Englewood Cliffs, N.J.: Prentice-Hall.

Simon H. A. (1957) *Administrative Behavior* 2nd ed., New York: Macmillan.

Simon H. A. (1965) *The Shape of Automation*, New York: Harper & Row.

Sloan A. P. (1963) *My Years with General Motors*, Garden City, N.Y.: Doubleday.

Sorenson T. C. (1963) *Decision-making in the White House*, New York: Columbia University Press.

Spencer L. M. (1955) "10 Problems that Worry Presidents," *Harvard Business Review, 33*, November–December: 75–83.

Starbuck W. H. (1965) "Organizational Growth and Development" in J. G. March, ed. *Handbook of Organizations*, Chicago: Rand McNally.

Steiner G. A. (1969) *Top Management Planning*, New York: Macmillan.

Stewart R. (1963) *The Reality of Management*, London: Heinemann.

Stewart R. (1965) "The Use of Diaries to Study Managers' Jobs," *The Journal of Management Studies, 2*:228–235.

Stewart R. (1967) *Managers and their Jobs*, London: Macmillan.

Stewart R. (1968a) "Management Education and our Knowledge of Managers' Jobs," *International Social Science Journal, 20*:77–89.

Stewart R. (1968b) "Diary Keeping as a Training Tool for Managers," *The Journal of Management Studies, 5*:295–303.

Stieglitz H. (1969) *The Chief Executive—And His Job*, New York: National Industrial Conference Board. Personnel Policy Study No. 214.

Stieglitz H. (1970) "The Chief Executive's Job—and the Size of the Company," *The Conference Board Record, 7*, September: 38–40.

Stogdill R. M. (1965) *Managers, Employees, Organizations*, Columbus: Ohio State University, Bureau of Business Research. Research Monograph Number 125.

Stogdill R. M. and Coons A. E., eds. (1957) *Leader Behavior: Its Description and Measurement*, Columbus, Ohio: Ohio State University, Bureau of Business Research. Research Monograph Number 88.

Stogdill R. M., Goode O. S., and Day D. R. (1963) "The Leader Behavior of Corporation Presidents," *Personnel Psychology, 16*:127–132.

Stogdill R. M., Goode O. S., and Day D. R. (1963) "The Leader Behavior of United States Senators," *The Journal of Psychology, 56*:3–8.

Stogdill R. M., Goode O. S., and Day D. R. (1964) "The Leader Behavior of Presidents of Labor Unions," *Personnel Psychology, 17*:49–57.

Stogdill R. M., Scott E. L., and Jaynes W. E. (1956) *Leadership and Role*

Expectations, Columbus: Ohio State University, Bureau of Business Research. Research Monograph Number 86.

Stogdill R. M., Shartle C. L., and Associates (1956) *Patterns of Administrative Performance,* Columbus, Ohio: Ohio State University, Bureau of Business Research. Research Monograph Number 81.

Strong E. P. (1965) *The Management of Business: An Introduction,* New York: Harper & Row.

Strong L. (1955) "Every Day is Doomsday—the Ordeal of Executive Decision," *The Management Review, 44,* November: 746–755.

Stryker P. (1960) *The Men from the Boys,* New York: Harper and Row.

Sullivan J. W. (1967) "New Man on the Hill," *Wall Street Journal,* January 26: 1, 19.

Tannenbaum R. (1949) "The Manager Concept: A Rational Synthesis," *The Journal of Business, 22:*225–241.

Taylor F. W. (1947) *Scientific Management,* New York: Harper & Row. First published 1911.

Thomas E. J. and Biddle B. J. (1966) *Role Theory: Concepts and Research,* New York: Wiley.

Thomason G. F. (1966) "Managerial Work Roles and Relationships Part I," *The Journal of Management Studies, 3:*270–284.

Thomason G. F. (1967) "Managerial Work Roles and Relationships Part II," *The Journal of Management Studies, 4:*17–30.

Tilles S. (1963) "The Manager's Job—A Systems Approach," *Harvard Business Review, 41,* January–February: 73–81.

Urwick L. F. (1954) *The Load on Top Management—Can it be Reduced?* London: Urwick, Orr and Partners Ltd.

U.S. News & World Report (1966) "A Look at the Inner Workings of the White House: Interview with Bill D. Moyers, Top Aide to the President," June 13: 78–85.

Walker C. R., Guest R. H., and Turner A. N. (1956) *The Foreman on the Assembly Line,* Cambridge, Mass.: Harvard University Press.

The Wall Street Journal (1967) "Portrait of a Company President: Younger, More Highly Educated," September 29: 12.

Warner W. L. and Abegglen J. C. (1955) *Big Business Leaders in America,* New York: Harper & Row.

Warner W. L. and Martin N. H., eds. (1959) *Industrial Man: Businessmen and Business Organizations,* New York: Harper & Row.

Weber M. (1950) *The Theory of Social and Economic Organization,* New York: Free Press. First published 1927.

Weick K. E. (1968) "Systematic Observational Methods" in G. Lindzey and E. A. Aronson, eds. *The Handbook of Social Psychology,* 2nd ed., Reading, Mass.: Addison-Wesley.

Whistler T. L. (1956) "The Assistant-to: the Man in Motley," *The Journal of Business, 29:*274–279.

Whistler T. L. (1960) "The 'Assistant-to' in Four Administrative Settings," *Administrative Science Quarterly, 5:*181–216.

Whyte W. F. (1955) *Street Corner Society* 2nd ed., Chicago: University of Chicago Press.

Whyte W. H., Jr. (1954) "How Hard Do Executives Work?" *Fortune*, January: 108–111, 148, 150–152.

Wikstrom W. S. (1967) *Managing at the Foreman's Level*, New York: National Industrial Conference Board. Personnel Policy Study No. 205.

Wirdenius H. (1958) *Supervisors at Work*, Stockholm: The Swedish Council for Personnel Administration.

Wong N. L. (1970) *A Programmed View of Managerial Work*, Montreal: McGill University, Unpublished M.B.A. thesis.

Woodward J. (1965) *Industrial Organization: Theory and Practice*, London: Oxford University Press.

Wrapp H. E. (1967) "Good Managers Don't Make Policy Decisions," *Harvard Business Review, 45*, September–October: 91–99.

Index

91 30 29 28 27 26 25 24 23 22 21